Android™
Application Development
FOR
DUMMIES®
2ND EDITION

Android™
Application Development
FOR
DUMMIES®
2ND EDITION

by Michael Burton and Donn Felker

WILEY

John Wiley & Sons, Inc.

Android™ Application Development For Dummies®, 2nd Edition

Published by
John Wiley & Sons, Inc.
111 River Street
Hoboken, NJ 07030-5774

www.wiley.com

Copyright © 2012 by John Wiley & Sons, Inc., Hoboken, New Jersey

Published by John Wiley & Sons, Inc., Hoboken, New Jersey

Published simultaneously in Canada

For general information on our other products and services, please contact our Customer Care Department within the U.S. at 877-762-2974, outside the U.S. at 317-572-3993, or fax 317-572-4002.

For technical support, please visit www.wiley.com/techsupport.

Wiley publishes in a variety of print and electronic formats and by print-on-demand. Some material included with standard print versions of this book may not be included in e-books or in print-on-demand. If this book refers to media such as a CD or DVD that is not included in the version you purchased, you may download this material at http://booksupport.wiley.com. For more information about Wiley products, visit www.wiley.com.

Library of Congress Control Number: 2012948923

ISBN: 978-1-118-38710-8 (pbk); ISBN 978-1-118-41745-4 (ebk); ISBN 978-1-118-42190-1 (ebk); ISBN 978-1-118-43327-0 (ebk)

Manufactured in the United States of America

10 9 8 7 6 5 4 3 2 1

WILEY

About the Authors

Michael Burton is the Lead Android Engineer at Groupon. He wrote the Groupon, Digg, TripIt, and OpenTable Android apps, among others. He's flown a project on the Space Shuttle. He's spoken on Android application development at conferences in London, Boston, Silicon Valley, Rio de Janeiro, and elsewhere. He's also the author of RoboGuice, the open-source dependency injection framework used by Google, Facebook, and others. Follow Michael on Twitter (@roboguice) or check out RoboGuice at `http://roboguice.org`.

Donn Felker is a recognized leader in the development and consultation of state-of-the-art, cutting-edge software in the mobile and web fields. He is an independent consultant with over 10 years of professional experience in various markets that include entertainment, health, retail, insurance, financial, and real estate. He is a mobile junkie, serial entrepreneur, and creative innovator in all things mobile and web. He is the founder of Agilevent, an innovative creative development firm that has done work for small startups as well as Fortune 500 companies. He is a Microsoft ASP Insider, an MCTS for .NET Framework 2.0 and 3.5 Web Applications, and a certified ScrumMaster. He's a national speaker on topics that include Android, .NET, and software architecture. He is the author of the TekPub.com Introduction to Android video series. He is a writer, presenter, and consultant on various topics ranging from architecture to development in general, agile practices, and patterns and practices. Follow Donn on Twitter (@donnfelker) or read his blog at `http://blog.donnfelker.com`.

Dedication

To BugDroid.

Author's Acknowledgments

Thanks to Donn Felker for writing the initial version of this book and tossing the project my way. Here's hoping we work on many successful projects in the future!

A big thank you to the extended Android open source community, including Carlos Sessa, Manfred Moser, Donn, and Jake Wharton among others, who contributed their code, expertise, and reviews of this book.

Thank you to my great team at Groupon, Chris, Alex, Robyn, Eric, Aubrey, and David, who have pushed me to understand the Android platform deeper than I would have on my own.

And finally, thank you to my friends and family who have supported me through the evenings I spent working on this project. The loaner puppy and the per-chapter treats were all I needed to push through those long weekends!

Publisher's Acknowledgments

We're proud of this book; please send us your comments at http://dummies.custhelp.com. For other comments, please contact our Customer Care Department within the U.S. at 877-762-2974, outside the U.S. at 317-572-3993, or fax 317-572-4002.

Some of the people who helped bring this book to market include the following:

Acquisitions and Editorial

Project Editor: Rebecca Senninger

Acquisitions Editor: Kyle Looper

Copy Editor: Rebecca Whitney

Technical Editor: Krista Dombroviak

Editorial Manager: Leah Michael

Editorial Assistant: Leslie Saxman

Sr. Editorial Assistant: Cherie Case

Cover Photo: © istockphoto.com/Palto

Cartoons: Rich Tennant (www.the5thwave.com)

Composition Services

Project Coordinator: Patrick Redmond

Layout and Graphics: Jennifer Creasey, Corrie Niehaus

Proofreader: Lisa Young Stiers

Indexer: Sharon Stock

Publishing and Editorial for Technology Dummies

    Richard Swadley, Vice President and Executive Group Publisher

    Andy Cummings, Vice President and Publisher

    Mary Bednarek, Executive Acquisitions Director

    Mary C. Corder, Editorial Director

Publishing for Consumer Dummies

    Kathleen Nebenhaus, Vice President and Executive Publisher

Composition Services

    Debbie Stailey, Director of Composition Services

Contents at a Glance

Table of Contents

Introduction

*W*elcome to *Android Application Development For Dummies!*

When Android was acquired by Google in 2005 (yes, Android was a start-up company at one point), a lot of people didn't have much interest in it because Google hadn't yet entered the mobile space. Fast-forward to a few years later, when Google announced its first Android phone: the G1. It was the start of something huge.

The G1 was the first publicly released Android device. It didn't match the rich feature set of the iPhone at the time, but a lot of people believed in the platform. As soon as Donut (Android 1.6) was released, it was evident that Google was putting some effort into the product. Immediately after version 1.6 was released, talk of 2.0 was already on the horizon.

Today, we're on version 4.1 of the Android platform, with no signs that things are slowing down. Without doubt, this is an exciting time in Android development.

About This Book

Android Application Development For Dummies is a beginner's guide to developing Android applications. You don't need any Android application development experience under your belt to get started. You can approach this material as a blank slate because the Android platform accomplishes various mechanisms by using different paradigms that most programmers aren't used to using — or developing with — on a day-to-day basis.

The Android platform is a *device-independent* platform, which means that you can develop applications for various devices. These devices include, but aren't limited to phones, e-book readers, netbooks, televisions, and GPS devices.

Finding out how to develop for the Android platform opens a large variety of development options for you. This book distills hundreds, if not thousands, of pages of Android documentation, tips, tricks, and tutorials into a short, digestible format that allows you to springboard into your future as an

Android developer. This book isn't a recipe book, but it gives you the basic knowledge to assemble various pieces of the Android framework to create interactive and compelling applications.

Conventions Used in This Book

Throughout the book, you use the Android framework classes, and you will be creating Java classes and XML files.

Code examples in this book appear in a monospace font so that they stand out from other text in the book. This means that the code you'll see looks like this:

```
public class MainActivity
```

Java is a high-level programming language that is case-sensitive, so be sure to enter the text into the editor *exactly* as you see it in the book as it follows standard Java conventions. Therefore, you can transition easily between the book examples and the example code provided by the Android Software Development Kit (SDK). All class names, for example, appear in `PascalCase` format, and all class-scoped variables start with `m`.

All the URLs in the book appear in monospace font as well:

```
http://d.android.com
```

Foolish Assumptions

To begin programming with Android, you need a computer that runs one of the following operating systems:

- ✔ Windows XP (32 bit), Vista (32 or 64 bit), or Windows 7 or 8 (32 or 64 bit)
- ✔ Mac OS X (Intel) 10.5.8 or later (x86 only)
- ✔ Linux (i386)

You also need to download the Android SDK (which is free) and the Java Development Kit (or JDK, which is also free), if you don't already have them on your computer. Chapter 2 outlines the entire installation process for all the tools and frameworks.

Because Android applications are developed in the Java programming language, you need to understand the Java language. Android also uses XML quite heavily to define various resources inside the application, so you should understand XML too. You don't have to be an expert in these languages, however.

You don't need a physical Android device, because all the applications you build in this book work on an emulator.

How This Book Is Organized

Android Application Development For Dummies has five parts, described in the following sections.

Part 1: The Nuts and Bolts of Android

Part I introduces the tools and frameworks that you use to develop Android applications. It also introduces the various SDK components and shows you how they're used in the Android ecosystem.

Part II: Building and Publishing Your First Android Application

Part II introduces you to building your first Android application: the Silent Mode Toggle application. After you build the initial application, you create an app widget for the application that you can place on the Home screen of an Android device. Then you publish your application to the Google Play Store.

Part III: Creating a Feature-Rich Application

Part III takes your development skills up a notch by walking you through the construction of the Task Reminder application, which allows users to create various tasks with reminders. You implement an SQLite content provider in this multiscreen application. You also see how to use the Android status bar to create notifications that can help increase the usability of your application.

Part IV: Tablets

Part IV takes the phone app you built in Part III and tweaks it to work on an Android tablet. You also find out how to bring your applications to non-Google Android devices such as the Amazon Kindle Fire.

Part V: The Part of Tens

Part V gives you a tour of sample applications that prove to be stellar launching pads for your Android apps, and useful Android libraries that can make your Android development career a lot easier.

Icons Used in This Book

This icon indicates a useful pointer that you shouldn't skip.

This icon represents a friendly reminder about a vital point you should keep in mind while proceeding through a particular section of the chapter.

This icon signifies that the accompanying explanation may be informative but isn't essential to understanding Android application development. Feel free to skip these snippets, if you like.

This icon alerts you to potential problems that you may encounter along the way. Read and remember these tidbits to avoid possible trouble.

Where to Go from Here

It's time to explore the Android platform! If you're a bit nervous, let me assure you that you don't have to worry; you should be nervous only because you're excited.

This book includes some extras online:

- ✔ Find the cheat sheet for this book at www.dummies.com/cheatsheet/androidapplicationdevelopment.

- ✔ Don't want to type all the code in the book? You can download it from the book's website at www.dummies.com/go/androidappdevfd2e.

- ✔ If there are ever updates to this book, you can find them at www.dummies.com/go/androidappdevfdupdates2e.

Part I
The Nuts and Bolts of Android

The 5th Wave   By Rich Tennant

"A snakebite app is what we should develop, I said. But no, you insisted on a butterfly identification app instead."

In this part . . .

Part I introduces you to the Android platform and describes what makes a spectacular Android application. You explore various parts of the Android software development kit (SDK) and explain how you can use them in your applications. You install the tools and frameworks necessary to develop Android applications.

Chapter 1

Developing Spectacular Android Applications

In This Chapter

▶ Seeing reasons to develop Android apps

▶ Starting with the basics of Android development

▶ Working with the hardware

▶ Getting familiar with the software

Google rocks! Google acquired the Android project in 2005 (see the sidebar "The roots of Android," later in this chapter) to ensure that a mobile operating system (OS) can be created and maintained in an open platform. Google continues to pump time and resources into the Android project, which has already proved to be beneficial. Though devices have been available only since October 2008, as of today about a million Android devices are activated daily. In only a few years, Android has already made a *huge* impact.

It has never been easier for Android developers to make money developing apps. Android users trust Google. Because your app resides in the Google Play Store — which Google controls — many Android users assume that your application is trustworthy, too.

Why Develop for Android?

The real question is, "Why *not* develop for Android?" If you want your app to be available to millions of users worldwide or you want to publish apps as soon as you finish writing and testing them or you like developing on an open platform, you have your answer. But in case you're still undecided, continue reading.

Market share

As a developer, you have an opportunity to develop apps for a fairly new — and booming — market. Many analysts believe that the number of Android devices in use is greater than the number of devices on all other mobile operating systems combined. The Google Play Store puts your app directly and easily into a user's hands (or, more accurately, device). Users don't have to search the Internet to find an app to install — they can simply go to the preinstalled Google Play Store on their devices and have access to all your apps. Because the Google Play Store comes preinstalled on most Android devices (see Chapter 19 for some exceptions), users typically search the Google Play Store for all their application needs. It isn't unusual to see an app's number of downloads soar in only a few days.

Time to market

Because of all the application programming interfaces (APIs) packed into Android, you can easily develop full-featured applications in a relatively short time frame. After you register as a developer at the Google Play Store, simply upload your apps and publish them. Unlike other mobile marketplaces, the Google Play Store has no app approval process. All you have to do is write apps and publish them.

Though anyone can publish any type of app (technically speaking), maintain your good karma — and your compliance with the Google terms of service — by producing family-friendly apps. Android has users from diverse areas of the world and in all age categories.

Open platform

The Android operating system is an *open platform:* Any hardware manufacturer or provider can make or sell Android devices. As you can imagine, the openness of Android has allowed it to gain market share quickly. Feel free to dig into the Android source code — at http://source.android.com — to see how certain tasks are handled, for example. By using open source code, manufacturers can even create custom user interfaces (UIs) and add built-in features to certain devices.

The roots of Android

Though most people aren't aware of it, Google didn't start the Android project. The initial version of the Android operating system was created by Android, Inc., a small start-up company in Silicon Valley that was purchased by Google in July 2005. The founders (who worked for various Internet technology companies, such as Danger, Wildfire Communications, T-Mobile, and WebTV) became part of the Google team that helped create what is now the full-fledged Android mobile operating system.

Cross-compatibility

Android is *cross-compatible:* It can run on devices of many different screen sizes and resolutions, including phones and tablets. In addition, Android comes supplied with tools to help you develop cross-compatible applications. Google allows apps to run only on Android-compatible devices, however. If your app requires a front-facing camera, for example, only phones with front-facing cameras can "see" your app in the Google Play Store — an arrangement known as *feature detection.* (For more information on publishing your apps to the Google Play Store, see Chapter 8.)

Mashup capability

A *mashup* combines two or more services to create an application. You can create a mashup by using the camera and the Android location services, for example, to take a photo with the exact location displayed on the image. Or you can use a map's API with the Contacts list, for example, to show all contacts on a map. You can easily make apps by combining services or libraries in countless new and exciting ways. A few other types of mashups that can help your brain juices start pumping out ideas

- ✔ **Geolocation and social networking:** Suppose that you want to write an app that tweets a user's current location every ten minutes throughout the day. Using the Android location services and a third-party Twitter API (such as iTwitter), you can do it easily.

✔ **Geolocation and gaming:** Location-based gaming, which is increasingly popular, is a helpful way to inject players into the thick of a game. A game might run a background service to check a player's current location and compare it with other players' locations in the same area. If a second player is within a specified distance, the first one could be notified to challenge her to a battle. All this is possible because of GPS technology on a strong platform such as Android.

✔ **Contacts and Internet:** With all the useful APIs at your disposal, you can easily make full-featured apps by combining the functionality of two or more APIs. You can combine the Internet and names from the Contacts list to create a greeting-card app, for example. Or you may simply want to add an easy way for users to contact you from an app or enable them to send your app to their friends. (See "Google APIs," later in this chapter, for more information on the APIs.)

Developers can make Android do almost anything they want, so use your best judgment when creating and publishing apps for mass consumption. Just because you want live wallpaper to highlight your version of the hula in your birthday suit doesn't mean that anyone else wants to see it.

Android Development Basics

Thank goodness you don't have to be a member of Mensa to develop Android applications! Developing in Android is simple because its default language is Java. Though writing Android applications is fairly easy, developing alone can be a difficult task to conquer.

If you've never developed applications before, this book isn't the best place to start reading about app development. Pick up a copy of *Beginning Programming with Java For Dummies,* by Barry Burd (John Wiley & Sons, Inc.) to learn the ropes. After you have a basic understanding of Java under your belt, you should be ready to tackle this book.

Although the Android operating system consists primarily of Java code, small parts of the framework aren't included. Android uses the XML language as well as basic Apache Ant scripting for build processes. You need to cement your basic understanding of XML before delving into this book.

If you need an introduction to XML, check out *XML For Dummies,* by Lucinda Dykes and Ed Tittel (John Wiley & Sons, Inc.).

If you already know how to use Java and XML, congratulations — you're ahead of the curve.

Java: Your Android programming language

Android applications are written in Java — not the full-blown version of Java that's familiar to developers using Java Platform, Enterprise Edition (J2EE), but a subset of the Java libraries that are specific to Android. This smaller subset of Java excludes classes that aren't suitable for mobile devices. If you have experience in Java, you should feel right at home developing apps in Android.

Even with a Java reference book on hand, you can always search at www. google.com to find information about topics you don't understand. Because Java isn't a new language, you can find plenty of examples on the web that demonstrate how to do virtually anything.

Not every class that's available to Java programmers is available also on Android. Verify that it's available to you before you start trying to use it. If it's not, an alternative is probably bundled with Android that can work for your needs.

Activities

An Android application can consist of only a single activity or several. An activity serves as a container for both the user interface and the code that runs it. You can think of activities as *pages* of your app — one page in your app corresponds to one activity. Activities are discussed in more detail in Chapters 3 and 5.

Intents

Intents make up the core message system that runs Android. An intent is composed of two elements:

- **An action:** The general action to be performed (such as view, edit, or dial) when the intent is received
- **Data:** The information that the action operates on, such as the name of a contact

Intents are used to start activities and to communicate among various parts of the Android operating system. An application can either broadcast an intent or receive an intent.

Sending messages with intents

When you *broadcast* an intent, you send a message telling Android to make something happen. The intent can tell Android to start a new activity from within your application or to start another application.

Registering intent receivers

Sending an intent doesn't make something happen automatically. You have to register an *intent receiver* that listens for the intent and then tells Android what to do — whether the task is starting a new activity or another app. If more than one receiver can accept a given intent, a chooser can be created to allow the user to choose which app to use to complete the activity — such as how the YouTube app allows the user to choose whether to watch videos in the YouTube app or in a browser.

Various registered receivers, such as the Gmail and the Messaging apps, handle image-sharing intents by default. When you find more than one possible intent receiver, a chooser opens with a list of options to choose from and asks what to do: Use e-mail, messaging, or another application, as shown in Figure 1-1.

Figure 1-1:
A chooser.

Follow best practice and create choosers for intents that don't target other activities within your application. If the Android system cannot find a match for an intent that was sent, and if a chooser wasn't created manually, the application crashes after experiencing a run-time exception — an unhandled error in the application. (Android expects developers to know what they're doing.)

Cursorless controls

Unlike the PC, where you manipulate the mouse to move the cursor, an Android device lets you use your fingers to do nearly anything you can do with a mouse. Rather than right-click in Android, however, you long-press an element until its context menu appears.

As a developer, you can create and manipulate context menus. You can allow users to use two fingers on an Android device, rather than a single mouse cursor, for example. Fingers come in all sizes, so design the user interface in your apps accordingly. Buttons should be large enough (and have sufficient spacing) so that even users with larger fingers can interact with your apps easily, whether they're using your app on a phone or tablet.

Views

A *view*, which is a basic element of the Android user interface, is a rectangular area of the screen that's responsible for drawing and event handling. Views are a basic building block of Android user interfaces, much like paragraph <p> or anchor <a> tags are building blocks of an HTML page. Some common views you might use in an Android application might be a `TextView`, `ImageView`, `Layout`, and `Button`, but there are dozens more out there for you to explore.

Many more views are ready for you to use. For complete details about views, check out the `android.widget` and `android.view` packages in the Android documentation at `http://developer.android.com/reference/android/widget/package-summary.html`.

Asynchronous calls

You use the `AsyncTask` class in Android to run multiple operations at the same time without having to manage a separate thread yourself. The `AsyncTask` class not only lets you start a new process without having to clean up after yourself but also returns the result to the activity that started it — creating a clean programming model for asynchronous processing. In general, we use loaders in this book rather than `AsyncTasks`, but it's useful to know about `AsyncTasks` for those occasional cases where a loader won't do what you want.

A *thread* is a process that runs separately from, but simultaneously with, everything else that's happening.

You use asynchronous processing for tasks that might take more than a small fraction of a second, such as network (Internet) communication; reading from, or writing to, storage; or media processing. When users have to wait for your task to complete, use an asynchronous call and an element in the user interface to notify them that something is happening.

Failing to use an asynchronous programming model can cause users of your application to believe that it's buggy. Downloading the latest Twitter messages via the Internet takes time, for example. If the network slows and you aren't using an asynchronous model, the application will lock up and the user will likely assume that something is wrong because the application isn't responding to her interaction. If the application fails to respond within a reasonable length of time (defined by the Android operating system), the user sees the Application Not Responding (ANR) dialog box, as shown in Figure 1-2. The user can then choose whether to close the application or wait for it to recover.

Figure 1-2: The ANR dialog box.

> ⚠ Sorry!
>
> Activity Hello, Android (in application Hello, Android) is not responding.
>
> | Force close | Wait |

To follow the best practice, run CPU-intensive or long-running code inside another thread, as described in the Designing for Responsiveness page on the Android developer site (http://developer.android.com/guide/practices/design/responsiveness.html).

Background services

If you're a Windows user, you may already know what a *service* is: an application that runs in the background and doesn't necessarily have a user interface. A classic example is an antivirus application that usually runs in the background as a service. Even though you don't see it, you know that it's running.

Most music players that can be downloaded from the Google Play Store, for example, run as background services. Users can then listen to music while checking e-mail or performing other tasks that require the use of the screen.

Honeycomb, Ice Cream Sandwich, and Jelly Bean Features

Android 3.0, nicknamed Honeycomb, introduced the world to the Android tablet. Honeycomb and its subsequent 3.1 and 3.2 releases brought about a number of changes to support this new device class. Android 4.0 Ice Cream Sandwich and 4.1 Jelly Bean refined the ideas introduced in Honeycomb for tablets and brought them to phones, allowing developers to use the same code to support both phones and tablets in a single code base.

The following sections introduce you to some of the features in these three versions (that will be covered throughout this book).

Fragments

Every "page" in an Android application is a separate activity. In older versions of Android, you would place any element that you wanted to display onscreen directly into the activity class. This arrangement worked well when viewed on a phone's small screen, on which you typically can't see a lot of information at once. You may be able to see a list of tasks, or a task that you're editing, but cramming both elements onto the screen at the same time is impossible.

On a tablet, however, you're swimming in real estate. Not only does it make sense to let users see a list of tasks and edit them on the same page, but it also looks silly not to let them do so. The screen size on a table is simply too big to fill with a single long list of items or lots of empty space.

Android doesn't allow you to easily put two activities on the screen at the same time. What to do? The answer is the fragment.

Using fragments, a single list fragment can occupy half the screen, and an edit fragment can occupy the other half. You can find out how to use fragments in your phone application in Chapter 9 and how to scale your app to tablets in Chapter 17.

You can think of fragments as miniature activities: Because every fragment has its own lifecycle, you know when it's being created and destroyed, among other information. Fragments go inside activities.

Loaders

A fragment is often used to display data to the user. For example, you might list some tasks by loading the list from the database. However, it's important to never perform I/O operations on the main user interface thread. If you perform a database operation in the main user interface thread, the user may see the (dreaded) Application Not Responsive dialog box, which is intrusive and confusing and often looks like a crash to many users.

A *loader* provides an easy way to load data on a background thread so that you don't delay the user interface (UI) thread and hang your app. You can find out more about loaders in Chapter 10.

Android support library

Fragments and loaders are effective ways to add usefulness to Android 3.x and 4.x applications. However, you may need to support older devices that use Android 1.x and 2.x, which don't support these new features.

Luckily, Android provides a solution. You can use the Android support library to make fragments and loaders compatible with devices all the way back to the Android Stone Age (circa 2009 A.D.).

In addition to supplying fragments and loaders, the support library adds several other excellent features to old devices, such as:

- **ViewPager:** Swipes pages left and right
- **GridLayout:** A new way to lay out views
- **ShareCompat:** For sharing activities with your friends

Visit `http://developer.android.com/tools/extras/support-library.html` to see the complete list of features in the Android support library.

Action bar

The Menu button is an important element in any application using Android 1.x or 2.x. All Android phones have (unlike another popular type of smartphone) the hardware Menu button, which can be used to access functions that aren't otherwise shown onscreen.

Or, rather, all Android phones *did* have this button. Beginning with Android 3.0, Android has dropped the Menu button. It still shows up on a few devices, such as on the Samsung Galaxy S III, but for the most part it's a relic of the past. Generally speaking, elements placed on the Android menu weren't easy to find, and users even tended to forget that they were there.

In place of the menu in devices using Android 3.x and later, the *action bar* is almost always present across the top of the screen — and it's therefore extremely difficult *not* to notice. See Figure 1-3 for an example of the action bar from the YouTube application.

Figure 1-3:
The
YouTube
action bar
for a funny
cat video.

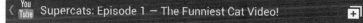

Check out these elements on the action bar:

- **Up Button, app logo:** Tap the Up button or the app logo on the action bar to move up one level.

  Note the subtle distinction between the Up button and the Back button: Pressing the Back button returns the user to the previous activity, regardless of which app is being used; pressing the Up button returns the user to the previous activity *in the current application*, even if that activity wasn't an activity the user was just performing.

  Suppose that you're viewing a web page in the Chrome browser and you tap a link to open the YouTube app. Pressing the Back button returns you to Chrome; pressing the Up button takes you to the YouTube app's home page.

- **Page:** Next to the application icon on the action bar is the title of the current page. If your application lets you filter data on the current page, you can add a drop-down menu there to allow users to change the filter.

- **Tab:** You can put tabs (rather than the page title) on the action bar to let users switch tabs in the current activity.

✔ **Action:** You can see, on the right end of the action bar, various actions that the user can perform. In the YouTube app shown in Figure 1-3, the user can add the video to a list, share the video, or search for more videos. Actions can take the form of text or icons (as shown in the figure) or both. You can add as many actions as you want. Actions that don't fit onscreen are placed on an overflow submenu on the right end.

✔ **Context action bar:** The action bar can change to show what the user is doing. For example, if a user chooses several items from a list, you can replace the standard action bar with a *contextual* action bar to let users choose actions based on those items. For example, if you want to allow bulk deletions, you can provide a Delete Items button on the contextual action bar.

Visit `http://developer.android.com/guide/topics/ui/actionbar.html` for more information about the versatility that this element of the user interface can add to your app.

The action bar doesn't exist at all on Android 2.x and earlier! It's not supported by the support library either. Any action bars you add to your application will not show up in these versions of Android. But don't dismay, the actions you put in your action bar will still show up under the Menu button for those devices, so users can still find them.

If you're interested in placing the action bar in an app running on an earlier version of Android (on an older phone or on the Kindle Fire, for example), try ActionBarSherlock at `http://actionbarsherlock.com`.

Holo

Android 3.0 adds three holographic themes to help you create beautiful Android applications:

✔ Holo Dark

✔ Holo Light

✔ Holo Light with dark action bars

These somewhat darker themes may require some getting used to, but they're much cleaner and more consistent than Android 2.x themes. The Holo themes are also visually less cluttered, which leaves more "real estate" for the important information you want your app to display.

The best quality of Holo is its consistency (at long last) across all Android devices and manufacturers — a manufacturer can't modify the Holo theme to make its version of Android look different.

Widgets, notifications, performance

The list of new features in Android 3.0, 4.0, and 4.1 seems endless. Here's a brief description of a few standouts:

- **Widgets:** Widgets are much improved in later versions of Android. They're easier to find, now that they've been moved to the Applications list. You can even add *list views* to widgets, to handle limited swiping and scrolling, and you can resize widgets to occupy more or less space. In fact, these user-friendly widgets automatically resize as they're dragged around the screen. These changes make them feel much more lively and responsive than in earlier versions.

- **Notifications:** Android 4.1 brings stylish new options to the formerly staid Android notification system. Because a notification is now expandable and collapsible, a user can see more information about it. For example, if your mother sends you a photo of her new puppy in a text message, you can see it directly in the notification without having to open the app. A notification about a new e-mail message can show a preview of the message text so that it can be read directly.

  In addition, a notification now also lets the user take action on it directly from whichever app is being used. To reply to a birthday e-mail from Grandma, for example, simply tap the Reply button on the notification to launch Gmail with an editor so that you can thank her.

- **Performance:** Android 4.1 brings significant performance improvements to the platform. You don't have to do anything special to benefit from a faster, smoother interface in your app — it will run smoothly on devices running Android 4.1 or later.

Hardware Tools

Google gives developers (even independent ones) the tools that are necessary to create top-notch, full-featured mobile apps. Google makes it simple to tap into, and make use of, all available hardware on a device.

To create a spectacular Android app, you should take advantage of all that the hardware has to offer. Don't get us wrong — if you have an idea for an app that needs no hardware assistance, that's okay, too.

Android devices come supplied with several hardware features that you can use to build apps. Table 1-1 describes the hardware features available on most Android devices.

Table 1-1	Android Device Hardware
Android Hardware Feature	*What It Does*
Accelerometer	Indicates whether the phone is moving
Bluetooth radio	Indicates whether a headset is connected
Built-in compass	Indicates in which direction the user is heading
Camera	Records video
GPS radio	Indicates the user's location
Proximity sensor	Indicates whether the device is facing up or down

Most Android devices are released with the hardware discussed in the following four sections, but not all devices are created equal. Android is free for hardware manufacturers to distribute, so it's used in a wide range of devices, including some made by small manufacturers overseas (and it isn't uncommon for some of these devices to be missing a feature or two).

Android devices come in all shapes and sizes: phones, tablets, and e-book readers. You will find many other implementations of Android in the future, such as Google TV (an Android-powered home appliance) as well as cars with built-in, Android-powered, touchscreen computers. The engineers behind Android provide tools that let you easily deploy apps on multiple screen sizes and resolutions. Don't worry — the Android team has done all the hard work for you. Chapter 4 covers the basics of screen sizes and densities.

Touchscreen

The Android touchscreen opens a ton of possibilities to enhance users' interaction with your apps. Users can swipe, flip, drag, or pinch to zoom, for example, by moving a finger on the touchscreen. You can even supply custom gestures in your app, which opens even more possibilities.

Android also supports *multitouch* capability, which lets a user touch the entire screen with more than one finger at a time.

Hardware buttons are old news. You can place buttons of any shape anywhere on the screen to create the user interface best suited for your app.

GPS

Combining the Android operating system with the GPS radio on a device lets the developer access, and track, a user's location at any time. The Foursquare social networking app is a good example — it uses the GPS feature to determine the user's location and then accesses the web to determine the closest venues to the user.

Another helpful example is the Maps application's ability to pinpoint a user's location on a map and provide directions to that person's destination. Combining Android with GPS hardware gives you access to the user's exact GPS location. Many apps use this combination to show users where the nearest gas station, coffeehouse, or even restroom is located.

Accelerometer

An *accelerometer* is a device that measures acceleration, and Android comes packed with accelerometer support. The accelerometer tells you whether a user's device is being moved or shaken, and even in which direction it's being turned. You can then use this information as a way to control your application.

You can use the accelerometer to perform simple tasks, such as determine when the device has been turned upside down and then complete an action. For example, you can immerse users in game play by having them shake their device to roll the dice. This level of usefulness is setting mobile devices apart from typical desktop personal computers.

SD card

Android gives you the tools you need to access (save and load) files on the device's *SD card* — a portable storage medium that you can insert into compatible phones, tablets, and computers. Starting with Android version 2.2 (Froyo), if a device is equipped with an SD card, you can use the card to store and access files that are needed by your application. To avoid bloating your app with extra required resources and hogging limited built-in memory, you can download some or all of your application's resources from your web host and save them to the device's SD card (which makes users less likely to uninstall your app when they need to clear space on their devices).

Not every device has an SD card preinstalled, though most do. Always ensure that a device has an SD card installed and that adequate space is available before trying to save files to it.

Software Tools

Various Android tools are at your disposal while you're writing Android applications. The following sections outline some of the most popular tools to use in your day-to-day Android development process.

Internet

Thanks to the Internet capabilities of Android devices, users can find real-time information on the Internet, such as the next showing of a new movie or the next arrival of a commuter train. As a developer, you can have your apps use the Internet to access real-time, up-to-date data, such as weather, news, and sports scores, or (like Pandora and YouTube) to store your application's icons and graphics.

You can even offload your application's more intense processes to a web server whenever appropriate, to save processing time or to streamline the app. In this well-established software architecture, known as *client–server computing*, the client uses the Internet to make a request to a server that's ready to perform some work for your app. The built-in Maps app is an example of a client that accesses map and GPS data from a web server.

Audio and video support

Including audio and video in your apps is a breeze in the Android operating system. Many standard audio and video formats are supported, and adding multimedia content to your apps — such as sound effects, instructional videos, background music, and streaming video and audio from the Internet — couldn't be easier. Be as creative as you want to be. The sky's the limit.

Contacts

Your app can access a user's Contacts list, which is stored on the device, to display the contact information in a new or different way or you can create your own Contacts list. You might even write an app that couples the contact information with the GPS system to alert the user whenever she's near a contact's address.

Don't use information from the Contacts list in a malicious way. Use your imagination, but be responsible about it. (See the next section "Security.")

Security

Suppose that someone releases an app that sends a user's entire Contacts list to a server for malicious purposes. For this reason, most functions that modify a user's Android device or access its protected content need specific *permissions*. For example, if you want to download an image from the web, you need permission to use the Internet so that you can download the file to your device, and you need a separate permission to save the image file to an SD card. When your app is being installed, the user is notified of the permissions your app is requesting and can decide whether to proceed. Though asking for permission isn't optional, it's as easy as implementing a single line of code in your application's manifest file. (Manifest files are described in Chapter 3.)

Google APIs

Users of the Android operating system aren't limited to making calls, organizing contacts, or installing apps. As a developer, you have great power at your fingertips — you can even integrate maps into your application, for example. To do so, you use the Maps APIs that contain map widgets.

Pinpointing locations on a map

Perhaps you want to write an app that displays a user's current location to friends. You can spend hundreds of hours developing a mapping system, or you can use the Android Maps API, which Google provides for use in your apps. You can embed the API in your application and you don't have to invest hundreds of development hours or even a single cent. Using the Maps API, you can find almost anything that has an address. The possibilities are endless — a friend's location, the nearest grocery store, or your favorite gas station, for example.

The KISS principle

The most difficult task in developing applications is remembering the KISS principle: Keep It Simple, Stupid. One way to unnecessarily complicate the code you create is to dive into development before understanding the role of the built-in APIs. Choosing this route may take more of your time than simply glossing over the Android documentation; you don't have to memorize the documentation, but do yourself a favor and at least skim it. Then you can see how easily you can use the built-in functionality — and how much time it can save you. You can easily write multiple lines of code to complete a one-line task. Changing the volume of the media player or creating a menu, for example, is a simple process, but if you don't know how to use the APIs, you may cause more problems by having to rewrite them.

Another way to muck things up is to add unnecessary functionality — give users the simplest way to operate their devices. For example, avoid designing a fancy, custom-tab layout when a couple of menu items will suffice. Also, Android comes supplied with enough widgets (built-in controls) to help you accomplish virtually any task. Using these controls makes your app even easier for users to work with because they already know and love them.

Showing your current location to friends is cool, but the Android Maps API can also access the Google Navigation API, to pinpoint your location and show your users how to reach it.

Messaging in the clouds

Suppose that your application's data is stored in the cloud (the Internet) and you download all its assets the first time it runs. And then you realize, after the fact, that an image is outdated. To update the image, the app needs to know that the image has changed. You can use the Google Cloud Messaging framework to send a cloud-to-device notification (a message from the web server to the device) to direct the app to update the image. This process works even if your app isn't running. When the device receives the message, it dispatches a message to start your app so that it can take the appropriate action.

Chapter 2

Prepping Your Development Headquarters

In This Chapter

▶ Becoming an Android application developer

▶ Collecting your tools of the trade

▶ Downloading and installing the Android software development kit

▶ Getting and configuring Eclipse

▶ Working with the Android development tools

All the software that you need to develop Android applications is *free*. That's where the beauty of developing Android applications lies. The basic building blocks you need to develop rich Android applications — the tools, the frameworks, and even the source code — are free. No one gives you a free computer, but you get to set up your development environment and start developing applications for free, and you can't beat free. Well, maybe you can — if someone pays you to write an Android application, but you'll reach that point soon enough.

This chapter walks you through the necessary steps to install the tools and frameworks so that you can start building kick-butt Android applications.

Developing the Android Developer Inside You

Becoming an Android developer isn't a complicated task. And it's likely simpler than you believe. To see what's involved, ask yourself these questions:

- ✔ Do I want to develop Android applications?
- ✔ Do I like free software development tools?
- ✔ Do I like to pay no developer fees?
- ✔ Do I have a computer to develop on?

If you answered yes to every question, today is your lucky day — you're ready to become an Android developer. You may be wondering what we mean by *pay no developer fees.* You're reading that question correctly: You pay no fees to develop Android applications.

There's always a catch, right? You can develop for free to your heart's content, but as soon as you want to publish your application to the Google Play Store, where you upload and publish your apps, you need to pay a small, nominal registration fee. At this writing, the fee is $25.

If you're developing an application for a client, you can publish your application as a redistributable package to give to him. Then your client can publish the application to the Google Play Store, using his Google account, to ensure that you don't have to pay a fee for client work. You can then be a bona fide Android developer and never have to pay a fee. That's *cool.*

Assembling Your Toolkit

After you know that you're ready to be an Android developer, grab your computer and get cracking on installing the tools and frameworks necessary to build your first blockbuster application.

Linux 2.6 kernel

Android was created on top of the open source Linux 2.6 kernel. The Android team chose to use this kernel because it provided proven core features on which to develop the Android operating system. The features of the Linux 2.6 kernel include (but aren't limited to)

- **Security model:** The Linux kernel handles security between the application and the system.

- **Memory management:** The kernel handles memory management, leaving you free to develop your app.

- **Process management:** The Linux kernel manages processes well, allocating resources to processes as they need them.

- **Network stack:** The Linux kernel also handles network communication.

- **Driver model:** The goal of Linux is to ensure that the application works. Hardware manufacturers can build their drivers into the Linux build.

You can see a good sampling of the Linux 2.6 feature set in Figure 2-1.

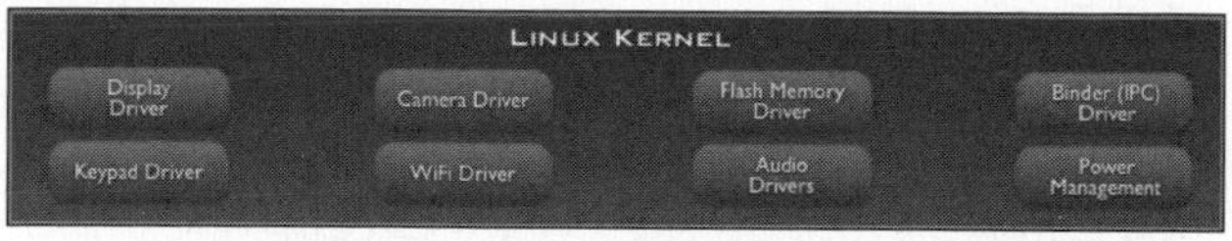

Figure 2-1:
Some Linux
kernel
features.

Android framework

Atop the Linux 2.6 kernel, the Android framework was developed with various features. These features were pulled from numerous open source projects. The output of these projects resulted in these elements:

- **The Android runtime:** The Android runtime is composed of Java core libraries and the Dalvik virtual machine.

- **Open GL (graphics library):** This cross-language, cross-platform application program interface (API) is used to produce 2D and 3D computer graphics.

- **WebKit:** This open source web browser engine provides the functionality to display web content and to simplify page loading.

- **SQLite:** This open source relational database engine is designed to be embedded in devices.

- **Media frameworks:** These libraries allow you to play and record audio and video.

- **Secure Sockets Layer (SSL):** These libraries are responsible for Internet security.

See Figure 2-2 for a list of common Android libraries.

Android source code

You should be aware that the full Android source code is open source, which means that it's not only free to use but also free to modify. If you want to download the Android source code and create a new version of Android, you're free to do so. Check the Android Open Source Project at http://source.android.com.

Figure 2-2:
Android
and other
third-party
libraries sit
atop the
Linux 2.6
kernel.

Application framework

If you've read the preceding section, you may say, "Well, that's all nice and well, but how do these libraries affect me as a developer?" It's simple: All these open source frameworks are available to you via Android. You don't have to worry about how Android interacts with SQLite and the surface manager; you use them as tools in your Android tool belt. The Android team has built on a known set of proven libraries, built in the background, and has given them to you, all exposed through Android interfaces. These interfaces wrapped up the various libraries and made them useful to the Android platform and to you as a developer. You benefit from these features because you don't have to build any of the functionality they provide:

- ✔ **Activity manager:** Manages the activity life cycle.
- ✔ **Telephony manager:** Provides access to telephony services as well as to certain subscriber information, such as phone numbers.
- ✔ **View system:** Handles the views and layouts that make up your user interface (UI).
- ✔ **Location manager:** Finds the device's geographic location.

Take a look at Figure 2-3 to see the libraries that make up the application framework.

Figure 2-3:
A glimpse
at part of
the Android
application
framework.

From kernel to application, the Android operating system has been developed with proven open source technologies. You, as a developer, can therefore build rich applications that have been fostered in the open source community. See Figure 2-4 for a full picture of how the Android application framework stacks up. The Applications section is where your application sits.

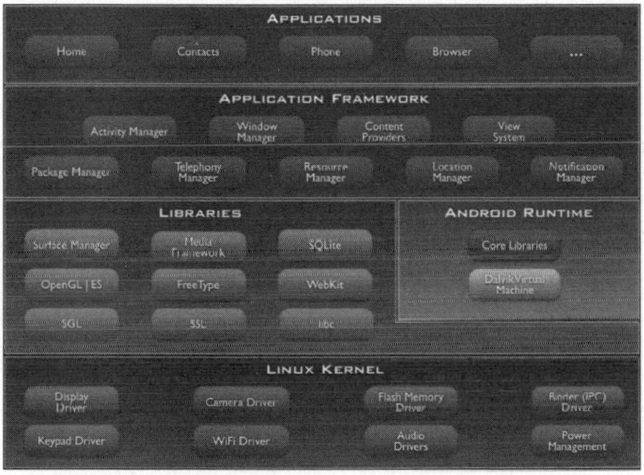

Figure 2-4:
How the
Android
application
framework
stacks up.

Sometimes when you're developing an Android application, you want to use the same resource as in the core Android system. A good example is an icon for a Settings menu option. By accessing the Android source code, you can browse the various resources and download the resources you need for your project. Having access to the source code also allows you to dig in and see exactly how Android does what it does. Be aware though that you need to follow Google's branding guidelines when borrowing these resources. Find out more at http://developer.android.com/distribute/googleplay/promote/brand.html.

Open Handset Alliance libraries

Huh? You didn't join an "alliance," so what's the Open Handset Alliance about? Don't worry — you don't have to use The Force to battle Darth Vader. It's not that big of a deal, and it's even kind of cool, like a bunch of smart companies combining their efforts to achieve the same goal.

The Open Handset Alliance (OHA) was announced in November 2007. At the time, the alliance consisted of 34 members, led by Google. With 84 members at the time this book was published, this group of technology and mobile companies (including T-Mobile, Sprint, LG, Motorola, HTC, NVidia, and Texas Instruments) have come together to pursue innovation in the mobile field and make the world a better place. Their goal is to provide users with comprehensive, compelling, and useful handsets. You can read more about the OHA at www.openhandsetalliance.com.

You should be aware of the OHA because all the libraries that comprise the Android operating system are based on open source code. Every member contributes in its own, special way. Chip manufacturers ensure that chipsets support the platform; hardware manufacturers build devices; and other companies contribute intellectual property (code and documentation, for example). The goal is to make Android a commercial success.

As these members contribute, they also start to innovate on the Android platform. Some of this innovation is incorporated into the Android source code, and some of it remains the intellectual property of the alliance members as decided by the OHA.

Just because one device has a fancy doohickey on it doesn't mean that another device will. The only thing you can count on as a developer is the core Android framework. OHA members may have added an extra library to help facilitate something on a device, but you have no guarantee that this library will be available on another device in, say, Turkey or England. An exception occurs if you're developing for a particular device, and only that device, such as an e-book reader. If that hardware has the sole function of reading books, you can program it for that specific purpose. Such as the Barnes & Noble Nook, which is powered by Android. It has special Forward and Back buttons that other Android devices don't have. Therefore, you'd program for these buttons because this device is a special case (if you're developing for the Nook), but you can't expect these buttons to be used on other devices.

Java knowledge

The Java programming language is one of the glorious tools that make programming Android a breeze compared with programming for other mobile platforms. Whereas other languages insist that you manage memory, deallocate and allocate bytes, and then shift bits around like a game of dominoes, Java's little buddy, the Java Virtual Machine (JVM), helps take care of that for you. The JVM allows you to focus on writing code to solve a business problem by using a clean, understandable programming language (or to build that next cool first-person shooter game you've been dreaming of) instead of focusing on the "plumbing" just to get the screens to show up.

You're expected to understand the basics of the Java programming language before you write your first Android application. If you're feeling rusty and need a refresher course on Java, you can visit the Java tutorials site at `http://docs.oracle.com/javase/tutorial`.

Though you find a little Java information in this book, you may want to spend some time with a good book like *Java All-in-One For Dummies,* by Doug Lowe (John Wiley & Sons, Inc.), if you have no Java experience.

Tuning Up Your Hardware

You can develop Android applications on various operating systems, including Windows, Linux, and Mac OS X. In this book, you find a combination of the Windows 7 operating system and Mac OS X, but you can use Linux as well.

Operating system

Android supports these platforms:

- ✔ Windows XP or later
- ✔ Mac OS X 10.5.8 or later (x86 only)
- ✔ Ubuntu Linux

Note that 64-bit Linux distributions must be capable of running 32-bit applications. Visit `http://developer.android.com/sdk/installing/index.html` for more details.

Throughout this book, some examples use Windows 7 64-bit Edition. Windows paths look similar to this:

```
c:\path\to\file.txt
```

Some examples use Mac OS X; a Mac or Linux path looks similar to this:

```
/path/to/file.txt
```

Computer hardware

Before you start installing the required software, make sure that your computer can run it adequately. Just about any desktop or laptop computer manufactured in the past four years will suffice. A laptop with a 1.6GHz Pentium D processor with 1GB of RAM running Windows XP and Windows 7 can run and debug Eclipse applications with no problem. (Eclipse — the software you use to develop your applications — should run smoothly on whatever computer you use.)

To ensure that you can install all the tools and frameworks you'll need, make sure that you have enough hard drive space to accommodate them. The Android developer site has a list of hardware requirements, outlining how much hard drive space each component requires, at `http://developer.` `android.com/sdk/requirements.html`.

To save you time, you need about 3GB of free hard drive space to install all the tools and frameworks necessary to develop Android applications.

Installing and Configuring Your Support Tools

It's time to put these exciting Android concepts into action, but before you can do so, you need to install and configure a few tools, including the software development kits (SDKs):

- ✔ **Java JDK:** Lays the foundation for the Android SDK.
- ✔ **Android SDK:** Provides access to Android libraries and allows you to develop for Android.
- ✔ **Eclipse IDE (integrated development environment):** Brings together Java, the Android SDK, and the Android Android Development Tools (ADT) and provides tools for you to write Android programs.
- ✔ **Android ADT:** Does a lot of the grunt work for you, such as creating the files and structure required for an Android app.

The following sections show you how to acquire and install all these tools.

A benefit of working with open source software is that, most of the time, you can get the tools to develop the software for free. Android is no exception to that rule. All the tools that you need to develop rich Android applications are free.

Getting the Java Development Kit

For some reason, the folks responsible for naming the Java SDK decided that it would be more appropriate to name it the Java Development Kit, or JDK.

The following steps work for Windows machines, but the steps are similar for Macs or Linux machines. Follow these steps to install the JDK:

1. **Go to** www.oracle.com/technetwork/java/javase/downloads/index.html.

   The Java SE downloads page appears. See Figure 2-5.

2. **Click the Download button for the Java Platform (JDK).**

   A new Java SE Downloads page appears, asking you to specify which platform (Windows, Linux, or Mac) you're using for your development work.

   The web page shown in Figure 2-5 may look different in the future. To ensure that you're visiting the correct page, visit the Android SDK System Requirements page in the online Android documentation for a direct link to the Java SDK download page. View the requirements page at http://developer.android.com/sdk/requirements.html.

Figure 2-5: Select JDK.

Click to download JDK.

3. **Click the Download link for the particular operating system you're using.**

   On Windows, choose the 32-bit install. If you're on a 64-bit machine, you can install both the 32-bit (x86) and 64-bit (x64) JDKs if you like, but you must install the 32-bit to develop with Android.

   Windows may open a message box with a security warning.

4. **In the Save As dialog box, select the location where you want to save the file, and click Save.**

5. **When the download is complete, double-click the file to install the JDK.**

   A dialog box asks whether you want to allow the program to make changes to your computer.

6. **Click the Yes button.**

   If you click the No button, the installation stops.

7. **When you're prompted to do so, read and accept the license agreement.**

That's all there is to it. You have the JDK installed and are ready to move to the next phase.

Acquiring the Android SDK

The Android SDK is composed of a debugger, Android libraries, a device emulator, documentation, sample code, and tutorials. You can't develop Android apps without the SDK.

Downloading the Android SDK

To download the Android SDK, follow these steps:

1. **Go to** `http://developer.android.com/sdk/index.html`.

2. **Choose the latest version of the SDK starter package for your platform to download the SDK.**

   You've just downloaded the Android SDK.

3. **Open SDK Manager.**

   - *Windows:* Run the SDK Installer and install the SDK to the default location. When finished, check the Start SDK Manager check box and click Finish. If you're prompted to accept the authenticity of the file, click Yes. The Android SDK Manager dialog box opens.

- *Mac:* Double-click the SDK file to unzip it. Move the resulting `android-sdk-mac_x86` directory to a safe place, such as your Applications directory. Open the Terminal and enter `cd` to go to the `android-sdk-mac_x86` directory, and then run `tools/android`. You may be prompted to install Java at this point if you don't already have it. If so, click Install.

4. **Select the SDK Platform Android 4.1 check box.**

   For the purposes of this book, select version 4.1, as shown in Figure 2-6. At this writing, 4.1 is the latest and greatest version of Android. You should also select the check boxes for the documentation and samples that correspond with Android version 4.1 (API 16).

   Every time a new version of the Android operating system is released, Google also releases an SDK that contains access to the added functionality in that version. If you want to include Bluetooth functionality in your app, for example, make sure that you have Android SDK version 2.0 or later because this functionality isn't available in earlier versions.

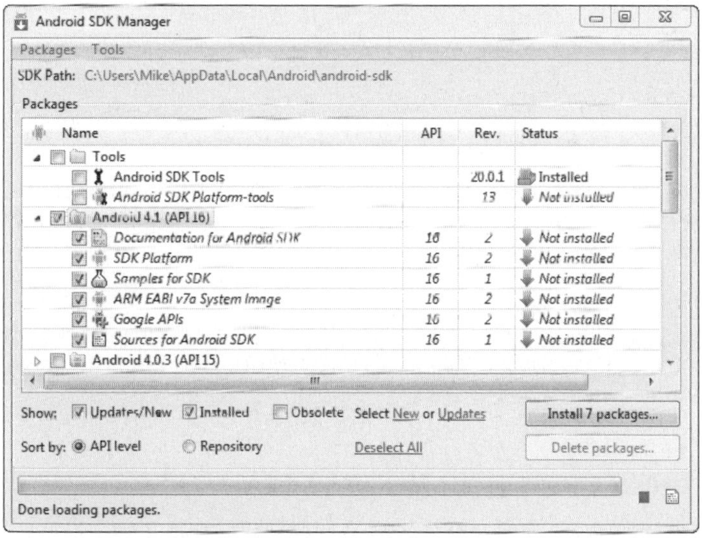

Figure 2-6: Choose packages to install.

5. **Click Install packages.**

   The Choose Packages to Install dialog box opens.

6. **Select the Accept radio button to accept the license, and then click Install, as shown in Figure 2-7.**

   The Installing Archives dialog box opens, displaying a progress bar.

7. **When the archives installation is complete, click the Close button.**

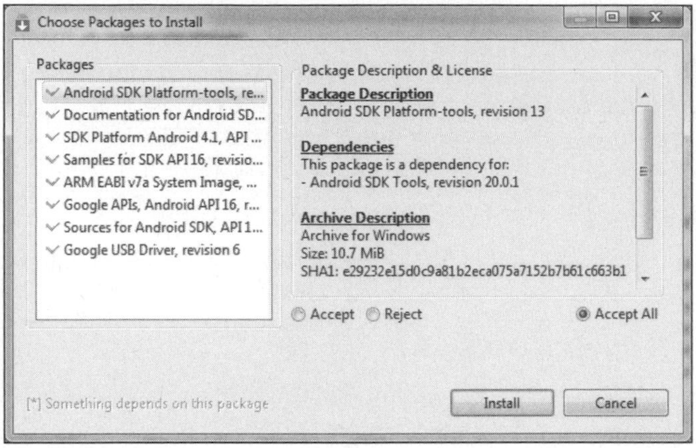

Figure 2-7:
The Choose
Packages to
Install
dialog box.

While the Android SDK is attempting to connect to the servers to obtain the files, you may occasionally see the `Failure to fetch URL` error. If this happens to you, navigate to Settings, select Force https://... Sources to Be Fetched Using http://, and then attempt to download the available packages again.

Following and setting your tools path

Setting the tools path is optional, but doing so saves you from having to remember and type the full path when you're accessing the Android Debug Bridge (adb) via the command line.

The adb lets you manage the state of an emulator or Android device so that you can debug your application or interact with the device at a high level. The adb tool has a lot of capabilities. For detailed information, see the Android documentation.

Adding the optional Android NDK

The set of tools known as the Android Native Development Kit (NDK) is a set of tools that allows lets you to embed components that use native code — code that you've written in a native language such as C or C++. Most developers won't ever need the NDK to build their apps.

If you decide to take on the NDK, you still have to download the SDK. The NDK isn't a replacement for the SDK. It's an added functionality set that complements the SDK.

To add the Android tools to your system-path variable on a Windows machine, follow these steps:

1. **Open Control Panel, and double-click the System icon to open System Preferences.**

2. **Click the Advanced System Settings link to open the System Properties window.**

3. **Click the Environment Variables button to open the Environment Variables dialog box.**

4. **Click the New button.**

   The New System Variable dialog box opens, as shown in Figure 2-8.

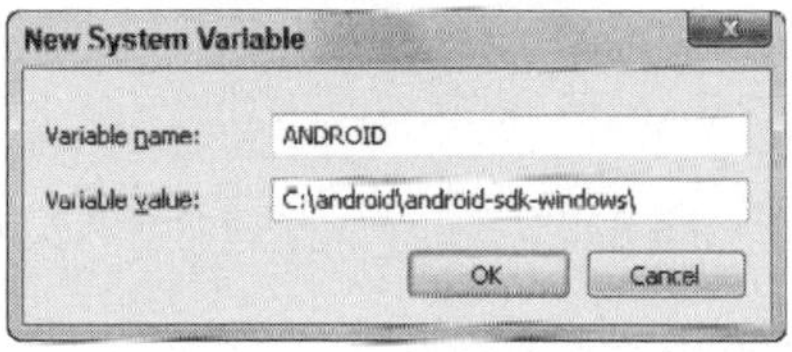

Figure 2-8:
The Environment Variables dialog box.

5. **In the Variable Name field, type** ANDROID.

6. **Type the full path to the SDK directory (**`c:\android\android-sdk-windows\`**) in the Variable Value field.**

7. **Click OK.**

   The Environment Variables dialog box opens, as shown in Figure 2-9.

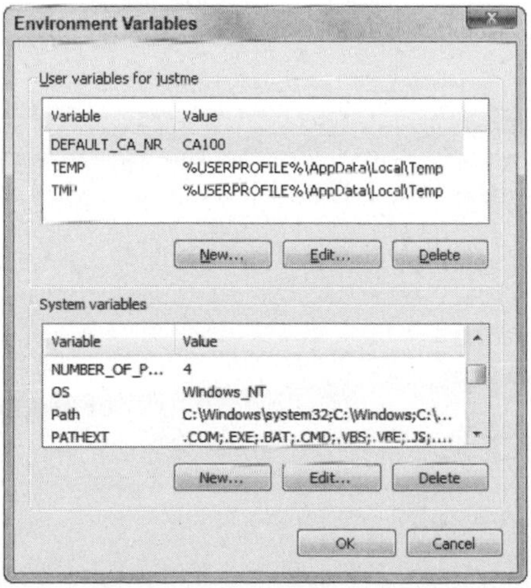

Figure 2-9:
Editing the PATH variable.

8. **In the System Variables section, select the PATH variable.**

9. **Click Edit and then type the following text at the end of the Variable Value field and click OK:**

```
;%ANDROID%/tools;%ANDROID%/platform-tools
```

If you're on a Mac, open the .profile file in your home directory (/Users/ *<your username>*) using TextEdit. If you can't see it, press ⌘+Shift+ period in the Open File dialog box to show hidden files. At the end of .profile, add the following:

```
export ANDROID=<full path to Android SDK, eg. /Applications/android-sdk-mac_x86>
export PATH=$PATH:$ANDROID/tools:$ANDROID/platform-tools
```

Then save the file and restart your Mac.

That's it — you're done. Now any time you access the Android tools directory, simply use your newly created environment variable.

In most operating systems, the system PATH variable won't be updated until you log out of and log back on to your operating system. If you find that your PATH variable values aren't present, try logging out of your computer and logging back on to your computer.

Getting the Total Eclipse

After you have the SDK, you need an integrated development environment (IDE) to use it. It's time to download Eclipse!

Installing Eclipse

To download Eclipse, navigate to the Eclipse downloads page at www. eclipse.org/downloads. Select Eclipse IDE for Java Developers (Eclipse IDE for JAVA EE Developers works as well) and download the zip file.

To install Eclipse, extract the contents of the Eclipse .zip file to the location of your choice, such as C:\Program Files\Eclipse on Windows or in your Applications folder on a Mac.

On Windows, once you unzip Eclipse, pin a shortcut to your Start menu instead so that Eclipse is easy to find when you need it.

To start Eclipse, follow these steps:

1. To run Eclipse, double-click the Eclipse icon.

If you're running a recent version of Windows, the first time you run Eclipse, a Security Warning dialog box may appear, as shown in Figure 2-10. It tells you that the publisher hasn't been verified and asks whether you still want to run the software. Clear the Always Ask Before Opening This File check box, and click the Run button.

Figure 2-10:
The
Windows
security
warning.

2. Set your workspace.

When Eclipse starts, the first thing you see is the Workspace Launcher dialog box, as shown in Figure 2-11. You can modify your workspace there, if you want, but for this book, you can stick with the default:

```
c:\users\<username>\workspace
```

on Windows, or

```
\Users\<username>\workspace
```

on a Mac

Leave the Use This As the Default and Do Not Ask Again check box deselected, and click the OK button.

If you plan to develop multiple applications, use a separate workspace for each project. If you store multiple projects in one workspace, maintaining organization becomes difficult, and you can easily change a similarly named file in a different project. Keeping projects in their own workspaces makes it easier to find the project when you have to go back to it to fix bugs.

When Eclipse finishes loading, you see the Eclipse welcome screen, shown in Figure 2-12.

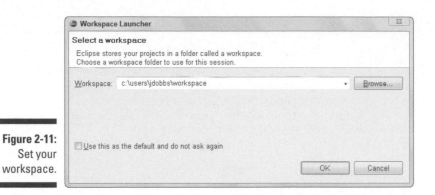

Figure 2-11:
Set your
workspace.

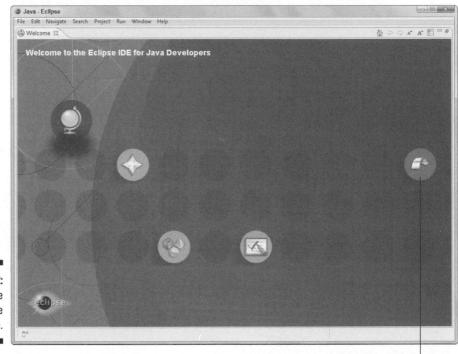

Figure 2-12:
The Eclipse
welcome
screen.

Click the arrow to go to the workbench.

3. **Click the curved-arrow icon on the right side of the screen to go to the workbench.**

   Eclipse is installed and easily accessible. You configure it in the next section.

Configuring Eclipse

The Android Development Tools (ADT) plug-in adds functionality to Eclipse to do a lot of the work for you. The ADT allows you to

- Create new Android projects easily.
- Start coding your application quickly because it creates all the necessary base files.
- Debug your application using the Android SDK tools.
- Export a signed application file, known as an Android Package (APK), right from Eclipse, eliminating the need for some command-line tools.

  Programmers used to need various command-line utilities to build an APK. Although that task wasn't difficult, it was tedious and sometimes frustrating. The ADT eliminates this frustrating process by guiding you through it "wizard style" from within Eclipse. Flip to Chapter 8 to export a signed APK.

Setting up Eclipse with the ADT

To set up Eclipse with the ADT, follow these steps:

1. **Start Eclipse, if it's not already running.**

2. **Choose Help⇨Install New Software.**

   The Install window opens. You use this window to install new plug-ins in Eclipse.

3. **Click the Add button to add a new site.**

   A *site* is a web address where software is hosted on the Internet. Adding a site to Eclipse makes it easier for you to update the software when a new version is released.

   The Add Repository window opens, as shown in Figure 2-13.

Figure 2-13: Enter the name and location of the site.

Add Repository	
Name: Android ADT	Local...
Location: https://dl-ssl.google.com/android/eclipse/	Archive...
?	OK Cancel

 4. **Type a name in the Name field.**

    This name can be anything you choose, but an easy one to remember is Android ADT.

 5. **Type** https://dl-ssl.google.com/android/eclipse/ **in the Location field.**

 6. **Click OK.**

    Android ADT is selected in the Work With drop-down menu, and the available options are displayed in the Name and Version window of the Install Details dialog box, as shown in Figure 2-14.

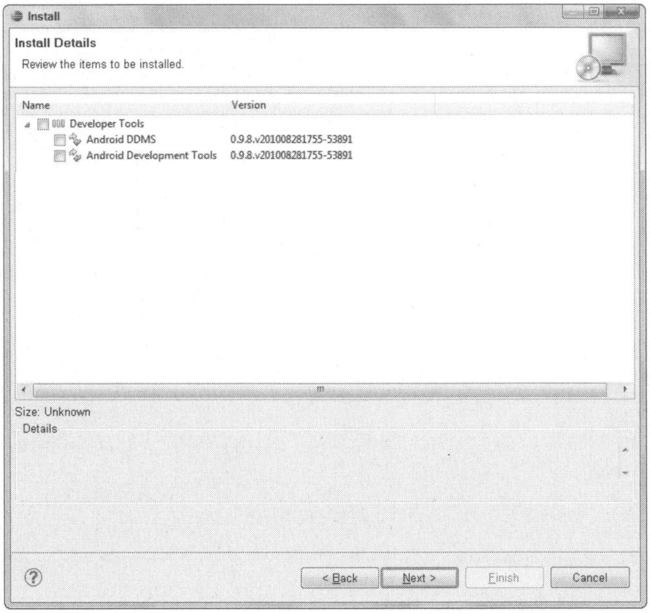

Figure 2-14:
Select
Developer
Tools.

 7. **Select the check box next to Developer Tools, and click the Next button.**

    The Install Details dialog box should list both the Android DDMS (see "Getting physical with a real Android device," later in this chapter) and the ADT. See Figure 2-15.

 8. **Click the Next button to review the software licenses.**

 9. **Click the Finish button.**

 10. **When you're prompted to do so, click the Restart Now button to restart Eclipse.**

    The ADT plug-in is installed.

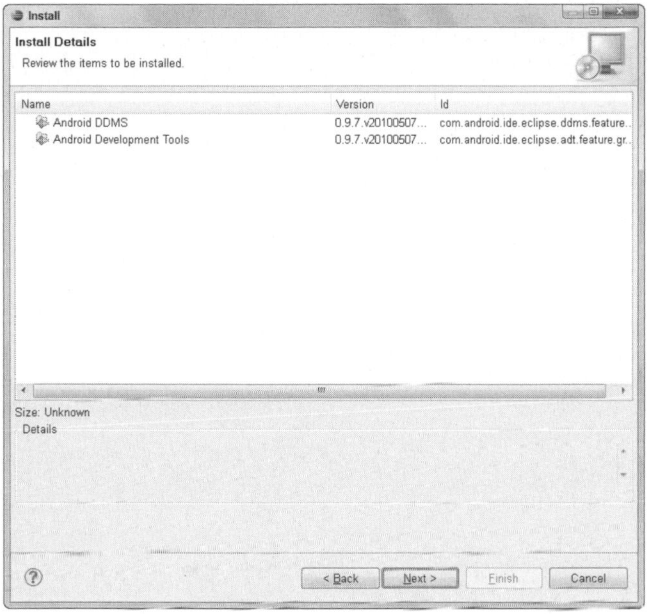

Figure 2-15:
DDMS and
ADT listed
in the Install
Details
dialog box.

If you're having difficulty downloading the tools from `https://dl-ssl.
google.com/android/eclipse`, **try removing the** s **from** `https://`, **like
this:** `http://dl-ssl.google.com/android/eclipse`.

Setting the location of the SDK

This section guides you through the configuration process. Completing it
seems like a lot to do, but you're almost done, and you have to do this work
only once. Follow these steps:

1. **Choose Window⇔Preferences.**

   The Preferences dialog box opens, as shown in Figure 2-16.

2. **Select Android in the left pane.**

3. **Set the SDK Location to the folder to which you saved the Android
   SDK.**

   If you saved Android SDK to `c:\android` on your computer, the location is `c:\android\android-sdk-windows`.

4. **Click OK.**

Eclipse is configured, and you're ready to start developing Android apps.

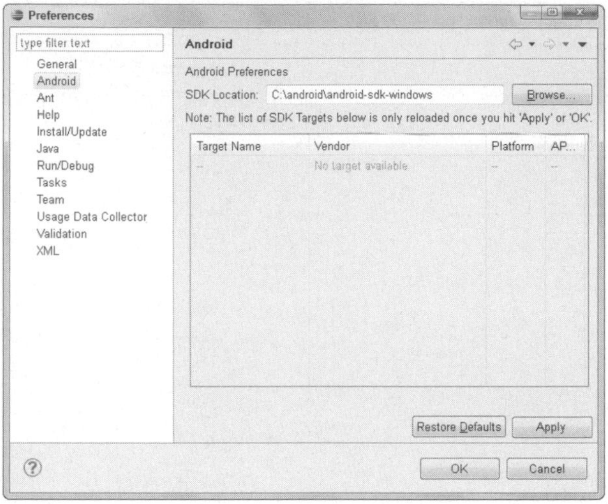

Figure 2-16:
Specify
the loca-
tion of the
SDK in the
Preferences
dialog box.

Navigating the Android SDK

Whoa — you find a lot of folders in the SDK! Don't worry: The folder structure of the Android SDK is easy to understand when you get the hang of it. You need to understand the structure of the SDK to be able to master it. Table 2-1 outlines the content of each folder.

Table 2-1	Folders in the Android SDK
SDK Folder	*What It Contains*
usb_driver	Drivers for Android devices. If you connect your Android device to the computer, install this driver so that you can view, debug, and push applications to your phone via the ADT.
	The usb_driver folder isn't visible until you install the USB driver.

SDK Folder	What It Contains
`tools` and `platform-tools`	Various tools that are available for use during development — such as for debugging, view management, and building.
`temp`	A temporary swapping location for the SDK when it needs a temporary space to perform work.
`samples`	Sample projects for you to play with. Full source code is included.
`platforms`	The platforms you target when you build Android applications, such as folders named `android-16` (which is Android 4.1) and `android-8` (which is Android 2.2).
`docs`	A local copy of the Android SDK documentation.
`add-ons`	Additional APIs that provide extra functionality. The Google APIs in this folder include mapping functionality. This folder remains empty until you install any of the Google Maps APIs.

Targeting Android Platforms

Android platform is a fancy way of saying *Android version*. At this writing, many versions of Android are available, ranging up through version 4.1. You can target any platform you choose.

Several versions of Android are still widely used on phones. If you want to reach the largest number of users, target an earlier version. If your app requires functionality that older platforms can't support, however, by all means target the newer platform. It would make no sense to write a Bluetooth toggle widget targeting any platform earlier than 2.0 because earlier platforms can't use Bluetooth.

Figure 2-17 shows the percentage of each platform in use as of May 2012. To view current platform statistics, visit `http://developer.android.com/resources/dashboard/platform-versions.html`.

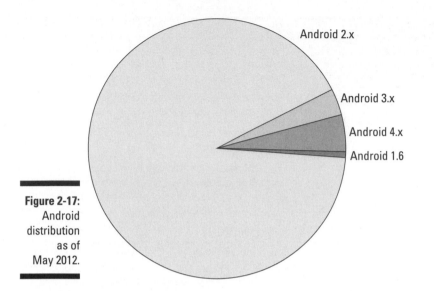

Android 2.x

Android 3.x

Android 4.x

Android 1.6

Figure 2-17:
Android
distribution
as of
May 2012.

Using SDK Tools for Everyday Development

The SDK tools are the building blocks you use in developing Android apps. New features packed into every release enable you to develop for the latest version of Android.

Saying hello to the emulator

Google provides not only the tools you need to develop apps but also an awesome little emulator to test your app. The emulator has some limitations (for example, it cannot emulate certain hardware components, such as the accelerometer) but not to worry — plenty of apps can be developed and tested using only an emulator.

When you're developing an app that uses Bluetooth, for example, you should use a physical device that has Bluetooth on it. If you develop on a speedy computer, testing on an emulator is fast; on slower machines, however, the emulator can take a long time to complete a seemingly simple task. If you're developing on an older machine, use a physical device. When you're developing on a newer, faster machine, use the emulator.

The emulator is handy for testing apps at different screen sizes and resolutions. It isn't always practical or possible to have several devices connected to your computer at the same time, but you can run multiple emulators with varying screen sizes and resolutions.

Getting physical with a real Android device

The emulator is awesome, but sometimes you need a physical device for testing. The Dalvik Debug Monitor Server, or DDMS, allows you to debug your app on an actual device, which comes in handy for developing apps that use hardware features that aren't, or can't be, emulated. Suppose that you're developing an app that tracks the user's location. You can send coordinates to the device manually, but at some point in your development, you probably want to test the app to find out whether it, in fact, displays the correct location. Using an actual device is the only way to do it.

If you develop on a Windows machine and you want to test your app on a real-life device, you need to install a driver. If you're on a Mac or Linux machine, you can skip this section because you don't need to install the USB driver.

To download the Windows USB driver for Android devices, follow these steps:

1. **In Eclipse, choose Window⇨Android SDK Manager.**

   The Android SDK Manager dialog box opens, as shown in Figure 2-18.

2. **Expand the Extras repository, and select the Google USB Driver package.**

3. **Click the Install Packages button.**

   The Choose Packages to Install dialog box opens, as shown in Figure 2-19.

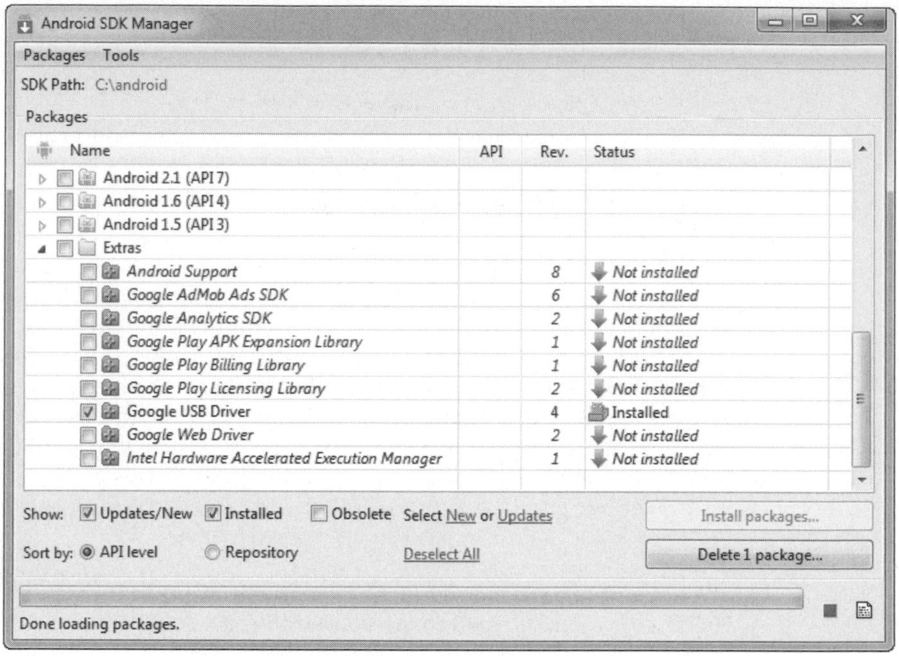

Figure 2-18:
Available
packages.

4. **Select the Accept radio button to accept the license, and then click the Install button.**

   The Installing Archives dialog box opens, displaying a progress bar.

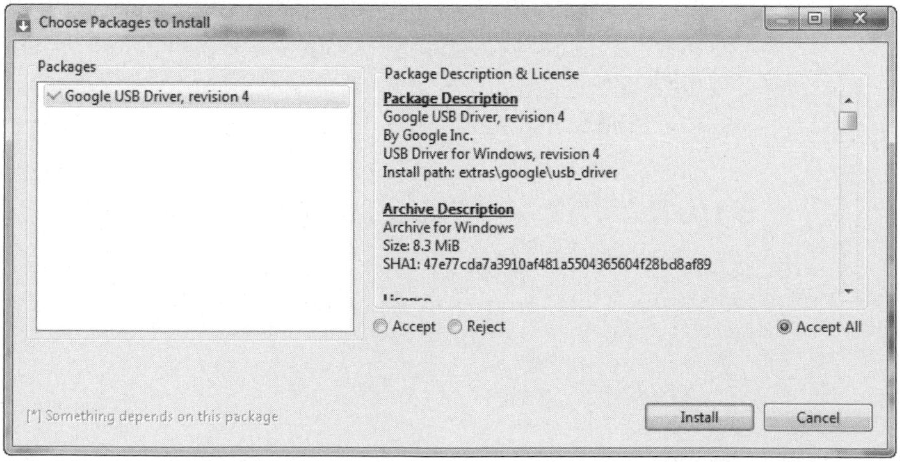

Figure 2-19:
Click the
Install
button.

5. When the package finishes downloading and installing, click the Close button.

6. Exit the Android SDK Manager dialog box.

Debugging your work

The DDMS equips you with the necessary tools to find those pesky bugs, allowing you to go behind the scenes as your app is running to see the state of its hardware, such as the wireless radio. But wait — there's more! The DDMS also simulates actions normally reserved for physical devices, such as sending global positioning system (GPS) coordinates manually, simulating phone calls, or simulating text messages. Get all the DDMS details at `http://developer.android.com/guide/developing/debugging/ddms.html`.

Trying out the API and SDK samples

The API and SDK samples are provided to demonstrate how to use the functionality provided by the API and SDK. If you're ever stuck and can't figure out how to make something work, visit `http://developer.android.com/resources/samples/index.html` to find samples of almost *anything*, from using Bluetooth to making a two-way text application or a 2D game.

You also have a few samples in your Android SDK. Simply open the Android SDK and navigate to the `samples` directory, which contains various samples that range from interacting with services to manipulating local databases. Spend some time playing with the samples — the best way to learn to develop Android applications is to look at existing working code bases and then experiment with them in Eclipse.

Giving the API demos a spin

The API demos inside the `samples` folder in the SDK are a collection of apps that demonstrate how to use the included APIs. You can find sample apps with a ton of examples, such as

✔ Notifications

✔ Alarms

✔ Intents

✔ Menus

✔ Search

✔ Preferences

✔ Background services

If you get stuck or you simply want to prepare yourself for writing your next spectacular Android application, check out the complete details at `http://developer.android.com/resources/samples/ApiDemos/index.html`.

Part II

Building and Publishing Your First Android Application

The 5th Wave   By Rich Tennant

"Stop working on the Priority Parking Spot Allocation program. They want to fast track the Coffee Pot/Cubicle Proximity program."

In this part . . .

Part II walks you through developing a useful Android application. You start with the basics of the Android tools and then delve into developing the screens and home-screen widgets that users will interact with. When the application is complete, you sign your application digitally so that you can deploy it to the Google Play Store. You finish by publishing your application to the Google Play Store.

Chapter 3

Your First Android Project

*B*efore you start creating that next blockbuster Android application, we walk you through creating your first Android application to help solidify a few key aspects in the Android project-creation process. In this chapter, you create a simple "Hello Android" application that requires no coding whatsoever. What — no coding? How is that possible? Follow along as we show you.

Starting a New Project in Eclipse

First things first: Start Eclipse. You should see a screen that looks similar to the one shown in Figure 3-1. Now you're ready to start cooking with Android.

If you haven't set up your development environment yet, turn to Chapter 2. It shows you how to set up all the tools and frameworks necessary to develop Android applications and, in the process, install the Eclipse Android Development Tools (ADT) plug-in. It gives you the power to generate new Android applications directly from within the Eclipse File menu.

Figure 3-1:
The Eclipse
develop-
ment
environment.

Follow these steps to create your first Android application project:

1. **In Eclipse, choose File⇨New⇨Other. Select Android Application Project.**

   The New Android App Wizard opens, as shown in Figure 3-2.

2. **Enter** Hello Android **as the application name.**

   The application name is the name of the application as it pertains to Android. When the application is installed on the emulator or physical device, this name appears in the application launcher.

   The Project and Package names should autocomplete for you. The Project Name field is important. The descriptive name you provide identifies your project in the Eclipse workspace. After your project is created, a folder in the workspace is named with the project name you define.

   When you set up Eclipse in Chapter 2, the Eclipse system asks you to set your default workspace. The workspace usually defaults to your *home directory,* where the system places files pertinent to you and where you can find your home directory listed in the Location field.

   If you would rather store your files in a location other than the default workspace location, deselect the Create Project in Workspace check box, which enables the Location text box. Click the Browse button, and select a location where you want your files to be stored.

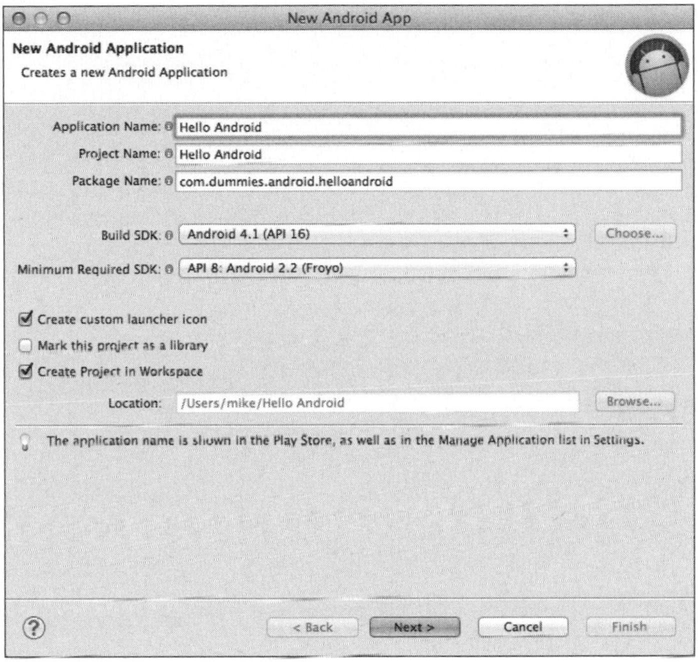

Figure 3-2:
The New
Android App
Wizard.

3. In the Package Name box, type com.dummies.android.helloandroid.

This is the name of the Java package. (See the nearby sidebar "Java package nomenclature.")

Java package nomenclature

A *package* in Java is a way to organize Java classes into namespaces similar to modules. Each package must have a unique name for the classes it contains. Classes in the same package can access one another's package-access members.

Java packages have a naming convention defined as the hierarchical naming pattern. Each level of the hierarchy is separated by periods. A package name starts with the highest-level domain name of the organization; then the subdomains are listed in reverse order. At the end of the package name, the company can choose what it wants to call the package. The package

name `com.dummies.android.hello android` is the name used in this example.

Notice that the highest-level domain is at the front of the package name (`com`). Subsequent subdomains are separated by periods. The package name traverses through the subdomains to get to the final package name of `helloandroid`.

A great example of another use for a package is having a Java package for all your web-related communications. Any time you needed to find a web-related Java class, you can open that Java package and work on your web-related Java classes. Packages allow you to keep your code organized.

Understanding Android versioning

Version codes aren't the same as version names. (Huh?) Android has version names and version codes. Each version name has a single version code associated with it. The following table outlines the version names and their respective version code. You can also find this information in the Build Target section of the New Android Project dialog box.

Version Name (Platform Level)	Version Code (API Level)
2.0	5
2.0.1	6
2.1	7
2.2	8
2.3.0–2.3.2	9
2.3.3 - 2.3.4	10
3.0	11
3.1	12
3.2	13
4.0.0 - 4.0.2	14
4.0.3	15
4.1	16

4. **Select Android 4.1 from the Build SDK drop-down list and API 8: Android 2.2 from the Minimum Required SDK drop-down list, and then click Next.**

The Build SDK drop-down list identifies which application programming interface (API) you want to develop for this project. Always set the Build Target SDK to the latest version that you've tested your app on. When you select Android 4.1, you build and test your app on devices going up to Android 4.1. Doing so allows you to develop with the Android 4.1 APIs, which include new features such as Android Beam. If you had selected Android 2.2 as the target, you wouldn't be able to use any features supported by version 4.1 (or 3.1).

Setting the Minimum Required SDK version lower than the Build Target SDK means that your app still runs on older devices, all the way down to Android 2.2 in this case.

When you set the build target and minimum required SDKs to different values, you can't use any APIs newer than the minimum required SDK on old devices. For example, you can't use Android Beam on an Android 2.2 device; the app will crash.

For more information, see the section "Understanding the Build Target and Min SDK Version settings," later in this chapter.

The Android Application Icon Editor appears.

5. **(Optional) Create an application icon for your project and click Next.**

6. **In the Create Activity box, choose BlankActivity and click Next.**

The New Blank Activity screen appears, as shown in Figure 3-3.

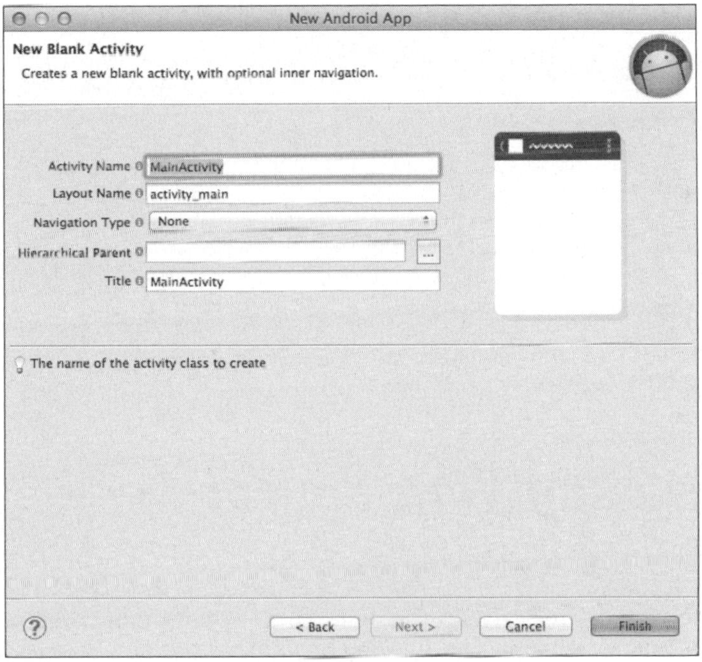

Figure 3-3: Set up your new activity.

7. **Enter** MainActivity **in the Activity Name box.**

The New Blank Activity screen defines what the initial activity is called — the entry point to your application. When Android runs your application, this file is the first one to be accessed. A common naming pattern for the first activity in your application is `MainActivity.java`. (How creative.)

8. **Click the Finish button.**

You're done! You should see Eclipse with a single project in the Package Explorer. For the purpose of this book, Package Explorer and Project Explorer (which is showing in Figure 3-4) are the same thing. Different names; same function.

Deconstructing Your Project

The Android project generated by Eclipse is a fresh, clean project with no compiled binary sources. Sometimes, Eclipse takes a second to catch up to you, so you may notice minor oddities about the system. You also need to understand what happens under the hood of Eclipse at a high level. That's what you find in the next couple of sections.

Responding to error messages

If you were quick enough to look (or if your computer runs on the slower edge of the spectrum), you may have noticed, immediately after you clicked the Finish button, a little red icon hovering over the Hello Android folder icon in the Package Explorer in your Eclipse window. (See Figure 3-5.) That icon is Eclipse's way of letting you know that something is wrong with the project in the workspace.

Figure 3-5:
A project
with errors
in Eclipse.

Package Explo ⋈	Hierarchy	Navigator

Hello Android

A project with errors in Eclipse

By default, Eclipse is set up to let you know with this visual cue when an error is found within a project. How can you have an error with this project? You just created the project using the New Android Project Wizard — what gives? Behind the scenes, Eclipse and the Android Development Tools do a few things for you:

- **Provide workspace feedback:** This feedback lets you know when a problem exists with any project in the workspace. You receive notification in Eclipse via icon overlays, such as the one shown in Figure 3-5. Another icon overlay you may see often is a small yellow warning icon, which alerts you to some warnings in the contents of the project.

- **Automatically compile:** By default, Eclipse autocompiles the applications in your workspace when any files within them are saved after a change.

If you don't want automatic recompilation turned on, you can turn it off by choosing Project⇒Build Automatically. This command disables the automatic building of the project. If this option is deselected, build your project manually by pressing Ctrl+B every time you change your source code.

So why are you getting an error in the first build? When the project was added to your workspace, Eclipse took over and, in conjunction with the ADT, determined that the project in the workspace had an error. The issue that raised the error in Eclipse was that neither the gen folder nor its contents were present. (See the section "Understanding Project Structure," later in this chapter, for information about the gen folder.)

The gen folder is automatically generated by Eclipse and the ADT when the compilation takes place. The process works like this:

1. As soon as the New Android Project Wizard finishes, Eclipse creates and saves the new project in its workspace.

2. Eclipse sees the new project and says, "Hey! I see some new files in my workspace. I need to report any errors I find and compile the project."

3. Eclipse reports the errors by placing an error icon over the folder. (Refer to Figure 3-5.)

4. Eclipse compiles the project.

   During the compilation step, the gen folder is created by Eclipse, and the project is successfully built.

5. Eclipse recognizes that the project has no more errors and removes the error icon from the folder.

   You're left with a clean workspace and a clean folder icon, as shown in Figure 3-6.

Figure 3-6:
A project in
the Package
Explorer
that has no
errors.

A project without any errors

Understanding the Build Target and Min SDK Version settings

The *build target* is the operating system in which you write code. If you choose 4.1, you can write code with all the APIs in version 4.1. If you choose 2.2, you can write code only with the APIs that are in version 2.2. You can't use the Wi-Fi Direct APIs in version 2.2, for example, because they weren't introduced until version 4.0. If you're targeting 4.1, you can write with the Wi-Fi Direct APIs.

Know which version you want to target before you start writing your Android application. Identify which Android features you need to use to ensure that your app functions as you expect. If you're positive that you need Bluetooth support, target at least version 2.0. If you're not sure which versions support the features you're looking for, you can find that information on the platform-specific pages in the SDK section of http://d.android.com. The Android 4.1 platform page is at http://d.android.com/sdk/android-4.1.html.

Android operating system (OS) versions are backward-compatible. If you target Android version 2.2, for example, your application can run on Android 4.x, 3.x, and of course 2.2. The benefit of targeting the 2.2 framework is that your application is exposed to a much larger market share. Your app can be installed on devices with version 2.2, 3.0, or 4.0 (and on future versions, assuming that no breaking framework changes are introduced in future Android OS releases). Selecting an older version isn't free of consequences, however. By targeting an older framework, you're limiting the functionality you have access to. By targeting 2.2, for example, you don't have access to the social media APIs.

Version codes and compatibility

The Min SDK Version is also used by the Google Play Store (covered in detail in Chapter 8) to help identify which applications to show users based on which version of Android they're running. If a user's device is running version code 8 (Android 2.2), you want your app to show up if it's compatible with version code 3, not with version code 16 (Android 4.1) apps. The Google Play Store manages which apps to show to each user via the Min SDK Version setting.

If you're having trouble deciding which version to target, the current version distribution chart can help you decide: `http://developer. android.com/about/dashboards`.

A good rule is to analyze the distribution chart to determine which version will give your app the best market share. The more devices you can target, the wider your audience; the more installs you have, the more successful your app.

The Min SDK Version setting is the minimum version of Android that the user must be running for the application to run properly on the device. This field isn't required to build an app, but if you don't indicate the Min SDK Version, a default value of 1 is used, indicating that your application is compatible with all versions of Android.

If your application is *not* compatible with all versions of Android (for example, if it uses APIs that were introduced in version code 5 — Android 2.0) and you haven't declared the Min SDK Version, when your app is installed on a system with an SDK version code of less than 5, your application will crash at runtime when it attempts to access the unavailable APIs. As a best practice, always set the Min SDK Version in your application to prevent these types of crashes.

Setting Up an Emulator

You're almost ready to run your application in Eclipse. You have one final thing to set up, and then you get to see all your setup work come to life in the Hello Android application. To see this application in a running state, you need to know how to set up an emulator through the various launch configurations.

You need to create an Android Virtual Device (AVD), also known as an emulator. An AVD is a virtual Android device that looks, acts, walks, and talks (well, maybe not walks and talks) like a physical Android device. AVDs can be configured to run any particular version of Android as long as the SDK for that version is downloaded and installed.

It's time to get reacquainted with the old standbys Android SDK and AVD Manager. Follow these steps to create your first AVD:

1. **Click the icon on the Eclipse toolbar, shown in Figure 3-7.**

   The AVD Manager dialog box opens.

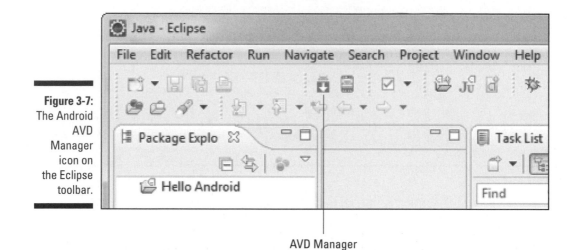

Figure 3-7: The Android AVD Manager icon on the Eclipse toolbar.

AVD Manager

AVD nomenclature

Be careful when naming AVDs. Android is available on many devices in the real world, such as phones, e-book readers, and netbooks. The time will come when you have to test your app on various configurations; therefore, adhering to a common nomenclature when creating AVDs can later help you recognize which AVD is intended for what purpose. The following line can help you remember the purpose of an AVD:

    {TARGET_VERSION}_{SKIN}_{SCREENSIZE}[{_Options}]

The AVD

    4_1_Default_WVGA

has the `TARGET_VERSION` value of Android 4.1. The version name 4.1 is transformed into `4_1`. The underscores are used in place of periods to keep the name of the AVD combined. Creating an AVD name as a single combined word helps when you're working in advanced scenarios with AVDs via the command line.

`SKIN` is the name of the skin of the emulator. Emulators can have various skins that make them look like actual devices. The default skin is provided by the Android SDK.

The `SCREENSIZE` value is the size of the screen with regard to the Video Graphics Array (VGA) size. The default is WVGA800. Other options are QVGA and HVGA.

2. **Click the New button.**

   The Create New Android Virtual Device (AVD) dialog box opens, as shown in Figure 3-8.

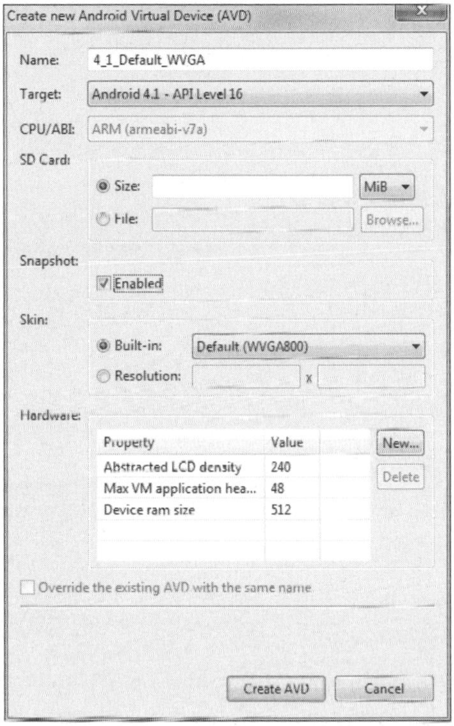

Figure 3-8:
The Create
New
Android
Virtual
Device
(AVD)
dialog box.

3. **For this AVD, in the Name field, type** 4_1_Default_WVGA.

   For more information on naming your AVDs, see the nearby sidebar "AVD nomenclature."

4. **In the Target box, select Android 4.1 — API Level 16.**

5. **In the SD Card section, leave the fields blank.**

   You have no use for an SD Card in the Hello Android application. You would use the SD Card option if you needed to save data to the SD card. If you want to have an emulator in the future, insert the size of the SD card in megabytes (MB) that you want to have created for you. At that time, an emulated SD Card will be created and dropped in your local file system.

6. **Leave the Skin option set to Default (WVGA800).**

7. **Don't select new features in the Hardware section.**

   The Hardware section outlines the hardware features your AVD should emulate. You don't need extra hardware configuration for the Hello Android application.

8. **Click the Create AVD button.**

   Figure 3-9 shows the completed AVD Manager dialog box.

Figure 3-9:
The recently created AVD in the Android SDK and AVD Manager dialog box.

9. **Close the Android SDK and AVD Manager dialog box.**

You may see this error message after you create your AVD:

```
Android requires .class compatibility set to 5.0. Please
        fix project properties
```

If so, you can fix it by right-clicking the project in Eclipse and choosing Android Tools⇨Fix Project Properties from the context menu.

Creating Launch Configurations

You're almost at the point where you can run the application. A *run configuration* specifies the project to run, the activity to start, and the emulator or device to connect to. Whoa! That's a lot of stuff happening quickly. Not to worry — the ADT can help you by automating many key steps so that you can get up and running quickly.

The Android ADT gives you two options for creating launch configurations:

- ✔ **Run configuration:** You need to run your application on a given device. You'll use run configurations most of the time during your Android development career.

- ✔ **Debug configuration:** You're debugging your application while it's running on a given device. You can find out how to debug in Chapter 5.

When you first run a project as an Android application by choosing Run⇨Run, the ADT automatically creates a run configuration for you. The Android Application option is visible when you choose Run⇨Run. After the run configuration is created, it's the default run configuration, now used every time you choose Run⇨Run.

If you're feeling ambitious and decide that you want to create a run configuration manually, follow along here. Don't worry — following these steps is simple:

1. Choose Run⇨Run Configurations.

The Run Configurations dialog box opens, as shown in Figure 3-10. In this dialog box, you can create many types of run configurations. The left side of the dialog box lists many types of configurations, but focus on these:

- • Android Application

- • Android JUnit Test

2. Select the Android Application item, and click the New Launch Configuration icon.

Or right-click Android Application and choose New from the context menu.

The New Launch Configuration window opens.

3. Type ExampleConfiguration **in the Name field.**

If you want to start from an existing launch configuration, right-click it, and choose Duplicate from the context menu. Change the name of the run configuration by entering a name in the Name field. You can then change various settings to give the launch configuration a unique configuration.

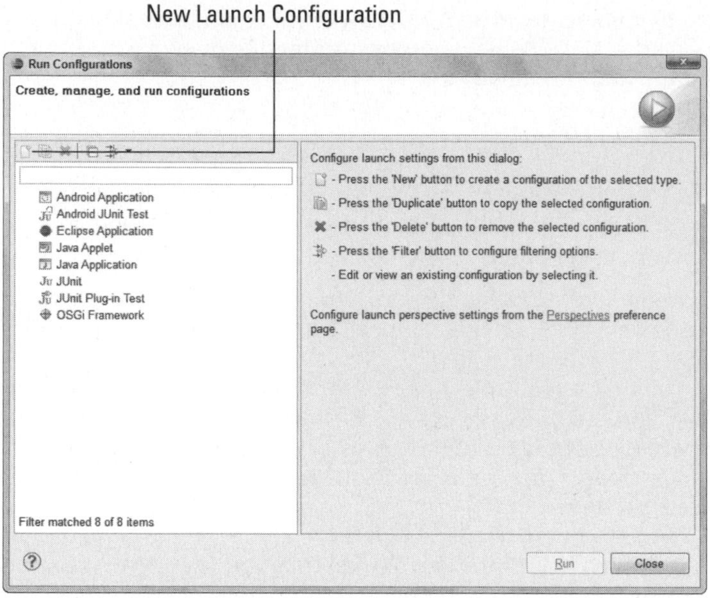

New Launch Configuration

Figure 3-10:
The Run
Config-
urations dia-
log box.

4. **On the Android tab, click the Browse button to select the project you're creating this launch configuration for.**

The Project Selection dialog box opens, as shown in Figure 3-11.

Figure 3-11:
Selecting
the project
for the new
launch con-
figuration.

5. **Select Hello Android and click OK.**

   The Run Configurations dialog box reopens.

6. **On the Android tab, leave the Launch Action option set to Launch Default Activity.**

   In this case, the default activity is `MainActivity`, which you set up in "Starting a New Project in Eclipse," earlier in this chapter.

7. **On the Target tab, shown in Figure 3-12, leave Automatic selected.**

   Notice that an AVD is listed in the Select a Preferred Android Virtual Device for Deployment section.

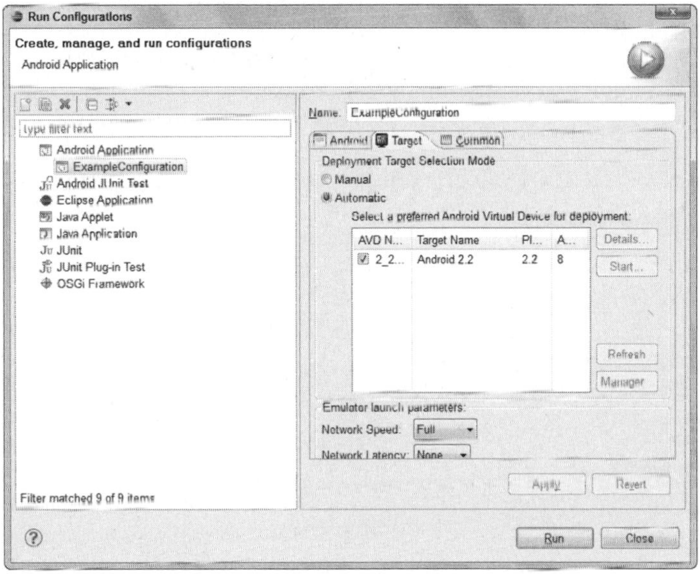

Figure 3-12:
A new, manually created launch configuration.

8. **Select the 4_1_Default_WVGA device.**

   This device is the AVD you created earlier. By selecting it, you're instructing this launch configuration to launch this AVD when a user runs the app by choosing Run➪Run. This view has both manual and automatic options. The manual option lets you choose which device to connect to when using this launch configuration. Automatic sets a pre-defined AVD to use when launching in the current launch configuration.

9. **Leave the rest of the settings alone, and click the Apply button.**

When you have no need for a launch configuration, select it in the left panel and click the Delete button on the toolbar, or right-click it and choose Delete from the context menu.

Running the Hello Android App

Understanding the basics of how to get an Android application up and running is a simple yet detailed process. You're now ready to see your hard work in action. You've created a launch configuration and Android Virtual Device; now it's time to get the application running. Finally!

Running the app in the emulator

Running the application is simple. Upon your instruction, the ADT launches an emulator with the default launch configuration you build earlier in this chapter. Starting your application is as simple as choosing Run⇨Run or pressing Ctrl+F11. Either action launches the application in an emulator using the default launch configuration — in this case, ExampleConfiguration. The ADT compiles your application and then deploys it to the emulator.

If you didn't create a launch configuration, you see the Run As dialog box, shown in Figure 3-13. Choose Android Application, and a launch configuration is created for you.

Figure 3-13:
The Run As
dialog box
appears
when a
launch con-
figuration
isn't set up.

If you created the ExampleConfiguration, you see the emulator loading, as shown in Figure 3-14.

Port number

AVD name

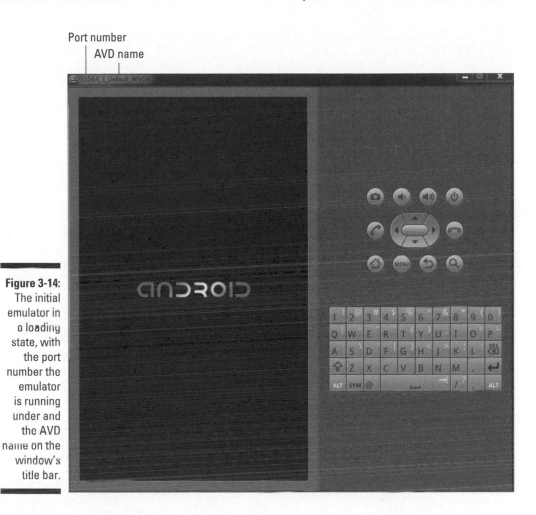

Figure 3-14:
The initial
emulator in
a loading
state, with
the port
number the
emulator
is running
under and
the AVD
name on the
window's
title bar.

Help! If your emulator never loads and stays stuck on the ANDROID screen(s), there's no need to worry, comrade. The first time the emulator starts, the emulator can take upward of ten minutes to finish loading, because you're running a virtual Linux system in the emulator. The emulator has to boot up and initialize. The slower your computer, the slower the emulator is in its boot process.

Figure 3-14 shows the emulator boot screen. The window's title bar contains the port number that the emulator is running on your computer (5554) and the AVD name (4_1_Default_WVGA). The Android logo is the same one that users of the default Android operating system see when they boot their phones (if a device manufacturer hasn't installed its own user interface customizations, as on the HTC Sense).

The third and final screen you see is the loaded emulator, shown in Figure 3-15.

Save valuable time by leaving the emulator running. The emulator doesn't have to be loaded every time you want to run your application. After the emulator is running, you can change your source code and then rerun your application. The ADT finds the running emulator and deploys your application to the emulator.

Figure 3-15:
The loaded
4_1_
Default_
WVGA
emulator.

When the emulator completes its loading phase, the default locked Home screen appears, as shown in Figure 3-16.

To unlock the Home screen, click and drag the Lock icon to the right side of the screen. When the icon reaches the far side of the Android screen, release the icon. During the drag, the icon's background turns green and its label changes to Unlock.

Figure 3-16:
Unlocking
a locked
Home
screen.

After the emulator is unlocked, the Home screen appears, as shown in Figure 3-17.

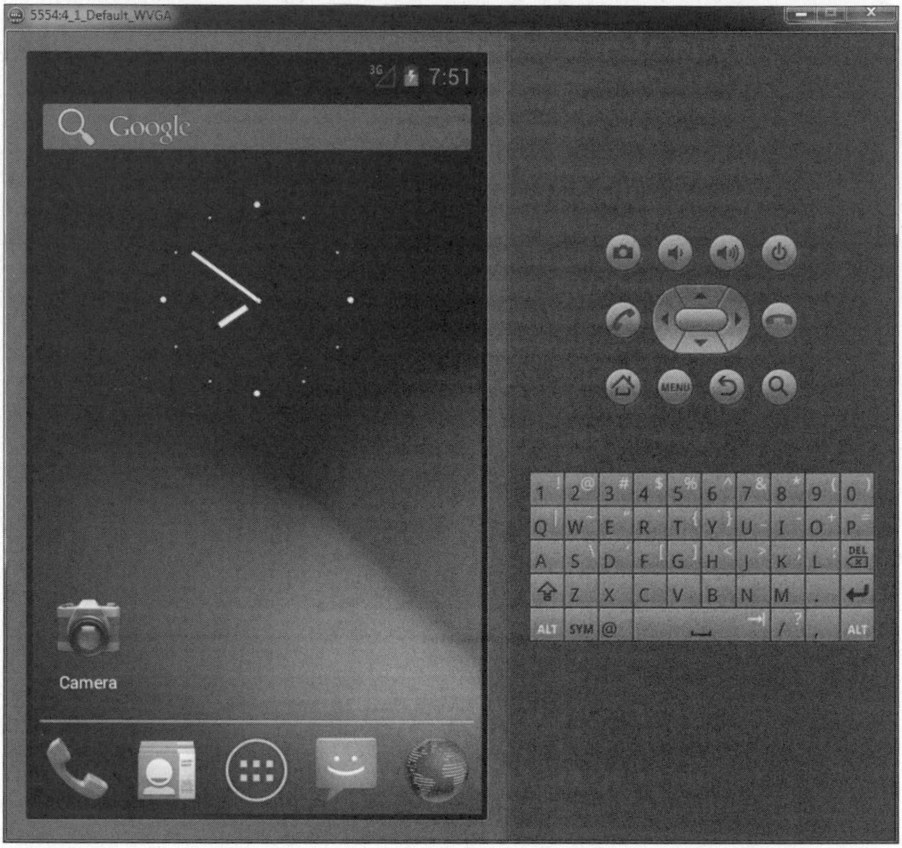

Figure 3-17:
The emula-
tor Home
screen.

Immediately thereafter, the ADT starts the Hello Android application for you. You see an empty screen containing the words `Hello world!`, as shown in Figure 3-18.

You've just created and started your first Android application.

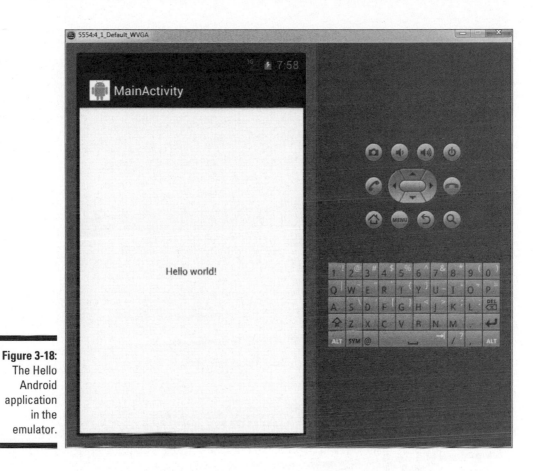

Figure 3-18:
The Hello
Android
application
in the
emulator.

 If you don't unlock the screen when the emulator starts, the ADT can't start the application. If you unlock the Home screen and your application doesn't start within five to ten seconds, simply run the application from Eclipse again by choosing Run⇨Run. The application is redeployed to the device, and it starts running.

You can view the status of the installation via the Console view in Eclipse, as shown in Figure 3-19.

The Console

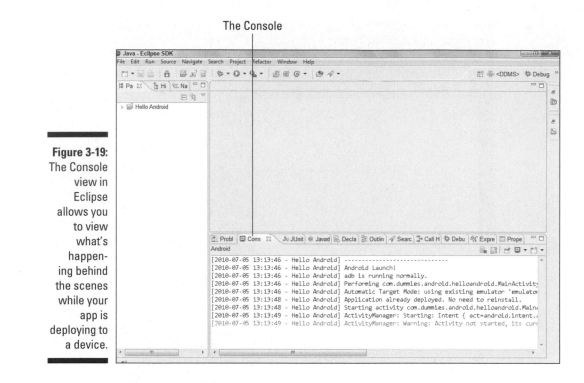

Figure 3-19:
The Console view in Eclipse allows you to view what's happening behind the scenes while your app is deploying to a device.

Checking deployment status

Inside Console view, you can see information regarding the state of your application deployment. Here's the full text of that information:

```
[2012-07-05 13:13:46 - Hello Android] ------------------------------
[2012-07-05 13:13:46 - Hello Android] Android Launch!
[2012-07-05 13:13:46 - Hello Android] adb is running normally.
[2012-07-05 13:13:46 - Hello Android] Performing com.dummies.android.
            helloandroid.MainActivity activity launch
[2012-07-05 13:13:46 - Hello Android] Automatic Target Mode: using existing
            emulator 'emulator-5554' running compatible AVD '4_1_Default_WVGA'
[2012-07-05 13:13:48 - Hello Android] Application already deployed. No need to
            reinstall.
[2012-07-05 13:13:48 - Hello Android] Starting activity com.dummies.android.
            helloandroid.MainActivity on device
[2012-07-05 13:13:49 - Hello Android] ActivityManager: Starting: Intent {
            act=android.intent.action.MAIN cat=[android.intent.category.
            LAUNCHER] cmp=com.dummies.android.helloandroid/.MainActivity }
[2012-07-05 13:13:49 - Hello Android] ActivityManager: Warning: Activity not
            started, its current task has been brought to the front
```

TIP

Console view provides valuable information on the state of the application deployment. It lets you know it's launching an activity; shows which device the ADT is targeting; and shows warning information, as presented in the last line of Console view:

```
[2012-07-05 13:13:49 - Hello Android] ActivityManager: Warning: Activity not
                started, its current task has been brought to the front
```

ADT informs you that the activity — MainActivity, in this case — hasn't been started because it was already running. Because the activity was already running, ADT brought that task to the foreground (the Android screen) for you to see.

Understanding Project Structure

You've created your first application. You even did it without coding. It's nice that the ADT provides you with the tools to fire up a quick application, but that won't help you create your next blockbuster application. The beginning of this chapter walks you through how to create a boilerplate Android application by using the New Android Project Wizard. The rest of this chapter shows you how to use the file structure that the Android wizard created for you.

WARNING!

The following sections aren't ones you should skim (they're vital!), because you'll spend your entire Android development time navigating these folders. Understanding what they're for and how they got there is a key aspect of understanding Android development.

Navigating the app's folders

In Eclipse, the Package or Project Explorer expands the Hello Android project, as shown in Figure 3-20.

After the Hello Android project is expanded, the list of subfolders includes

- ✔ src
- ✔ gen
- ✔ The Android version, such as Android 4.1
- ✔ assets
- ✔ res

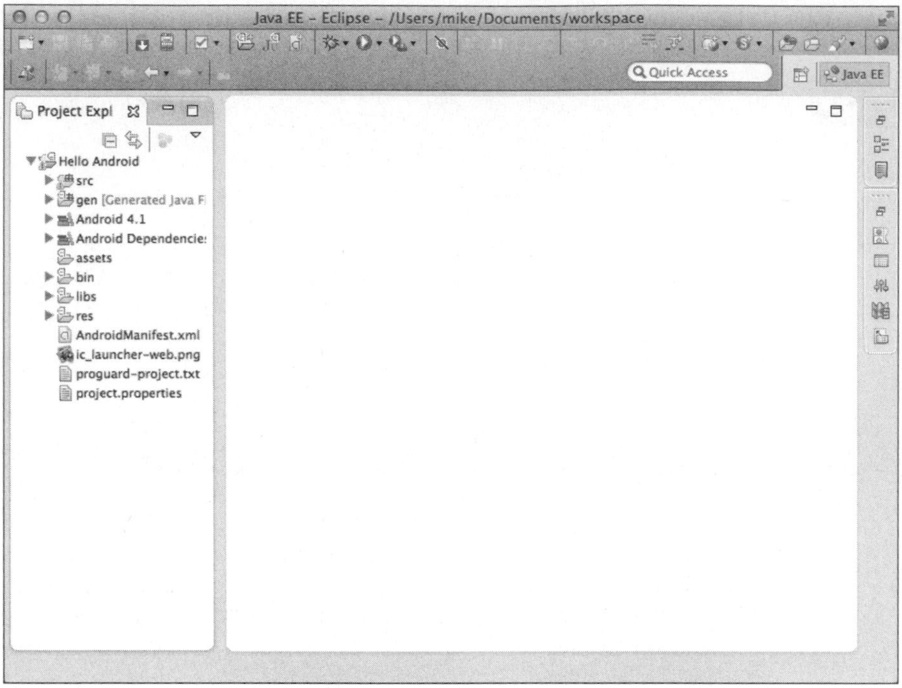

Figure 3-20:
The Project
Explorer
with the
Hello
Android
project
folder
structure
expanded.

These folders aren't the only ones you can have inside an Android project, but they're the default folders created by the New Android Project Wizard. Other folders include `bin`, `libs`, and Android Dependencies.

Two important files in the project are `AndroidManifest.xml` and `project. properties`. The `AndroidManifest.xml` file helps you identify the components that build and run the application, whereas the `project. properties` file helps you identify the default properties of the Android project (such as the Android version).

The following sections discuss all these folders and files.

Source (src) folder

The source folder — known as the `src` folder in Android projects — includes your stub `MainActivity.java` file, which you create in the New Android Project Wizard, earlier in this chapter. To inspect the contents of the `src` folder, you must expand it. Follow these steps:

1. **Select the `src` folder, and click the small arrow to the left of the folder to expand it.**

   You see your project's default package: `com.dummies.android. helloandroid`.

2. **Select the default package, and expand it.**

    This step exposes the `MainActivity.java` file within the `com.dummies.android.helloandroid` package, as shown in Figure 3-21.

Figure 3-21:
The `src` folder expanded and showing the stub `MainActivity.java` file inside the default `com.dummies.android.helloandroid` Java package.

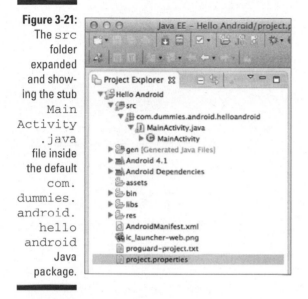

 You aren't limited to a single package in your Android applications. In fact, separating into packages the different pieces of core functionality in your Java classes is considered to be a best practice. An example is a class whose responsibility is to communicate with a web API via eXtensible Markup Language (XML). Also, your application might have `Customer` objects that represent a customer domain model, and those customers are retrieved via the web API classes. At this point, you might have two extra Java packages that contain the additional Java classes:

- ✔ `com.dummies.android.helloandroid.models`
- ✔ `com.dummies.android.helloandroid.http`

These packages would contain their respective Java components. `com.dummies.android.helloandroid.models` would contain the domain model Java classes, and `com.dummies.android.helloandroid.http` would contain the HTTP-related Java classes (web APIs). Figure 3-22 shows an Android project set up this way.

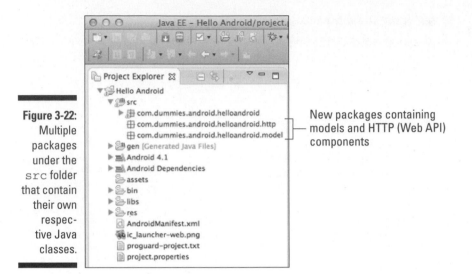

Figure 3-22:
Multiple
packages
under the
`src` folder
that contain
their own
respec-
tive Java
classes.

New packages containing
models and HTTP (Web API)
components

Target Android Library folder

The Target Android Library folder isn't a folder per se, but it's more along the
lines of an item in Eclipse presented through the ADT.

This item includes the `android.jar` file that your application builds against.
The version of this file was determined by the build target that you chose
in the New Android Project Wizard. Expanding the Android 4.1 item in the
project exposes the `android.jar` file and the path to where it's installed, as
shown in Figure 3-23.

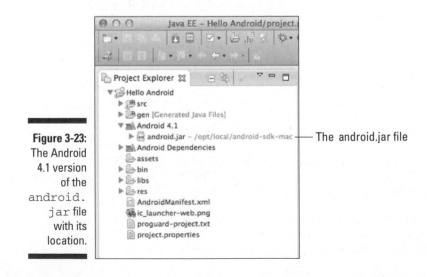

Figure 3-23:
The Android
4.1 version
of the
`android.
jar` file
with its
location.

The `android.jar` file

Assets (assets) folder

The `assets` folder is empty by default. This folder is used to store raw asset files.

A *raw asset file* can be one of many assets you may need for your application to work. A great example is a file that contains data in a proprietary format for consumption on the device. Android has the Asset Manager, which can return all assets in the `assets` directory. Upon reading an asset, your application can read the data in the file. If you create an application that has its own dictionary for word lookups (for autocomplete, perhaps), you may want to bundle the dictionary into the project by placing the dictionary file (usually, an XML or binary file such as a SQLite database) in the `assets` directory.

Android treats assets as a raw approach to resource management. You aren't limited in what you can place in the `assets` directory. Note, however, that working with assets can be a little more tedious than working with resources, because you're required to work with streams of bytes and convert them to the objects you're after — audio, video, or text, for example.

Assets don't receive resource IDs like resources in the `res` directory. You have to work with bits, bytes, and streams manually to access the contents.

Resources (res) folder

The `res` folder contains the various resources that your application can consume. Always externalize any resources that your application needs to consume. Classic examples of such resources include strings and images. As an example, you should avoid placing strings inside your code. Instead, create a string resource, and reference that resource from within code. (You find out how to do this later in this book.) These types of resources should be grouped in the `res` subdirectory that suits them best.

You should also provide alternative resources for specific device configurations by grouping them in specifically named resource directories. At runtime, Android determines which configuration the application is running in and chooses the appropriate resource (or resource folder) to pull its resources from. You may want to provide a different user interface (UI) layout depending on the screen size or different strings depending on the language setting, for example.

After you externalize your resources, you can access them in code via resource IDs that are generated by the ADT in the R class. (See "The mysterious gen folder," later in this chapter.)

You should place each resource in a specific subdirectory of your project's `res` directory. Table 3-1 lists the subdirectories that are the most common types of resource folders under the parent `res` directory.

Table 3-1 **Supported Subdirectories of the `res` Directory**

Directory	Resource Type
`anim/`	XML files that define animations.
`color/`	XML files that define a list of colors.
`drawable/`	Bitmap files (`.png`, `.9.png`, `.jpg`, `.gif`) or XML files that are compiled into the following drawable resources.
`drawable-xhdpi/`	Drawables for screens with extra-high resolution. The `xhdpi` qualifier stands for extra-high-density screens. This is the same as the `drawable/` resource folder except that all bitmap or XML files stored here are compiled into extra-high-resolution drawable resources.
`drawable-hdpi/`	Drawables for high-resolution screens. The `hdpi` qualifier stands for high-density screens, the same as the `drawable/` resource folder except that all bitmap or XML files stored here are compiled into high-resolution drawable resources.
`drawable-ldpi/`	Drawables for low-resolution screens. The `ldpi` qualifier stands for low-density screens. It's the same as the `drawable/` resource folder except that all bitmap or XML files stored here are compiled into low-resolution drawable resources.
`drawable-mdpi/`	Drawables for medium-resolution screens. The `mdpi` qualifier stands for medium-density screens. It's the same as the `drawable/` resource folder except that all bitmap or XML files stored here are compiled into medium-resolution drawable resources.
`layout/`	XML files that define a user interface layout.
`menu/`	XML files that represent application menus.
`raw/`	Arbitrary files to save in their raw form. Files in this directory aren't compressed by the system.
`values/`	XML files that contain simple values, such as strings, integers, and colors. Whereas XML resource files in other `res/` folders define a single resource based on the XML filenames, files in the `values/` directory define multiple resources for various uses. You should follow a few filename conventions, outlined in the nearby sidebar "Naming resources in the values directory," for the resources you can create in this directory.

Naming resources in the values directory

You should follow a few filenaming conventions for the resources you can create in the `values` directory:

✔ `arrays.xml` for resource arrays (storing like items, such as strings or integers, together)

✔ `colors.xml` for resources that define color values; accessed via the `R.color` class

✔ `dimens.xml` for resources that define dimension values (`20px` equals 20 pixels, for example); accessed via the `R.dimen` class

✔ `strings.xml` for string values; accessed via the `R.string` class

✔ `styles.xml` for resources that represent styles; accessed via the `R.style` class. A style is similar to a cascading style sheet in HTML. You can define many styles and have them inherit from one another.

WARNING!

Never save resource files directly in the `res` directory. If you do, a compiler error occurs.

The resources you save in the resource folders listed in Table 3-1 are known as *default* resources — they define the default design and layout of your Android application. Different types of Android-powered devices may need different resources, however. If you have a device with a larger-than-normal screen, for example, provide alternative layout resources to account for the difference.

A discussion of the powerful resource mechanism inside Android could require its own chapter, but this book covers the basics to get you up and running. The resource mechanism can help with internationalization (enabling your app for different languages and countries), device size and density, and even resources for the mode that the phone may be in. To dive into the ocean of resources, review the "Providing Resources" section of the Dev Guide in the Android documentation, at `http://d.android.com/guide/topics/resources/providing-resources.html`.

Bin, libs, and Referenced Libraries folders

Library folders aren't shown in your Hello Android application, but you should be aware of a couple of extra folders, one of which is the `libs/` directory. It can contain private third-party libraries that perform a function for you. An example is jTwitter, a third-party Java library for the Twitter API. If you were to use jTwitter in your Android application, you'd place the `jtwitter.jar` library in the `libs` directory.

After a library is placed in the `libs` directory, add it to your Java build path — the class path that's used for building a Java project. If your project depends on another third-party or private library, Eclipse should know where to find that library, and setting the build path via Eclipse does exactly that. Assuming that you added `jtwitter.jar` to your `libs` directory, you can add it to your build path easily by right-clicking the `jtwitter.jar` file and choosing Build Path➪Add to Build Path from the context menu. It's then listed in under the `libs` folder in Package Explorer, as shown in Figure 3-24.

You can find out more about jTwitter at `www.winterwell.com/software/jtwitter.php`.

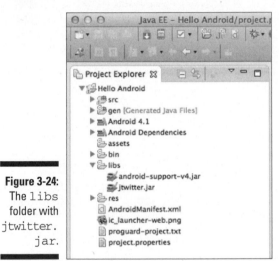

Figure 3-24:
The `libs`
folder with
`jtwitter.jar`.

We don't use the `libs` directory in this book, though developers commonly use third-party libraries in Android applications.

The mysterious gen folder

Ah, you finally get to witness the magic that is the `gen` folder. When you create an Android application, before the first compilation, the `gen` folder doesn't exist. Upon the first compilation, ADT generates the `gen` folder and its contents.

The `gen` folder contains Java files generated by ADT. The ADT creates an `R.java` file. (We tell you more about that topic in a moment.) The `gen` folder contains items generated from the `res` directory. Without a proper understanding of what the `res` folder is and what it contains, you have no clue what the `gen` folder is for. But because you're already an expert on the `res` folder, you can dive into the `gen` folder.

When you write Java code in Android, you reach a point when you need to reference the items in the res folder. You do this by using the R class. The R.java file is an index to all resources defined in your res folder. You use this class as a shorthand way to reference resources you've included in your project. This is particularly useful with the code-completion features of Eclipse because you can quickly identify the proper resource via code completion.

Expand the gen folder in the Hello Android project and the package name contained within the gen folder. Now open the R.java file by double-clicking it. You can see a Java class that contains nested Java classes. These nested Java classes have the same names as some of the res folders defined in the preceding res section. Under each of those subclasses, you can see members that have the same names as the resources in their respective res folders (excluding their file extensions). The Hello Android project's R.java file should look similar to the following code:

```
/* AUTO-GENERATED FILE.  DO NOT MODIFY.
 *
 * This class was automatically generated by the
 * aapt tool from the resource data it found.  It
 * should not be modified by hand.
 */

package com.dummies.android.helloandroid;

public final class R {
    public static final class attr {
    }
    public static final class drawable {
        public static final int ic_launcher=0x7f020000;
    }
    public static final class layout {
        public static final int main=0x7f030000;
    }
    public static final class string {
        public static final int app_name=0x7f040001;
        public static final int hello=0x7f040000;
    }
}
```

Whoa — what's all that 0x stuff? The ADT tool generates this code for you so that you don't have to worry about what's happening behind the scenes. As you add resources and the project is rebuilt, ADT regenerates the R.java file. This newly generated file contains members that reference your recently added resources.

You should never edit the R.java file by hand. If you do, your application may not compile, and then you're in a world of hurt. If you accidentally edit the R.java file and can't undo your changes, you can delete the gen folder and build your project. At this point, ADT regenerates the R.java file for you.

Viewing the application's manifest file

You keep track of everything you own and need through lists, don't you? Well, that's exactly what the Android manifest file does. It keeps track of everything your application needs, requests, and has to use to run.

The Android manifest file is stored at the root of your project and is named AndroidManifest.xml. Every application must have an Android manifest file in its root directory.

The application manifest file provides all essential information to the Android system — information that it must have before it can run any of your application's code. The application manifest file also provides

- ✔ The name of your Java package for the application, which is the unique identifier for your application in the Android system as well as in the Google Play Store
- ✔ The components of the application, such as the activities and background services
- ✔ The declaration of the permissions your application requires to run
- ✔ The minimum level of the Android API that the application requires

The Android manifest file declares the version of your application. You *must* version your application. How you version your application is similar to how the Android OS is versioned. It's important to determine your application's versioning strategy early in the development process, including considerations for future releases of your application. The versioning requirements are that each application has a version code and version name.

Version code

The *version code* is an integer value that represents the version of the application code relative to other versions of your application. This value is used to help other applications determine their compatibility with your application. Also, the Google Play Store uses it as a basis for identifying the application internally and for handling updates.

You can set the version code to any integer value you like, but you must make sure that each successive release has a version code greater than the previous one.

Typically, on the first release, you set the version code to 1. Then you mono-tonically increase the value in a given order with each release, whether the release is major or minor. This means that the version code doesn't have a strong resemblance to the application release version that's visible to the user, which is the version name. (See the next section.) The version code typically isn't displayed to users in applications.

Upgrading your application code and releasing the app without incrementing the version code causes different code bases of your app to be released under the same version. Consider a scenario in which you release your application with version code 1. This is your first release. A user installs your application via the Google Play Store and notices a bug in your application, and she lets you know. You fix the bug in the code, recompile, and release the new code base without updating the version code in the Android manifest file. At this point, the Google Play Store doesn't know that anything has changed because it's inspecting your version code in the application manifest. If the version code had changed to a value greater than 1, such as 2, the Google Play Store would recognize that an update had been made and would inform users who installed the version-code 1 app that an update is available. If you didn't update the version code, users would never get the update to your code base and would run a buggy app. No one likes that!

Version name

The *version name* is a string value that represents the release version of the application code as it should be shown to users. The value is a string that can be anything, but it typically follows a common release-name nomenclature that describes the application version:

```
<major>.<minor>.<point>
```

An example of this release-name nomenclature is 2.1.4 or, without the <point> value (4, in this case), 2.1.

The Android system doesn't use this value for any purpose other than to enable applications to display it to users.

The version name may be any other type of absolute or relative version identi-fier. The Foursquare application, for example, uses a version-naming scheme that corresponds to the date. An example of the version application name is 2012.05.02, which clearly represents a date. The version name is left up to you. You should plan ahead and make sure that your versioning strategy makes sense to you and your users.

Permissions

Assume that your application needs to access the Internet to retrieve some data. Android restricts Internet access by default. For your application to have access to the Internet, you need to ask for it.

In the application manifest file, you must define which permissions your application needs to operate. Table 3-2 lists some commonly requested permissions.

Table 3-2	Commonly Requested Application Permissions
Permission	*What It Means*
Internet	The application needs access to the Internet.
Write External Storage	The application needs to write data to the Secure Digital card (SD card).
Camera	The application needs access to the camera.
Access Fine Location	The application needs access to the global positioning system (GPS) location.
Read Phone State	The application needs to access the state of the phone (such as ringing).

Viewing the project.properties file

The project.properties file is used in conjunction with ADT and Eclipse. It contains project settings such as the build target. This file is integral to the project, so don't lose it.

The project.properties file should never be edited manually. To edit the contents of the file, use the editor in Eclipse: Right-click the project name in the Package Explorer and choose Properties from the context menu. This action opens the Properties editor, shown in Figure 3-25.

This editor allows you to change various properties of the project by selecting any of the options on the left. You can select the Android property and change the Android SDK, for example.

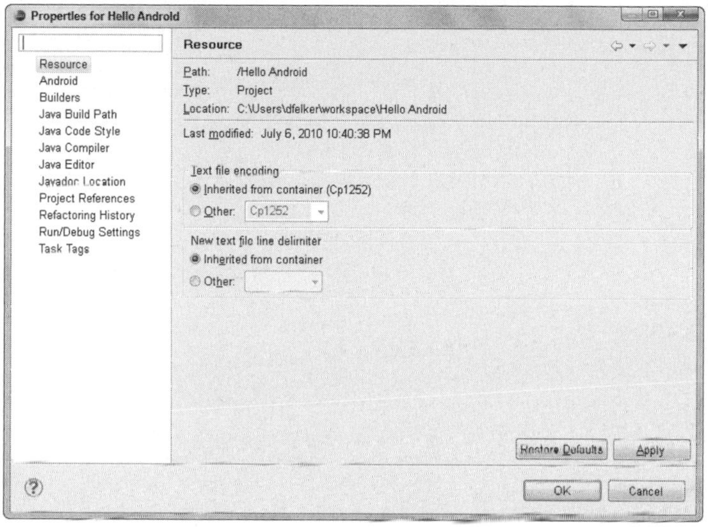

Figure 3-25:
The
Properties
editor in
Eclipse.

Closing Your Project

When you've created your application, you need to close any files you have open in Eclipse before you start your next application. You can do this by closing each file individually or by right-clicking the files and choosing Close All from the shortcut menu.

After you have closed all the files, you need to close the project itself. In Eclipse, in the Package Explorer, right-click the project and choose Close Project. By closing the project, you're telling Eclipse that you currently don't need to work with that project. This frees resources that Eclipse uses to track the project state, therefore speeding up your application.

Chapter 4

Designing the User Interface

*I*n Chapter 3, you discover what Android is and how to build your first application. This chapter helps you delve into the fun stuff: building a real application and publishing it to the Google Play Store.

The application you build in this chapter allows the user to toggle the ringer mode on the phone by simply pressing a button. This application seems simple, but it solves a real-world problem.

Imagine that you're at work and you're about to go to a meeting. You can turn down the volume on your phone to silence it and then attend the meeting. (You wouldn't want to be the one whose phone *always* rings during a meeting, would you?) The problem is that you like your ringer loud, but not too loud, so you use only the second-to-loudest setting. When you leave your meeting, you remember to restore the ringer volume, but you always have to move all the way to the maximum volume and then down one setting, to ensure that you have the correct one. Though this event isn't life changing, it's a nuisance to complete every time you need to silence your phone's ringer.

If an application would allow you to tap a button to turn off the ringer and then, when you leave the meeting, tap the button again to restore the ringer to the last state it was in, you would never have to readjust it again. That's the application you're about to build.

Creating the Silent Mode Toggle Application

Create the new application by choosing File⇨New Project. Choose Android Project from the list, and then click the Next button. Use Table 4-1 for your project settings.

Table 4-1	Project Settings for Silent Mode Toggle
Setting	*Value*
Application Name	Silent Mode Toggle
Project name	Silent Mode Toggle
Contents	Leave the default selected (create new project in workspace)
Build target	Android 4.1
Package name	`com.dummies.android.silentmodetoggle`
Create activity	`MainActivity`
Min SDK Version	8 (2.2)

Click the Finish button. You should now have the Silent Mode Toggle application in your Package Explorer, as shown in Figure 4-1.

If you receive an error that looks similar to this — "The project cannot be built until build path errors are resolved" — you can resolve it by right-clicking the project and choosing Android Tools⇨Fix Project Properties. This realigns your project with the IDE workspace.

Figure 4-1:
The Silent
Mode
Toggle
application
in Eclipse.

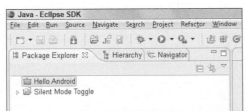

TIP

Notice how you set the build target to 4.1 and the minimum SDK to 2.2 (API level 8). What you have done is told Android that your code can run on any device that runs at least version code 8 (Android 2.2). If you were to change this to version code 16, you would be saying that your app can run on any device running version 16 (Android 4.1) or higher. When creating a new application, you should decide whether you want it to run on older versions.

If you need a refresher on how to create a new Android app in Eclipse, see Chapter 3.

Laying Out the Application

When you have the Silent Mode Toggle application created inside Eclipse, it's time for you to design the application's *user interface*, the part of an application where users interact with the app. This area of your application should be as snappy as possible.

Your application will have a single button centered in the middle of the screen to toggle silent mode. Directly above the button, an image will provide visual feedback to let the user know whether the phone is in silent mode or normal ringer mode. Figures 4-2 and 4-3 show what the finished application will look like.

Figure 4-2: The Silent Mode Toggle application in normal ringer mode.

Figure 4-3:
The Silent
Mode
Toggle
application
in silent
ringer mode.

Using the XML layout file

All layout files for an application are stored in the `res/layouts` directory of the Android project in Eclipse. When you create the Silent Mode Toggle application, the Android Development Tools (ADT) creates a file named `activity_main.xml` in the `res/layouts` directory. This default layout file is the one the ADT creates for you when you create a new application.

Double-click the file, click the `activity_main.xml` tab at the bottom of the screen, and you see some XML in the Eclipse editor window, as shown in Figure 4-4.

Figure 4-4 shows a simple layout in which a text value is in the middle of the screen. Your code should look like this:

```
<RelativeLayout xmlns:android="http://schemas.android.com/apk/res/android"
    xmlns:tools="http://schemas.android.com/tools"
    android:layout_width="match_parent"
    android:layout_height="match_parent" >

    <TextView
        android:layout_width="wrap_content"
        android:layout_height="wrap_content"
        android:layout_centerHorizontal="true"
        android:layout_centerVertical="true"
        android:padding="@dimen/padding_medium"
        android:text="@string/hello_world"
        tools:context=".MainActivity" />

</RelativeLayout>
```

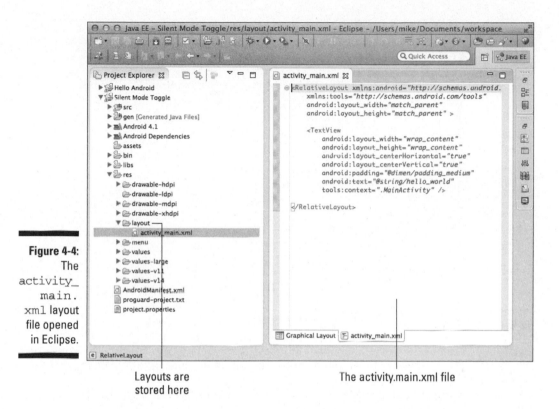

Q Quick Access | Java EE

Project Explorer ✕

▶ Hello Android
▼ Silent Mode Toggle
  ▶ src
  ▶ gen [Generated Java Files]
  ▶ Android 4.1
  ▶ Android Dependencies
  assets
  ▶ bin
  ▶ libs
  ▼ res
    ▶ drawable-hdpi
    drawable-ldpi
    ▶ drawable-mdpi
    ▶ drawable-xhdpi
    ▼ layout
      activity_main.xml
    ▶ menu
    ▶ values
    ▶ values-large
    ▶ values-v11
    ▶ values-v14
  AndroidManifest.xml
  proguard-project.txt
  project.properties

RelativeLayout

activity_main.xml ✕

```
<RelativeLayout xmlns:android="http://schemas.android.
    xmlns:tools="http://schemas.android.com/tools"
    android:layout_width="match_parent"
    android:layout_height="match_parent" >

    <TextView
        android:layout_width="wrap_content"
        android:layout_height="wrap_content"
        android:layout_centerHorizontal="true"
        android:layout_centerVertical="true"
        android:padding="@dimen/padding_medium"
        android:text="@string/hello_world"
        tools:context=".MainActivity" />

</RelativeLayout>
```

Graphical Layout | activity_main.xml

Figure 4-4:
The
`activity_main.xml` layout
file opened
in Eclipse.

Layouts are
stored here

The activity.main.xml file

This XML file defines exactly what the view should look like. The following sections break down this file, element by element.

Default XML declaration

The first element in the XML file provides the default XML declaration, letting text editors such as Eclipse and platforms such as Android know what type of file it is:

```
<?xml version="1.0" encoding="utf-8"?>
```

Layout type

The next element in the XML file defines the layout type. In this case, you're working with `RelativeLayout`, where children can be arranged relative to one another. `RelativeLayout` is a container for other items that show up onscreen:

```
<RelativeLayout xmlns:android="http://schemas.android.com/apk/res/android"
    xmlns:tools="http://schemas.android.com/tools"
    android:layout_width="match_parent"
    android:layout_height="match_parent" >
```

The closing `</RelativeLayout>` tag isn't showing because this tag is a container for other items. The close tag is inserted after all view items have been added to the container.

See Table 4-2, later in this chapter, for more information about layout types — `RelativeLayout` or otherwise.

Views

`RelativeLayout` can hold *views,* which are the basic building blocks of user interface components. The following code shows `TextView`, which is responsible for displaying text to the screen:

```
<TextView
    android:layout_width="wrap_content"
    android:layout_height="wrap_content"
    android:layout_centerHorizontal="true"
    android:layout_centerVertical="true"
    android:padding="@dimen/padding_medium"
    android:text="@string/hello_world"
    tools:context=".MainActivity" />
```

A view occupies a rectangular space on the screen and is responsible for drawing and event handling. All items that can show up on a device screen are views. The `View` class is the superclass that all items inherit from in Android.

At the end of the XML file, you have the closing tag for the `RelativeLayout`. This line closes the container:

```
</RelativeLayout>
```

The following section describes the forest that's filled with different types of layouts.

Using the Android SDK layout tools

When you create a user interface, you sometimes have to lay out components relative to each other or in a table or, under certain circumstances, even using absolute positioning. Thankfully, the engineering geniuses at Google who created Android thought of all this and provided the necessary tools to create those types of layouts. Table 4-2 briefly introduces the common types of layouts available in the Android Software Development Kit (SDK).

Table 4-2	Android SDK Layouts
Layout	*What It Does*
LinearLayout	Arranges its children in a single row or column.
RelativeLayout	Lets the positions of the children be described in relation to each other or to the parent.
FrameLayout	Designed to block out an area on the screen to display a single item. You can add multiple children to a FrameLayout, but all children are pegged to the upper-left area of the screen. Children are drawn in a stack, with the most recently added child at the top of the stack. This layout is commonly used as a way to lay out views in an absolute position.
GridLayout	Arranges its children into a grid.

Other, different types of layout tools exist, such as a TabHost for creating tabs and Sliding Drawer for finger-swiping motions that hide and display views. Programmers tend to use these layout tools in special-case scenarios. The items in Table 4-2 outline the most commonly used layouts.

Using the visual designer

Good news: Eclipse has a visual designer. Bad news: The designer is limited in what it can do (as are all visual designers).

Opening the visual designer

To view the visual designer, with the activity_main.xml file open in the Eclipse editor, click the Graphical Layout button, as shown in Figure 4-5.

Figure 4-5:
The
Graphical
Layout but-
ton, which
shows
the visual
designer.

Click this tab for the
visual designer.

The visual designer is now onscreen, as shown in Figure 4-6. From here, you can drag and drop items from the Layouts or Views toolboxes.

Inspecting a view's properties

Using the visual designer, you can view the properties of a given view by simply clicking it. Most likely, your Properties window is hidden. To look at properties, follow these steps:

1. **Choose Window⇨Show View⇨Other.**

2. **Expand General and choose Properties.**

   The Properties view opens in Eclipse, as shown in Figure 4-7.

3. **Select the "Hello world" view in the visual designer.**

   The view has a blue border, and the properties show up in the Properties window below it.

4. **Scroll the list of properties to determine which elements can be changed in the view.**

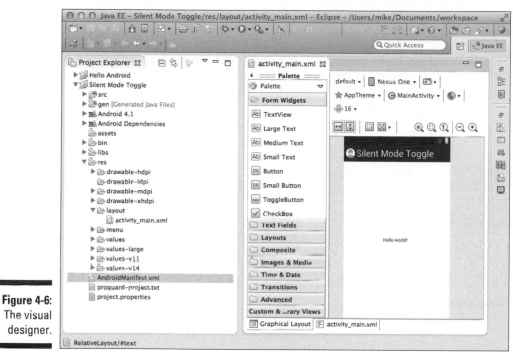

Figure 4-6:
The visual
designer.

If you're unsure which properties a view has, open the visual designer, click the Properties tab, and quickly inspect the Properties view to see what the view has to offer. If the Properties tab isn't visible, enable it by choosing Window⇨Show View⇨Other⇨General⇨Properties.

A view's available properties can change depending on its parent layout. For example, a `TextView` inside a `LinearLayout` has a different set of properties (for layout) than when it's inside a `RelativeLayout`.

The visual designer works well for simple scenarios where the contents are static in nature. But what happens when you need to draw items on the screen dynamically based on user input? The designer cannot help you in this scenario — it's best suited for a *static content scenario,* where you create your layout once and it doesn't update dynamically. The text of `TextViews` or images might change, but the actual layout of the views inside the layout doesn't change.

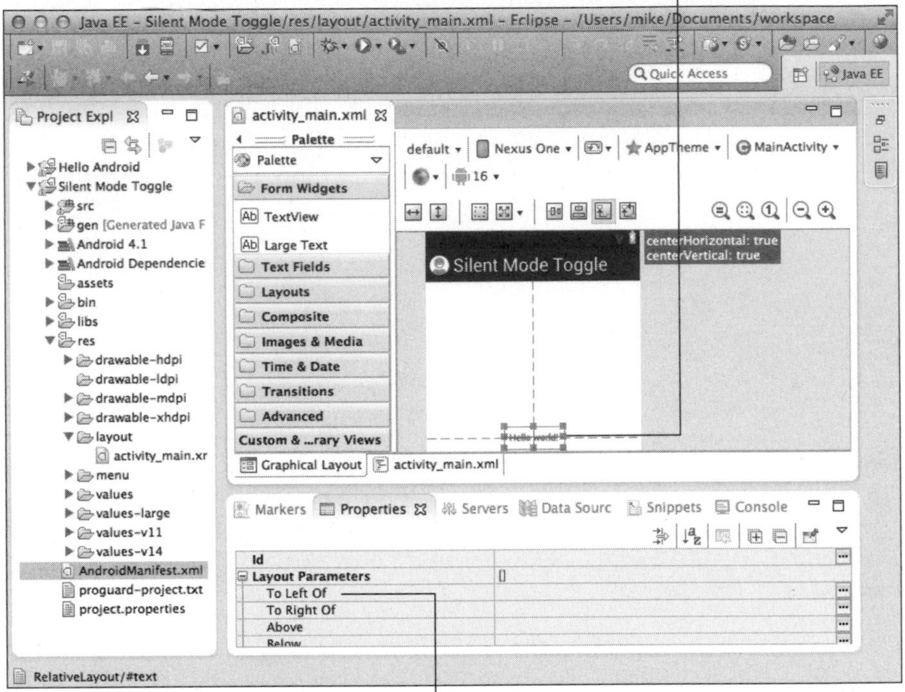

Blue line around
selected view

View properties

Figure 4-7:
A selected
item in
the visual
designer,
with some
properties
listed in the
Properties
window.

Developing the User Interface

Okay, it's time to start developing the user interface. First make sure that you're in XML view of your layout by clicking the `activity_main.xml` tab. When you're in XML view, delete the XML and replace it with the following. Your layout should now look like this:

```xml
<?xml version="1.0" encoding="utf-8"?>
<LinearLayout xmlns:android="http://schemas.android.com/apk/res/android"
    android:orientation="vertical"
    android:layout_width="match_parent"
    android:layout_height="match_parent"
    >

</LinearLayout>
```

Viewing XML layout attributes

Before continuing, you need to understand the attributes of the Android layout XML you're working with. See Table 4-3.

Table 4-3	XML Layout Attributes
Layout	*What It Does*
`xmlns:android="..."`	Defines the XML namespace that you use to reference part of the Android SDK
`android:orientation=` `"vertical"`	Informs Android that this view will be laid out vertically, such as in the portrait format in printing
`android:layout_width=` `"match_parent"`	Informs the view that it should fill as much horizontal space as it can, up to its parent, to make its own width the same as its parent's
`android:layout_height=` `"match_parent"`	Informs the view that it should fill as much vertical space as it can, up to its parent, to make its own height the same as its parent's

At this point, you have defined the layout to fill the entire screen by setting the width and height to `"match_parent"`.

Working with views

As stated earlier in this chapter, views in Android are the basic building blocks of user interface components. Anytime you implement a user interface component, such as a `Layout` or `TextView`, in the Android system, you're using a view. When you work with views in Java, you have to cast them to their appropriate type to be able to work with them.

Setting layout_width and layout_height values

Before a view can be presented to the screen, a couple of settings must be configured on the view so that Android knows how to layout the view on the screen. The attributes that are required, `layout_width` and `layout_height`, are known as `LayoutParams` in the Android SDK.

The `layout_width` attribute specifies the given width of a view, and the `layout_height` attribute specifies the given height of a view.

Setting match_parent and wrap_content values

The `layout_width` and `layout_height` attributes can take any pixel value or density-independent pixel value to specify their respective dimensions. However, two of the most common values for `layout_width` and `layout_height` are `match_parent` and `wrap_content` constants.

The `match_parent` value informs the Android system to fill as much space as possible on screen based on the available space of the parent layout. The `wrap_content` value informs the Android system to occupy only as much space as needed to show the view. As the view's contents grow, as would happen with a `TextView`, the view's viewable space grows, similar to the `Autosize` property in Windows forms development.

If you're using a static layout, these two attributes must be set in the XML layout. If you're creating views dynamically via code, the layout parameters must be set via Java code. Either way, you cannot be without them. To find out more about dynamic creation of views, see the API samples that come with the Android SDK.

If you forget to provide values for `layout_width` or `layout_height`, your Android application will crash when rendering the view. Thankfully, you find out quickly when you test your application.

Before Android 2.2, `match_parent` was named `fill_parent` (though its meaning remains the same). If you plan to support Android devices in versions earlier than 2.2, you need to use `fill_parent` instead of `match_parent`.

Adding an Image to Your Application

Although looking at text is fun, the truly interesting components are added via input mechanisms and images. The following sections demonstrate how to include images in your application — it's time to put some stuff on the screen!

Placing an image onscreen

The first element to add to the screen is the phone image (refer to Figures 4-2 and 4-3), so first you need the phone image, of course. You can download an image from this book's source code, available from this book's website, or you can use your own.

Why you should worry about density folders

Android supports various screen sizes and densities. Elsewhere in this chapter, we mention placing an image in the mdpi folder, which is for medium-density devices. What about small- and large-density devices? If Android cannot find the requested resource in the desired density, it opts for a density of the resource it can find. If your device has a high-density screen, the image is stretched out and most likely quite pixilated. If your device has a low-density device, the image is compressed to fit within the screen dimensions. To avoid this problem, create multiple versions of your image to target multiple screen densities. For more information, see the Supporting Multiple Screens page in the Android documentation at http://developer.android.com/guide/practices/screens_support.html.

Adding images to a project is simple: Drag them from the folder where they're stored to the res/drawable-mdpi folder, as shown in Figure 4-8.

For the Silent Mode Toggle application, you need two phone images: normal and silent. Be sure to put both images in the res/drawable-mdpi folder.

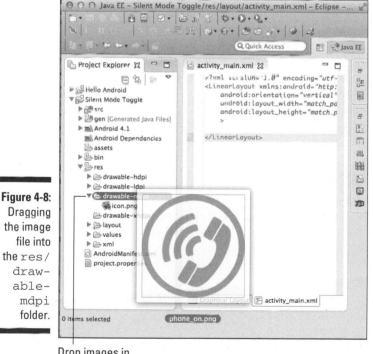

Figure 4-8: Dragging the image file into the res/drawable-mdpi folder.

Drop images in this folder.

To follow along in the rest of the chapter, be sure that the images are named this way:

- ✔ **Normal mode image:** `phone_on.png`
- ✔ **Silent mode image:** `phone_silent.png`

If your images aren't named correctly, you can rename them now. Your Eclipse project should then look like the one shown in Figure 4-9.

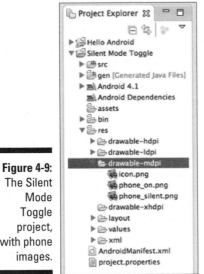

Figure 4-9:
The Silent
Mode
Toggle
project,
with phone
images.

When you drag images into Eclipse, the ADT recognizes that the project file structure has changed. The ADT then rebuilds the project because the Build Automatically selection is enabled on the Project menu. The `gen` folder, where the `R.java` file resides, regenerates, and the `R.java` file then includes a reference to the two new images you added.

You can use the references to these resources to add images to your layout in code or in XML definition. You declare them in the XML layout in the following section.

Adding the image to the layout

To add an image to the layout, type the following into the `activity_main.xml` file, overwriting the current content of the file:

```xml
<?xml version="1.0" encoding="utf-8"?>
<LinearLayout xmlns:android="http://schemas.android.com/apk/res/android"
    android:orientation="vertical"
    android:layout_width="match_parent"
    android:layout_height="match_parent"
    >
    <ImageView
            android:id="@+id/phone_icon"
            android:layout_width="wrap_content"
            android:layout_height="wrap_content"
            android:layout_gravity="center_horizontal"
            android:src="@drawable/phone_on" />

</LinearLayout>
```

This code adds the `ImageView` inside the `LinearLayout`. An `ImageView` allows you to project an image to the screen on the device.

Setting image properties

The `ImageView` contains a couple of extra parameters:

- ✔ **The** `android:id="@+id/phone_icon"` **property:** The id attribute defines the unique identifier for the view in the Android system. You can find an in-depth explanation of the `android:id` value nomenclature at `http://developer.android.com/guide/topics/ui/declaring-layout.html`.

- ✔ **The** `layout_gravity` **property:** This property defines how to place the view (both its x- and y-axes) with its parent. In this example, the value is defined as the `center_horizontal` constant. This value instructs the Android system to place the object in the horizontal center of its container, not changing its size. You can use many other constants, such as `center_vertical`, `top`, `bottom`, `left`, `right`, and many more. See the `LinearLayout.LayoutParams` Android documentation for a full list.

- ✔ **The** `android:src="@drawable/phone_on"` **property:** This property is a direct child of the `ImageView` class. You use this property to set the image that you want to show up on the screen.

Notice the value of the `src` property — `"@drawable/phone_on"`. What you're seeing is the use of the `R.java` file. You can reference drawable resources via XML by typing the at symbol (@) and the resource you want.

Certain Android attributes begin with the `layout_` prefix — `android:layout_width`, `android:layout_height`, `android:layout_gravity` are all examples. The `layout_` convention tells you that the attribute relates to the view's *parent*. Attributes that don't begin with `layout_` pertain to the view itself. So the `ImageView`'s `android:src` attribute tells the `ImageView` which image to use, but its `android:layout_gravity` tells the `ImageView`'s parent (the `LinearLayout`, in this case) to lay out the `ImageView` in the center of the parent.

Setting drawable resources

You don't type **@drawable-mdpi** for the drawable resource identifier, **@drawable**, because it's Android's job (not yours) to support multiple screen sizes. The Android layout system knows only about drawables — it knows nothing of low-, medium-, high-, or extra high density drawables during design time. At runtime, Android determines whether and when it can use low-, medium-, or high-density drawables.

For example, if the app is running on a high-density device and the requested drawable resource is available in the `drawable-hdpi` folder, Android uses that resource. Otherwise, it uses the closest match it can find. Support for various screen sizes and densities is a broad topic (and complex, in some aspects). For an in-depth view into this subject, read the "Managing Multiple Screen Sizes" article in the Android documentation at `http://developer.android.com/guide/practices/screens_support.html`.

The `phone_on` portion identifies the drawable you want to use. The image filename is `phone_on.png`. To stay within Java's member-naming guidelines, however, the file extension is removed, leaving `phone_on`. If you were to open the `R.java` file in the `gen` folder, you would see a member variable with the name `phone_on`, not `phone_on.png`.

Thanks to the ADT, you can see your available options for this property via code completion. Place the cursor directly after `@drawable/` in the `src` property of the `ImageView` in the Eclipse editor, and press Ctrl+spacebar. The code completion window opens, as shown in Figure 4-10. The other resource names in the window are other options you could choose for the `src` portion of the drawable definition.

```
*activity_main.xml ※
    <?xml version="1.0" encoding="utf-8"?>
    <LinearLayout xmlns:android="http://schemas.android.com/apk/res/android"
        android:orientation="vertical"
        android:layout_width="match_parent"
        android:layout_height="match_parent"
        >
        <ImageView
            android:id="@+id/phone_icon"
            android:layout_width="wrap_content"
            android:layout_height="wrap_content"
            android:layout_gravity="center_horizontal"
            android:src="@drawable/" />
    </LinearLayout>              @drawable/
                                @drawable/ic_launcher
                                @drawable/icon
                                @drawable/phone_on



 Graphical Layout    activity_main.xml
```

Figure 4-10:
Code com-
pletion, with
resources.

Creating a Launcher Icon
for the Application

When your app is installed, its icon helps users identify its presence in the
application launcher. When you create the Silent Mode Toggle application,
the ADT automatically includes a default launcher icon, as shown on the left
in Figure 4-11.

You should change this somewhat bland icon to one of your own. A round
phone icon works for the Silent Mode Toggle application, as shown on the
right in Figure 4-11. You can create your own (as shown in the following section) or use the one from the downloaded source code from this book's
website.

Figure 4-11:
The default
icon (left)
and a
unique icon
(right).

Designing a custom launcher icon

Creating your own launcher icons is fairly easy, thanks to the Android project. The article "Icon Design Guidelines" in the Android documentation covers all aspects of icon design — a how-to manual for creating icons for the Android platform, a style guide, a list of do's and don'ts, materials and colors, size and positioning guidelines, and (best of all) icon templates that you can use. You can find useful resources for designing icons at `http://d.android.com/guide/practices/ui_guidelines/icon_design.html` and `http://d.android.com/design/style/iconography.html`.

Working with templates

After you download the Android SDK, these icon templates and materials are available for you to use immediately on your computer's hard drive. Navigate to your Android SDK installation directory (see Chapter 2), and from there navigate to the `docs/shareables` directory. You'll find various `.zip` files that contain templates and samples. Open the templates in the image-editing program of your choice, and follow the design guidelines in the documentation to create your next rockin' icon set.

Matching icon sizes with screen densities

Because every screen density requires an icon in a different size, you, as the designer, need to know how large the icon should be. Each density must have its own icon size to look appropriate (no pixilation, stretching, or compressing) on the screen.

Table 4-4 summarizes the finished icon sizes for each of the three generalized screen densities.

Table 4-4	Finished Icon Sizes
Screen Density	Icon Size in Pixels
Low-density screen (ldpi)	36 x 36
Medium-density screen (mdpi)	48 x 48
High-density screen (hdpi)	72 x 72
Extra-high-density screen (xhdpi)	96 x 96

Adding a custom launcher icon

To place your custom launcher icon into the project, follow these steps:

1. **Rename the image icon to** ic_launcher.png.

2. **Drag your icon into the** drawable-mdpi **folder.**

   Eclipse asks whether you want to overwrite the existing ic_launcher. png.

3. **Click Yes.**

   The ic_launcher.png file is now in the drawable-mdpi folder.

You're not done yet! For the ldpi, hdpi and xhdpi folders, you need a low-, high-, and extra high density version of the icon. Copy the respective icons into the ldpi, hdpi, and xhdpi folders.

If you don't copy the icons of other densities into their respective folders, users who have a low- or high-density device receive the default launcher icon (refer to Figure 4-11), whereas the medium-density devices receive the new icon that you included in the project.

You dragged the file into the drawable-mdpi folder — what gives? Each of the other folders contains its own version of the icon. Open the drawable-hdpi, drawable-xhdpi, and drawable-ldpi folders in your Eclipse project, and you can see that each density has its own ic_launcher.png file. Be sure to place the correct icon in each density-specific folder.

Adding a Toggle Button View

Android devices come fully equipped with various views that include buttons, check boxes, and text-entry fields so that you can quickly build your user interface. Some views are more complex, such as a date picker, a clock, and zoom controls.

Views also provide user interface events that inform you when a user has interacted with the particular view, such as tapping a button.

You need to add a button view to your application so that you can toggle silent mode on the phone.

To add a button to your layout, type the following code after `ImageView`:

```
<Button
        android:id="@+id/toggleButton"
        android:layout_width="wrap_content"
        android:layout_height="wrap_content"
        android:layout_gravity="center_horizontal"
        android:text="Toggle Silent Mode"
    />
```

You have now added a button to your view with an ID resource of `toggle Button`. That's how you reference the button in the Java code. (Chapter 5 tackles coding.)

The height and width are set to `wrap_content`, which informs the Android layout system to place the view onscreen and occupy only as much usable space as it needs. The `layout_gravity` property is the same as the `ImageView` above it, centered horizontally.

The final property that has been introduced in this view is the `text` property of the button, which sets the button's text to `Toggle Silent Mode`.

Your full code base should now look like this:

```
<?xml version="1.0" encoding="utf-8"?>
<LinearLayout xmlns:android="http://schemas.android.com/apk/res/android"
    android:orientation="vertical"
    android:layout_width="match_parent"
    android:layout_height="match_parent"
    >
<ImageView
        android:id="@+id/phone_icon"
        android:layout_width="wrap_content"
        android:layout_height="wrap_content"
        android:layout_gravity="center_horizontal"
        android:src="@drawable/phone_on" />
    <Button
        android:id="@+id/toggleButton"
        android:layout_width="wrap_content"
        android:layout_height="wrap_content"
        android:layout_gravity="center_horizontal"
        android:text="Toggle Silent Mode" />

</LinearLayout>
```

Previewing the Application in the Visual Designer

To take a look at what the layout looks like in the visual designer, click the Graphical Layout tab to view it, as shown in Figure 4-12.

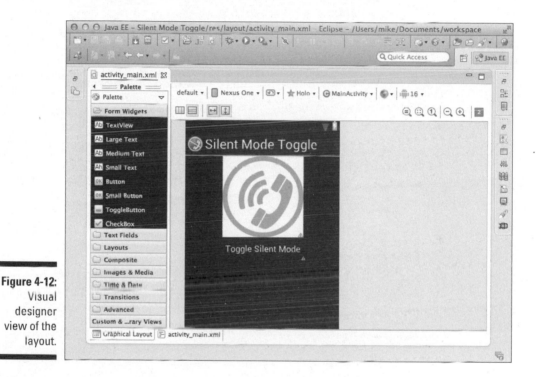

Figure 4-12:
Visual designer view of the layout.

Yuck! The background is black, and your image is white. It doesn't look right. You should make the background of your layout white to make the image blend into the background accordingly. Here's how to do it:

1. **Select the** `activity_main.xml` **tab.**

2. **Add the** `background` **property to your** `LinearLayout`**:**

   ```
   android:background="#ffffff"
   ```

The hexadecimal value of #ffffff is an opaque white color. You can type any color, such as #ff0000, which is red.

You can also set an image as a background, by using a resource.

3. **Verify that the definition of** LinearLayout **looks like this:**

```
<LinearLayout xmlns:android="http://schemas.android.
        com/apk/res/android"
    android:orientation="vertical"
    android:layout_width="match_parent"
    android:layout_height="match_parent"
    android:background="#ffffff">
```

4. **Save the file.**

5. **Select the Graphical Layout tab to view the visual designer.**

Figure 4-13 shows the final layout.

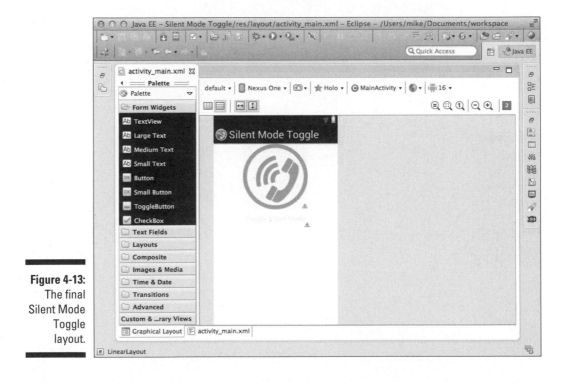

Figure 4-13:
The final
Silent Mode
Toggle
layout.

The ADT visual designer

The visual designer has many different configurations. By default, the designer is set to Nexus One, one of Google's first flagship smartphones. Selecting the Devices drop-down list in the visual designer shows you which devices you can simulate your layout on. The configurations represent the various possible configurations of the device. The Nexus One had two states that were valid at runtime.

✔ **Landscape:** The phone is in horizontal Landscape mode.

✔ **Portrait:** The phone is held in a vertical Portrait mode.

Each device on the Devices drop-down list has its own set of configurations. You can create your own, custom configurations by choosing Devices⇨Custom⇨Custom⇨New.

Chapter 5

Coding Your Application

*Y*ou're probably eager to start coding your application. In this chapter, you code it, from soup to nuts. Before you can start banging out bits and bytes, though, you need a firm understanding of activities.

Understanding Activities

An *activity* is a single, focused action that a user can take. For example, an activity might present a list of menu items that a user can choose from, or it might display photographs along with captions. An application may consist of only one activity or (like most applications in the Android system) several. Though activities may work together to appear to be one cohesive application, they work independently from each other.

An activity in Android is an important part of an application's overall life cycle, and the way the activities are launched and put together is a fundamental aspect of the Android application model. Every activity is implemented as an implementation of the Activity base class.

Almost all activities interact with the user, so the Activity class creates for you the window in which you can place your user interface (UI). Activities are most often presented in full-screen mode, but in some instances you can find an activity floating in a window or embedded inside another activity — known as an *activity group*.

Working with methods, stacks, and states

Two important methods that almost all activities implement are

- onCreate: Where the activity is initialized. Most importantly, it's where you tell the activity which layout to use by using a layout resource identifier — considered the entry point of your activity.

- onPause: Where you deal with the user leaving your activity. Any changes made by the user should be committed at this point (if you need to save them).

Activities in the system are managed as an *activity stack*. When a new activity is created, it's placed on top of the stack and becomes the running activity. The previous running activity always remains below it in the stack and returns to the foreground only when the new activity exits.

 To be a successful programmer, you must understand the importance of how and why the activity works behind the scenes. You can not only better understand the Android platform but also accurately troubleshoot your application's odd behavior at runtime.

An activity has essentially four states, as described in Table 5-1.

Table 5-1	Essential States of an Activity
Activity State	**Description**
Active/running	The activity is in the foreground of the screen (at the top of the stack).
Paused	The activity has lost focus but is still visible. (A new, non-full-size or transparent activity has the focus on top of your activity.) Because a paused activity is completely alive, it can maintain state and member information and remains attached to the window manager in Android. However, up through Gingerbread (3.0) the activity can be killed by the Android system in extreme low-memory conditions.
Stopped	If an activity becomes obscured by another activity, it's stopped. It retains all state and member information, but isn't visible to the user. Therefore, the window is hidden and will often be killed by the Android system when memory is needed elsewhere.
Created and resumed	The system has either paused or stopped the activity. The system can reclaim the memory by asking it to finish, or it can kill the process. When it displays the activity to the user, it must resume by restarting and restoring to its previous state.

Tracking an activity's life cycle

Figure 5-1 shows the important paths of an activity — the *activity life cycle*.

The rectangles represent callback methods you can implement to respond to events in the activity. The shaded ovals represent the major states of the activity.

The activity life cycle is a large and complex topic, and the following sections cover only the basics. If you want to read more about activity life cycles, check out the "Activity Life Cycle and Process Life Cycle" article in the Android documentation at `http://d.android.com/reference/android/app/Activity.html#ProcessLifecycle`.

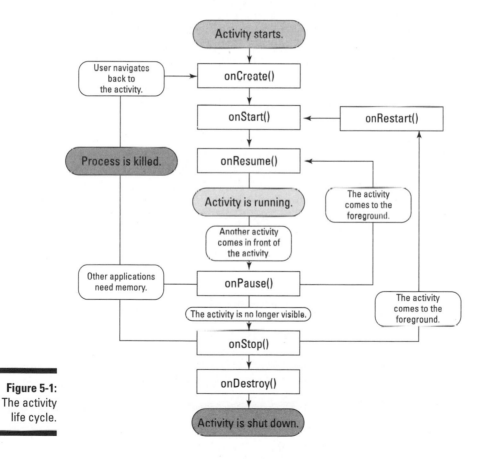

Figure 5-1:
The activity
life cycle.

Monitoring key loops

You may be interested in monitoring these three loops in your activity:

- ✔ The **entire lifetime** takes place between the first call to onCreate()
  and the final call to onDestroy(). The activity performs all global setup
  in onCreate() and releases all remaining resources in onDestroy().
  For example, if you create a thread to download a file from the Internet
  in the background, it may be initialized in the onCreate() method.
  That thread can be stopped in the onDestroy() method.

- ✔ The **visible lifetime** of the activity takes place between the onStart()
  and onStop() methods. During this time, the user can see the activity onscreen (though it may not be in the foreground interacting with
  the user, which can happen when the user is interacting with a dialog
  box). Between these two methods, you can maintain the resources
  that are needed to show and run your activity. For example, you can
  create an event handler to monitor the state of the phone. The phone
  state can change, and this event handler can inform the activity of the
  phone entering Airplane mode and react accordingly. You would set up
  the event handler in onStart() and tear down any resources you're
  accessing in onStop(). The onStart() and onStop() methods can
  be called multiple times as the activity becomes visible or hidden to the
  user.

- ✔ The **foreground lifetime** of the activity begins at the call to onResume()
  and ends at the call to onPause(). During this time, the activity is in
  front of all other activities and is interacting with the user. An activity
  normally toggles between onResume() and onPause() multiple times,
  for example, when the device goes to sleep or when a new activity handles a particular event — therefore, the code in these methods must be
  fairly lightweight.

Viewing activity methods

The entire activity life cycle boils down to these methods:

```
public class Activity extends ApplicationContext {
    protected void onCreate(Bundle savedInstanceState);
    protected void onStart();
    protected void onRestart();
    protected void onResume();
    protected void onPause();
    protected void onStop();
    protected void onDestroy();
}
```

All methods can be overridden, and custom code can be placed in all of
them. All activities implement onCreate() for initialization and may also
implement onPause() for clean-up. You should always call the superclass
(base class) when implementing these methods.

Following an activity's path

The movement of an activity throughout its life cycle looks like this:

- ✔ onCreate(): Called when the activity is first created. You initialize most of your activity's class-wide variables here. onStart() is always called next. Killable: No. Next: onStart().

- ✔ onRestart(): Called after your activity has been stopped before being started again. onStart() is always called next. Killable: No. Next: onStart().

- ✔ onStart(): Called when your activity is becoming visible to the user. Followed by onResume() if the activity is brought to the foreground or onStop() if it becomes hidden from the user. Killable: No. Next: onResume() or onStop().

- ✔ onResume(): Called when the activity will be available for interacting with the user. The activity is at the top of the activity stack at this point. Killable: No. Next: onPause().

- ✔ onPause(): Called when the system is about to resume a previous activity or if the user has navigated away to another portion of the system, such as by pressing the Home key. This stage is typically used to commit unsaved changes to data that needs to be persisted. If the activity is brought back to the foreground, onResume() is called; if the activity becomes invisible to the user, onStop() is called. Killable: Yes, but only on Gingerbread (2.3) or earlier. Next: onResume() or onStop().

- ✔ onStop(): Called when the activity is no longer visible to the user because another activity has resumed and is covering this one. This may happen because another activity has started or a previous activity has resumed and is now in the foreground of the activity stack. It's followed by onRestart() if this activity is returning to interact with the user or by onDestroy() if this activity is going away. Killable: Yes. Next: onRestart() or onDestroy().

- ✔ onDestroy(): The final call you receive before your activity is destroyed. This method gets called either because the activity is finishing (such as someone calling finish() on it) or because the system is temporarily destroying the activity to reclaim space. You can distinguish between these two with the isFinishing() method, which helps identify whether the method is finishing or the system is killing it. The isFinishing() method is often used inside onPause() to determine whether the activity is pausing or being destroyed. Killable: Yes. Next: Nothing.

The *killable* indicator at the end of each activity method description notes the activities the Android system can kill at any time and without notice. You should therefore use the onPause() method to complete any clean-up to write persistent data (such as user edits to data) to your storage mechanism.

Recognizing configuration changes

A configuration change is a change that's made to the screen orientation (for example, if the user moves the screen to the side and back or moves it from portrait to landscape mode or vice versa), the language, or an input device. A configuration change causes your activity to be destroyed while completing the normal activity life cycle: onPause() followed by onStop() and then onDestroy(). After the onDestroy() method is called, the system creates a new instance of the activity to be created, which takes place because resources and layout files and other elements might need to change depending on the current system configuration. For example, an application may look completely different if the user is interacting with it in Portrait mode, as compared to being displayed in Landscape mode (on its side).

Creating Your First Activity

You may have already created your first activity if you created a project using the New Android Project Wizard in Chapter 3: the MainActivity activity. Open the MainActivity.java file in your project to enhance it in the following sections.

Starting with onCreate

The entry point into your application is the onCreate() method. The code for the MainActivity.java file already contains an implementation of the onCreate() method. It's where you start writing code! For now, your code should look like this:

```
public class MainActivity extends Activity {
    /** Called when the activity is first created. */
    @Override
    public void onCreate(Bundle savedInstanceState) {
        super.onCreate(savedInstanceState);
        setContentView(R.layout.activity_main);
    }
}
```

You write the initialization code directly below the setContentView() method.

Be sure to always include this method call to your onCreate() method:

```
super.onCreate(savedInstanceState);
```

It's required for the application to run. This line directs the base Activity class to perform setup work for the MainActivity class. If you omit this line of code, you receive a runtime exception.

Telling Android to display the user interface

By default, an activity has no idea what its user interface is. It can be a simple form that allows the user to type information to be saved; a visual, camera-based, augmented, virtual reality application (such as Layar in the Google Play Store); or a drawn-on-the-fly user interface, such as in a 2D or 3D game. As a developer, it's your job to tell the activity which layout the activity should load.

To show the user interface onscreen, you have to set the content view for the activity, by adding this line of code:

```
setContentView(R.layout.activity_main);
```

R.layout.activity_main is the activity_main.xml file that's located in the res/layouts directory. It's the layout you define in the Chapter 4.

Handling user input

The Silent Mode Toggle application has little user interaction. The only user interaction that your application will have is a single button that the user taps to toggle silent mode.

To respond to this tap event, you need to register an *event listener,* which responds to an event in the Android system. Though you find various types of events in the Android system, two of the most commonly used are keyboard events and touch events (also known as clicks).

Keyboard events

A *keyboard event* occurs whenever a particular keyboard key is pressed. For example, if the user presses the Alt+E hot key in your application, you may want the view to toggle into Edit mode. Responding to keyboard events allows you to do this. If you need to override the onKeyDown method to use your own keyboard event, do it this way:

```
@Override
public boolean onKeyDown(int keyCode, KeyEvent event) {
        // TODO Auto-generated method stub
        return super.onKeyDown(keyCode, event);
}
```

Touch events

A *touch event* occurs whenever the user taps a widget on the screen. The Android platform recognizes each tap event as a click event. Examples of views that can respond to touch events include (but aren't limited to)

- ✔ Button
- ✔ ImageButton
- ✔ EditText
- ✔ Spinner
- ✔ ListView Rows
- ✔ MenuItem

All views in the Android system can react to a tap; however, some widgets have their *clickable* property set to false by default. You can override this setting in your layout file or in code to allow a view to be clickable by setting the clickable attribute on the view or the setClickable() method in code.

Writing your first event handler

For your application to respond to the click event of the user toggling silent mode, you respond to the click event that's exposed by the button.

Entering the code

Type into your editor the code shown in Listing 5-1. It demonstrates how to implement a click handler for `toggleButton`. The code consists of the entire `onCreate()` method with the new code. You can either fill in the button code (in bold) or overwrite your entire `onCreate` code.

Listing 5-1:   The Initial Class File with a Default Button OnClickListener

```
@Override
public void onCreate(Bundle savedInstanceState) {
    super.onCreate(savedInstanceState);
    setContentView(R.layout.activity_main);

    Button toggleButton = (Button)findViewById(R.id.toggleButton);
    toggleButton.setOnClickListener(new View.OnClickListener() {
        public void onClick(View v) {
        }
    });
}
```

This listing uses the `findViewById()` method, which is available to all activities in Android. This method, which allows you to find any view inside the activity's layout and do some work with it, always returns a `View` class that you must cast to the appropriate type before you can begin. In the following code (which is a line from Listing 5-1), you're casting the returned `View` from `findViewById()` to a `Button` (which is a subclass of `View`).

```
Button toggleButton = (Button)findViewById(R.id.toggleButton);
```

Immediately following this line of code, you start setting up the event handler.

The event handling code is placed inline after you retrieve the `Button` from the layout. Setting up the event handler is as simple as setting a new `View.OnClickListener`. This click listener contains an `onClick()` method that's called after the user taps the button. It's where you place the code to handle the silent mode toggle.

Be sure to cast to the appropriate type. If the type in your layout file is different from what you're casting it to (if you're trying to cast an `ImageView` in the layout file to `ImageButton`, for example), you'll crash your application.

When you type this code into your editor, you may see red, squiggly lines, as shown in Figure 5-2. These lines are Eclipse's way of telling you that it doesn't know what the "button" is.

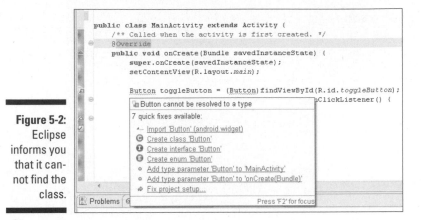

```
public class MainActivity extends Activity {
    /** Called when the activity is first created. */
    @Override
    public void onCreate(Bundle savedInstanceState) {
        super.onCreate(savedInstanceState);
        setContentView(R.layout.main);

        Button toggleButton = (Button)findViewById(R.id.toggleButton);
                                                          nClickListener() {
        Button cannot be resolved to a type

        7 quick fixes available:

          Import 'Button' (android widget)
        ⓒ Create class 'Button'
        ⓘ Create interface 'Button'
        Ⓔ Create enum 'Button'
        ○ Add type parameter 'Button' to 'MainActivity'
        ○ Add type parameter 'Button' to 'onCreate(Bundle)'
        ◈ Fix project setup...

    Problems    ◎                              Press 'F2' for focus
```

Figure 5-2:
Eclipse
informs you
that it can-
not find the
class.

Follow these steps to correct the problem:

1. **Place the cursor over the squiggly line and leave it there for a moment.**

   A small context window opens to give you several options. (Refer to Figure 5-2.)

2. **Select the first option — Import 'Button'.**

   The following import statement is added to the top of the file:

   ```
   import android.widget.Button;
   ```

   This import statement informs Eclipse where the Button is located in the Android packages.

Extracting the code to a method

The code is starting to become unwieldy and difficult to read. At this point, the best thing you can do is extract the new button code to a method that you can call from within onCreate(). To do it, you create a private void method named setButtonClickListener() that contains the button code you just typed. This new method is placed in the onCreate() method. The new code is shown in Listing 5-2.

Listing 5-2:   Button Listener Extracted to a Method

```
public class MainActivity extends Activity {
    /** Called when the activity is first created. */
    @Override
    public void onCreate(Bundle savedInstanceState) {
        super.onCreate(savedInstanceState);
        setContentView(R.layout.activity_main);

        setButtonClickListener();                                      →8
    }


    private void setButtonClickListener() {                           →11
            Button toggleButton = (Button)findViewById(R.id.toggleButton);
            toggleButton.setOnClickListener(new View.OnClickListener() {
                public void onClick(View v) {
                    // TODO Auto-generated method stub
                }
            });
    }
}
```

Listing 5-2 works this way:

→8   On this line, a method is called to set up the button click listener.

→11   The new method is getting called.

Now you can respond to the click event by providing code for the
onClick() method of your button.

Working with the Android Framework Classes

This section gets into the good stuff — the nitty-gritty of Android development and its Android framework classes! Yes, activities and views are integral parts of the system, but they're simply the "plumbing" that's required
in any modern operating system (in one capacity or another). The real fun is
just about to start.

The following sections describe how to check the state of the phone ringer to determine whether it's in normal mode (ringing loud and proud) or silent mode. At this point, you can begin to start toggling the phone's ringer mode.

Getting good service

To access the Android ringer, you'll need lots of access to the `AudioManager` in Android, which is responsible for managing the ringer state, so you should initialize it in `onCreate()`.

All important initialization needs to happen in `onCreate()`.

You first need to create a private class-level `AudioManager` variable by the name of `mAudioManager`. Type this name at the top of your class file, directly after the class declaration line, as shown in Listing 5-3.

Listing 5-3:   Adding the Class-Level AudioManager Variable

```
package com.dummies.android.silentmodetoggle;

import android.app.Activity;
import android.media.AudioManager;                                    →4
import android.os.Bundle;
import android.view.View;
import android.widget.Button;

public class MainActivity extends Activity {

    private AudioManager mAudioManager;                              →11

    @Override
    public void onCreate(Bundle savedInstanceState) {
        super.onCreate(savedInstanceState);
        setContentView(R.layout.activity_main);

        setButtonClickListener();

        mAudioManager = (AudioManager)getSystemService(AUDIO_SERVICE);   →20
    }

    private void setButtonClickListener() {
            Button toggleButton = (Button)findViewById(R.id.toggleButton);
            toggleButton.setOnClickListener(new View.OnClickListener() {
                public void onClick(View v) {
                    // TODO Auto-generated method stub
                }
            });
    }
}
```

This list briefly explains what the numbered lines:

→**4**   The `import` statement that brings in the necessary package so that you can use `AudioManager`.

→**11**   The `private` class-level `AudioManager` variable. Because it's class wide, you can have access to it in other parts of the activity.

→**20**   Initializes the `mAudioManager` variable by getting the service from the base `Activity` `getSystemService()` method call.

Whoa! What's `getSystemService()`? By inheriting from the base `Activity` class, `AudioManager` receives all the benefits of being an activity, including access to the `getSystemService()` method call. This method returns the base Java `Object` class, so you have to cast it to the type of service you're requesting.

This call returns all available system services that you might need to work with. All services that are returned can be found in the `Context` class in the Android documentation, at `http://d.android.com/reference/android/content/Context.html`. Popular system service types include

✔ `AUDIO_SERVICE`

✔ `LOCATION_SERVICE`

✔ `ALARM_SERVICE`

Toggling Silent mode with AudioManager

After you have a class-wide instance of `AudioManager`, you can start checking the state of the ringer and toggling the ringer. The code you need to add or modify is in bold in Listing 5-4.

Listing 5-4:   Adding the Application Toggle to the App

```
package com.dummies.android.silentmodetoggle;

import android.app.Activity;
import android.graphics.drawable.Drawable;
import android.media.AudioManager;
import android.os.Bundle;
import android.view.View;
import android.widget.Button;
import android.widget.ImageView;

public class MainActivity extends Activity {
```

(continued)

Listing 5-4 *(continued)*

```
private AudioManager mAudioManager;
private boolean mPhoneIsSilent;                                      →14

@Override
public void onCreate(Bundle savedInstanceState) {
    super.onCreate(savedInstanceState);
    setContentView(R.layout.activity_main);

    mAudioManager = (AudioManager)getSystemService(AUDIO_SERVICE);

    checkIfPhoneIsSilent();                                          →23

    setButtonClickListener()                                        →25
}

private void setButtonClickListener() {
        Button toggleButton = (Button)findViewById(R.id.toggleButton);
        toggleButton.setOnClickListener(new View.OnClickListener() {
            public void onClick(View v) {

            if (mPhoneIsSilent) {                                   →32
                // Change back to normal mode
                mAudioManager
                        .setRingerMode(AudioManager.RINGER_MODE_NORMAL);
                mPhoneIsSilent = false;
            } else {
                // Change to silent mode
                mAudioManager
                    .setRingerMode(AudioManager.RINGER_MODE_SILENT);
                    mPhoneIsSilent = true;
            }

            // Now toggle the UI again
            toggleUi();                                             →44
            }
    });
}

/**
 * Checks to see if the phone is currently in Silent mode.
 */
private void checkIfPhoneIsSilent() {                               →53
    int ringerMode = mAudioManager.getRingerMode();
    if (ringerMode == AudioManager.RINGER_MODE_SILENT) {
        mPhoneIsSilent = true;
    } else {
        mPhoneIsSilent = false;
    }
```

```
    }

    /**
     * Toggles the UI images from silent to normal and vice versa.
     */
    private void toggleUi() {                                          →66

        ImageView imageView = (ImageView) findViewById(R.id.phone_icon);
        Drawable newPhoneImage;

        if (mPhoneIsSilent) {
            newPhoneImage =
                getResources().getDrawable(R.drawable.phone_silent);

        } else {
            newPhoneImage =
                getResources().getDrawable(R.drawable.phone_on);
        }

        imageView.setImageDrawable(newPhoneImage);
    }

    @Override                                                          →84
    protected void onResume() {
        super.onResume();
        checkIfPhoneIsSilent();
        toggleUi();
    }
}
```

This list briefly explains what each new section of code does:

→**14**   Sets up a new class-level `boolean mPhoneIsSilent` variable to keep track of the ringer state.

→**23**   Calls the `checkIfPhoneIsSilent()` method to initialize `mPhone IsSilent`. The default value of a `boolean` is false — which can be wrong if the phone is in Silent mode. This line figures out what happens when the ringer mode is toggled.

→**25**   The button event-handling code was moved to the bottom of the `onCreate()` method because it depends on the setup of the `mPhoneIsSilent` variable. Even though nothing is likely to happen, you should keep the code organized.

Clean code is manageable code.

→**32**   The code between Lines 32 and 44 handles a user tap on the toggle button, by checking to see whether the ringer is enabled via the class-level `mPhoneIsSilent` variable.

If the ringer is silent, the code falls into the first `if` block and changes the ringer mode to RINGER_MODE_NORMAL, which turns the ringer back on. The mPhoneIsSilent variable is also changed to `false` for the next time this code runs.

If the ringer isn't silent, the code falls into the `else` code block. This code block turns the ringer mode from its current state to RINGER_MODE_SILENT, which turns off the ringer. The `else` block also sets the mPhoneIsSilent variable to `true` for the next time around.

→44 The toggleUi() method changes the user interface to give the user a visual identifier that the mode on the phone has changed. Anytime the ringer mode changes, the toggleUi() method needs to get called.

→53 The checkIfPhoneIsSilent() method initializes the mPhone IsSilent class-level variable in the onCreate() method. If you fail to do this, your application doesn't know what state the AudioManager's ringer is in. If the phone is silent, mPhoneIs Silent gets set to `true`; otherwise, it's `false`.

→66 This toggleUi() method changes the ImageView from the layout you created in Chapter 4, depending on the state of the ringer.

If the ringer is silent, the user interface displays an image showing that the phone ringer is off. If the phone's ringer is in Normal mode, the image indicates that the phone ringer is on.

Both these images are in the resource directories. (See Chapter 4.) The ImageView is found inside the layout, and after detecting the mode, the View is updated by pulling the correct image from getResources().getDrawable(...) and set with the set ImageDrawable(...) call on the ImageView. This method updates the image that's displayed on the ImageView onscreen.

→84 The onResume() method is overridden for your application to correctly identify its state. The mPhoneIsSilent variable keeps track of the phone's ringer state, but only for the class. The person using your application also needs to know what state the phone is in, so onResume() calls toggleUi() to toggle the user interface.

The toggleUi() call is strategically placed in the onResume() method for a simple reason: to assume that the user opens the Silent Toggle Mode application and then returns to the Home screen and turns off the phone using the phone controls. When the user returns to the activity, the activity is resumed and brought to the foreground. At that time, onResume() is called to check the state of the ringer mode and update the user interface accordingly. If the user changed the mode, the app reacts as the user would expect.

Installing Your Application

You've done it — you've written your first application. In the next sections, you install your app on the emulator and put that baby into action!

Running your app in an emulator

When you run your application in an emulator, the ADT is smart enough to remember the last launch configuration and uses it by default. (If you ever need to change the launch configuration — say to launch a different activity or application — turn to Chapter 3.)

The emulator and Eclipse speak to each other through the Android Debug Bridge (adb). You installed the adb with the Android Development Tools (ADT) in Chapter 2.

It's time to install this app on the emulator. Follow these steps:

1. **In Eclipse, choose Run⇨Run or press Ctrl+F11 to run the application.**

   You see the Run As window, shown in Figure 5-3.

2. **Choose Android Application and click OK to start the emulator.**

Figure 5-3:
The Run As configuration dialog box.

3. **Wait for the emulator to load and then unlock the emulator.**

   If you're unsure how to unlock the emulator, refer to Chapter 3. When the emulator is unlocked, your application starts and the emulator runs your program, as shown in Figure 5-4.

TIP

If your application doesn't start, rerun the application by choosing Run⇨Run or pressing Ctrl+F11.

Figure 5-4:
The emulator running the application.

4. **Click the Toggle Silent Mode button to see the image change to the phone in the red slashed circle, shown in Figure 5-5.**

   Notice the new icon on the notification bar — the Silent Notification icon.

   Silent notification icon

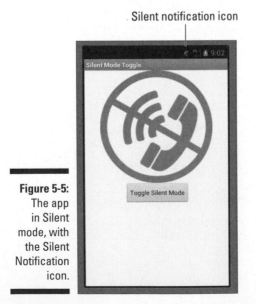

Figure 5-5:
The app in Silent mode, with the Silent Notification icon.

5. **Return to the Home screen by clicking the Home button on the emulator.**

6. **Open the application. (It's the center button at the bottom of screen.)**

    You see the application launcher icon in the list of applications.

After the emulator is running, it's running on its own. The emulator has no dependencies on Eclipse. In fact, you can close Eclipse and still interact with the emulator.

Installing on a physical Android device

Installing an application on a device is no different from installing it on the emulator, except for having to make a few small adjustments to get it to work. You likely installed the driver in Chapter 2, so the remaining steps are straightforward:

1. **From the Home screen of your phone, access the Settings panel.**

2. **Under Security for newer phones and Applications for older phones, select the Unknown Sources check box, as shown in Figure 5-6.**

    Select this setting to install applications that aren't in the Google Play Store.

Figure 5-6: This setting allows the installation of applications that don't originate in the Google Play Store.

3. **Choose Development and select the USB Debugging option, as shown in Figure 5-7.**

   This step allows you to debug your application on a device. (You can find more about debugging later in this chapter, in the "Using the Eclipse debugger" section.)

Figure 5-7:
Enabling
your device
to perform
USB
debugging.

4. **Connect your phone to the computer by using a USB cable.**

5. **When the phone is detected on your system, run the application by either choosing Run⇨Run or pressing Ctrl+F11.**

   The ADT recognizes another option for a launch configuration, so it asks you (in the Android Device Chooser dialog box, shown in Figure 5-8) on which device you want to run the application.

   The emulator doesn't show up in the list of available options unless it's running.

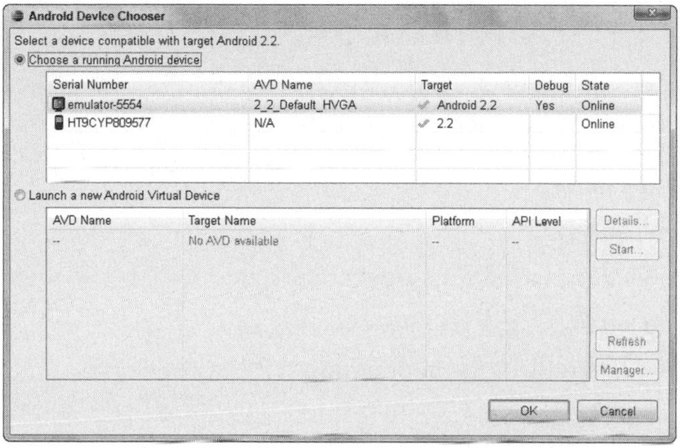

Figure 5-8:
The Android
device
chooser.

6. **Choose your phone from the list and click OK.**

   This step sends the application to your phone, and it launches it just as it would on the emulator. In a few seconds, the app should show up on your phone.

   You've now deployed the application to your phone.

If you change the app and you need to test it again, you have to reinstall it on your phone. It's a simple matter of plugging in your phone and choosing Run⇨Run or pressing Ctrl+F11.

Uh-Oh! (Responding to Errors)

You write perfect code, right? Even if it's perfect this time, though, the day will come when it isn't. When coding doesn't go as planned, you have to figure out the problem. To help developers in the dire situation of a random application crash, the ADT provides valuable tools to help debug applications.

Using the Dalvik Debug Monitor Server

The Dalvik Debug Monitor Server (DDMS) is a debugging tool that provides these features, among others:

- ✔ Port forwarding
- ✔ Screen capturing
- ✔ Thread and heap information on the device
- ✔ System log messages via LogCat
- ✔ Process and radio state information
- ✔ Incoming call and SMS spoofing
- ✔ Location data spoofing

DDMS, located in the Android SDK platform-`tools` directory, can work with an emulator and a connected device. In Chapter 2, you add the platform-`tools` directory to your path, so you should be able to access DDMS from the command line.

Why you should get to know DDMS

Debugging is rarely fun. Thankfully, DDMS provides the tools necessary to help you dig yourself out of a hole filled with bugs. One of the most commonly used features in DDMS is the LogCat viewer, which allows you to view the output of system log messages from your system, as shown in Figure 5-9.

This system log reports everything from basic information messages (which include the state of the application and device) to warning and error information. Seeing only an "Application Not Responding" or a force-close error message on the device doesn't clarify what has happened. Opening the DDMS and reviewing the entries in LogCat can help identify, down to the line number, where the exception is occurring.

DDMS doesn't solve the problem for you (darn it!), but it can make tracking down the root cause of the issue much easier.

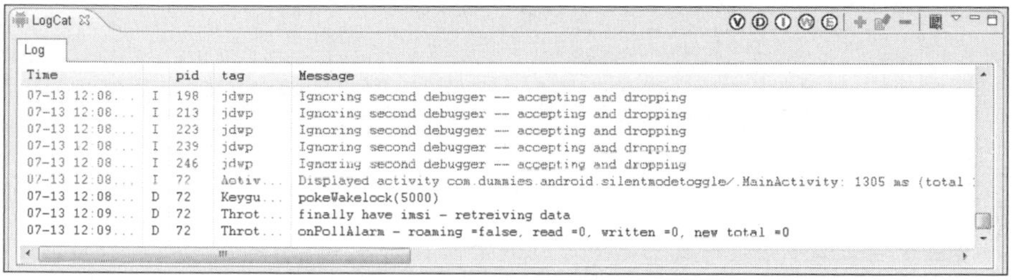

Figure 5-9:
A view of
LogCat.

DDMS is also useful in scenarios where you have no physical device for testing. For example, if your application is based on tracking a user who is moving across a map and the user's device has no GPS (or the user has no device), the task becomes nontrivial. Thankfully, DDMS is here to help. DDMS provides tools via location control. As a developer, you can manually provide GPS coordinates or a GPS eXchange Format (GPX) file or a Keyhole Markup Language (KML) file that represents points on a map that can be timed accordingly. For example, you might specify that the user stay at this point for 5 seconds, move to another point, move to the next point, and so on.

Displaying log messages in DDMS

Displaying log messages in DDMS is as simple as adding one line of code to your app. Open the `MainActivity.java` file, and at the bottom of the method, add a log entry, as shown in bold in Listing 5-5.

Listing 5-5:   The onCreate() Method

```
@Override
public void onCreate(Bundle savedInstanceState) {
    super.onCreate(savedInstanceState);
    setContentView(R.layout.activity_main);

    mAudioManager = (AudioManager)getSystemService(AUDIO_SERVICE);

    checkIfPhoneIsSilent();

    setButtonClickListener();

    Log.d("SilentModeApp", "This is a test");                    →12
}
```

Line 12 demonstrates how to output a message into the system log. SilentModeApp is known as the TAG that you're giving to this log entry; the second parameter to the log call is the message you want to output. The tag helps filter messages while looking at them in DDMS.

Declare a TAG constant in your code and use it instead of repeatedly typing the TAG, as in this example:

```
private static final String TAG = "SilentModeApp";
```

Notice the d in Log.d in Listing 5-5, indicating that this is a debug message. Other options are

- ✔ e: error
- ✔ i: info
- ✔ wtf: What a terrible failure (Yes, it's an option.)
- ✔ v: verbose

The various logging types exist for you to decide how various messages should be logged.

For logging to work, you have to import the android.util.Log package.

Viewing DDMS messages

You can view DDMS messages by either opening DDMS manually or opening the DDMS perspective in Eclipse:

- ✔ **Manually:** Navigate to wherever you installed the Android SDK. Inside the tools directory, double-click the ddms.bat file. The DDMS application opens outside the Eclipse IDE, as shown in Figure 5-10.

- ✔ **In Eclipse:** The ADT has installed a DDMS perspective. To open it, click the Open Perspective button (see Figure 5-11) and choose DDMS.

    If DDMS isn't visible in this view, select the Other option and then select DDMS, to add a DDMS perspective to the list of perspectives that you can easily toggle.

    If you prefer to move the LogCat window (usually near the bottom of the screen) to the main area of the screen, as shown in Figure 5-12, simply drag the LogCat tab title and drop it on the location you want.

Dalvik Debug Monitor

File   Edit   Actions   Device   Help

Name			
▲ 🖥 emulator-5554	Online		2_2_Def...
?	72	🐾	8600
?	118	🐾	8601
?	113	🐾	8602
?	121	🐾	8603
?	140	🐾	8604
?	153	🐾	8605

Info   Threads   VM Heap   Allocation Tracker   Sysinfo   Emulator Control   Event Log

DDM-aware?   -
App description: -
VM version: -
Process ID: -
Supports Profiling Control: -
Supports HPROF Control: -

Log

Time	pid	tag	Message
07-13 12:4... I	113	jdwp	Ignoring second debugger – accepting and dropping
07-13 12:4... I	121	jdwp	Ignoring second debugger – accepting and dropping
07-13 12:4... I	140	jdwp	Ignoring second debugger – accepting and dropping
07-13 12:4... I	153	jdwp	Ignoring second debugger – accepting and dropping
07-13 12:4... I	184	jdwp	Ignoring second debugger – accepting and dropping
07-13 12:4... I	195	jdwp	Ignoring second debugger – accepting and dropping
07-13 12:4... I	198	jdwp	Ignoring second debugger – accepting and dropping
07-13 12:4... I	213	jdwp	Ignoring second debugger – accepting and dropping
07-13 12:4... I	223	jdwp	Ignoring second debugger – accepting and dropping
07-13 12:4... I	239	jdwp	Ignoring second debugger – accepting and dropping
07-13 12:4... I	246	jdwp	Ignoring second debugger – accepting and dropping
07-13 12:4... I	252	jdwp	Ignoring second debugger – accepting and dropping
07-13 12:4... I	270	jdwp	Ignoring second debugger – accepting and dropping
07-13 12:4... D	72	SntpClient	request time failed: java.net.SocketException: Address family not supported by protocol

Filter

Figure 5-10:
An instance
of DDMS
running sep-
arately from
Eclipse.

Start the application by choosing Run⇨Run or pressing Ctrl+F11. When
your application is running in the emulator, open the DDMS perspective
and look for your log message. It should look somewhat similar to the
one shown in Figure 5-13.

You can now switch back to the Java perspective by clicking the Java
Perspective button. (Refer to Figure 5-11.)

Open Perspective button

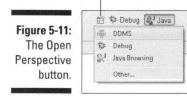

Figure 5-11:
The Open
Perspective
button.

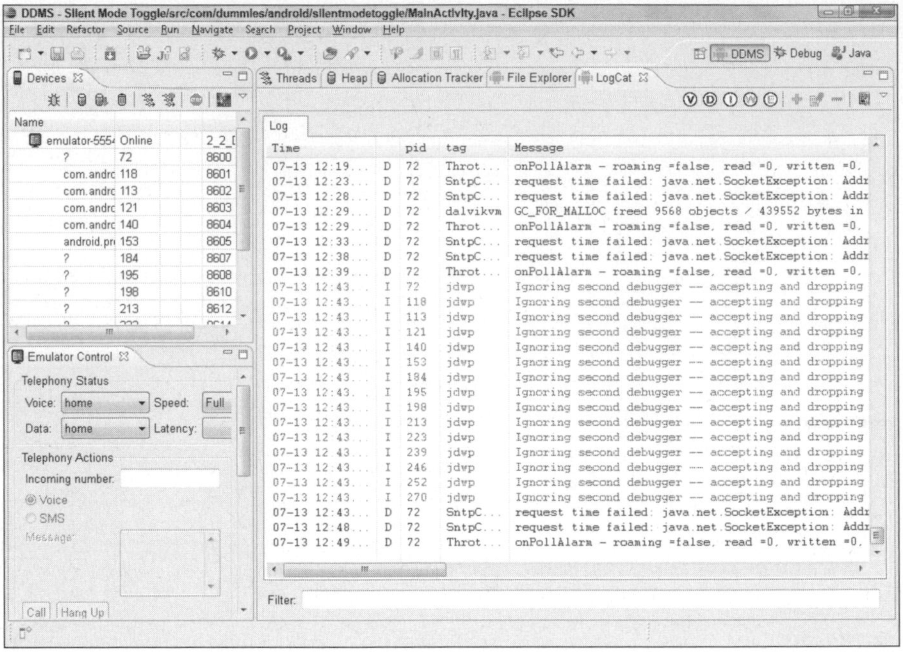

Figure 5-12:
The LogCat window, in the main viewing area of Eclipse.

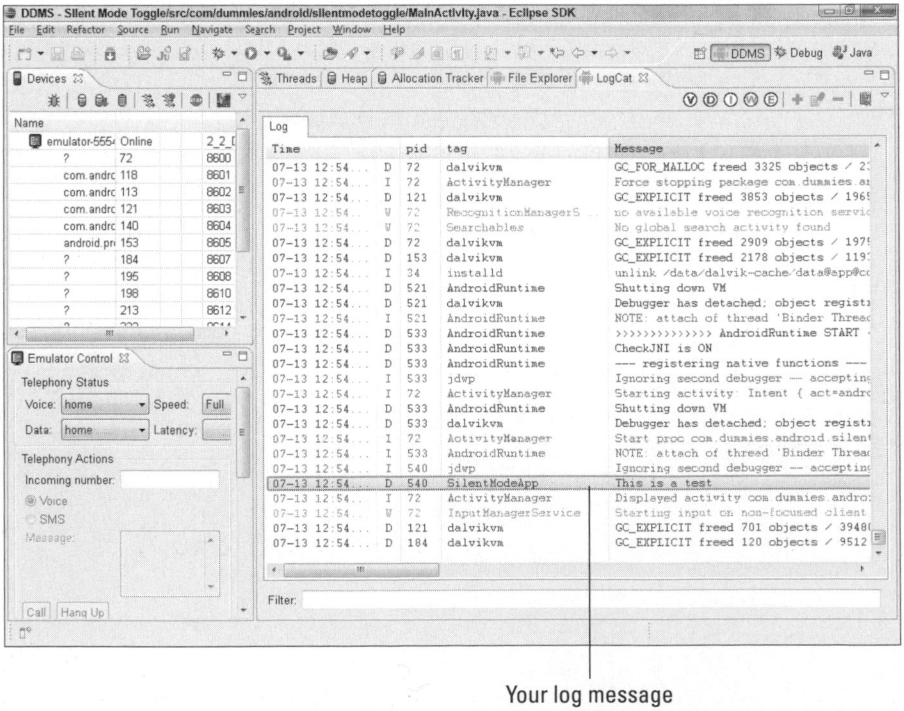

Figure 5-13:
Viewing your LogCat message in Eclipse via the DDMS perspective.

Your log message

Using the Eclipse debugger

Although DDMS might be one of your best allies, your number-one weapon in the battle against the army of bugs is the *Eclipse debugger,* which lets you set various breakpoints, inspect variables using the watch window, view LogCat, and much more. You use the debugger for either runtime errors or logic errors.

Eclipse catches errors in syntax. When the application doesn't compile, Eclipse alerts you by placing a colored, squiggly line underneath the problematic area.

Checking runtime errors

The *runtime error* is the Wicked Witch of the East — it comes out of nowhere and leaves everything a mess. In Android, runtime errors occur while an application is running. Your application might be humming along and, all of a sudden, your application crashes when you click a menu option or a button, for example. The possible reasons for this behavior are innumerable — perhaps you didn't initialize the AudioManager in the onCreate() method, and then you tried to access the variable later in the app, which would cause a run-time exception.

The debugger can help in this situation because you can set a breakpoint at the start of onCreate() that allows you to inspect the values of the variables through the debug perspective. You would likely then realize that you forgot to initialize the AlarmManager.

Listing 5-6 demonstrates what would create this scenario — commenting out the AlarmManager initialization causes an exception to be thrown at runtime.

Listing 5-6:   Commenting Out the AlarmManager Initialization

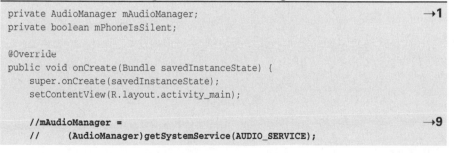

```
private AudioManager mAudioManager;                              →1
private boolean mPhoneIsSilent;

@Override
public void onCreate(Bundle savedInstanceState) {
    super.onCreate(savedInstanceState);
    setContentView(R.layout.activity_main);

    //mAudioManager =                                            →9
    //      (AudioManager)getSystemService(AUDIO_SERVICE);
```

(continued)

Listing 5-6 *(continued)*

```
        checkIfPhoneIsSilent();

        setButtonClickListener();

        Log.d("SilentModeApp", "This is a test");
    }
    /**
     * Checks to see if the phone is currently in silent mode.
     */
    private void checkIfPhoneIsSilent() {
        int ringerMode = mAudioManager.getRingerMode();            →22
        if (ringerMode == AudioManager.RINGER_MODE_SILENT) {
            mPhoneIsSilent = true;
        } else {
            mPhoneIsSilent = false;
        }

    }
```

Listing 5-6 works this way:

→**1**   The class-level `AudioManager` is introduced.

→**9**   This code, which is commented out, leaves the `mAudioManager` variable in a null state.

→**22**   When `onCreate()` called `checkIfPhoneIsSilent()`, the application threw a runtime exception because `mAudioManager` was null and the application tried to reference a member on an object that doesn't exist.

Attaching a debugger to the `onCreate()` method allows you to track down the root cause of the error.

Creating breakpoints

You have a couple ways to create a breakpoint, which will pause your application mid-execution and let you examine its running state:

✔ Choose the line where you want to place the breakpoint by clicking it with the mouse. Choose Run⇨Toggle Breakpoint, as shown in Figure 5-14, or press Ctrl+Shift+B.

✔ Double-click the left gutter in the Eclipse editor where you want to create a breakpoint.

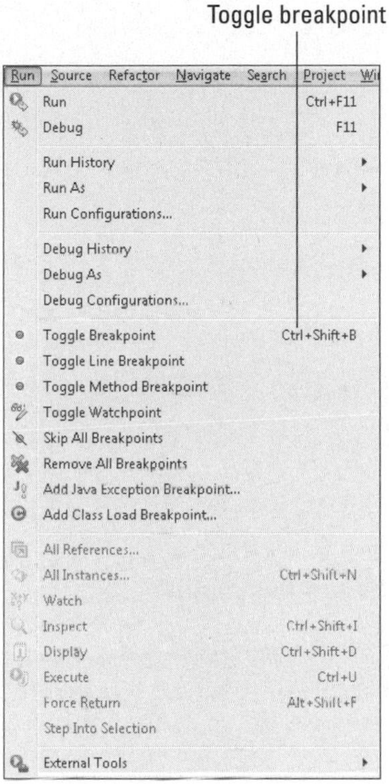

Toggle breakpoint

Toggle breakpoint

Figure 5-14:
Setting a
breakpoint
by using a
menu or hot
keys.

Either method creates a small, round icon in the left gutter of the Eclipse editor, as shown in Figure 5-15.

To try debugging in Eclipse, comment out line 3 of the onCreate() method, as shown in Listing 5-7.

Listing 5-7:   Commenting Out Code to Throw an Error

```
setContentView(R.layout.activity_main);

//mAudioManager = (AudioManager)getSystemService(AUDIO_SERVICE);          →3

checkIfPhoneIsSilent();                                                    →5
```

→3   The AudioManager is commented out.

→5   The method is called, which causes the application to fail.

Set a breakpoint on line 5.

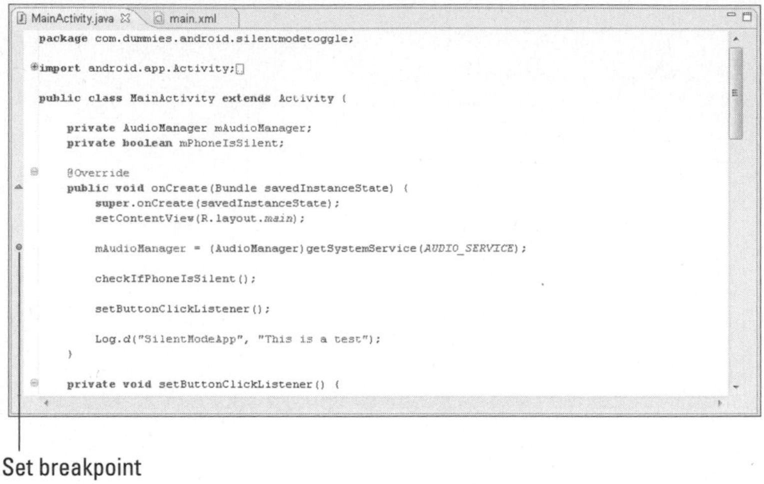

Figure 5-15:
A set break-
point in the
left gutter
of Eclipse's
editor
window.

Set breakpoint

Starting the debugger and the Debug perspective

You have one task to tend to before you start debugging: Tell the Android application that it's debuggable. To do so, open the `AndroidManifest.xml` file, select the Application tab at the bottom (see Figure 5-16), and then choose the debuggable property and set it to `true`, as shown in the figure. Then save the file.

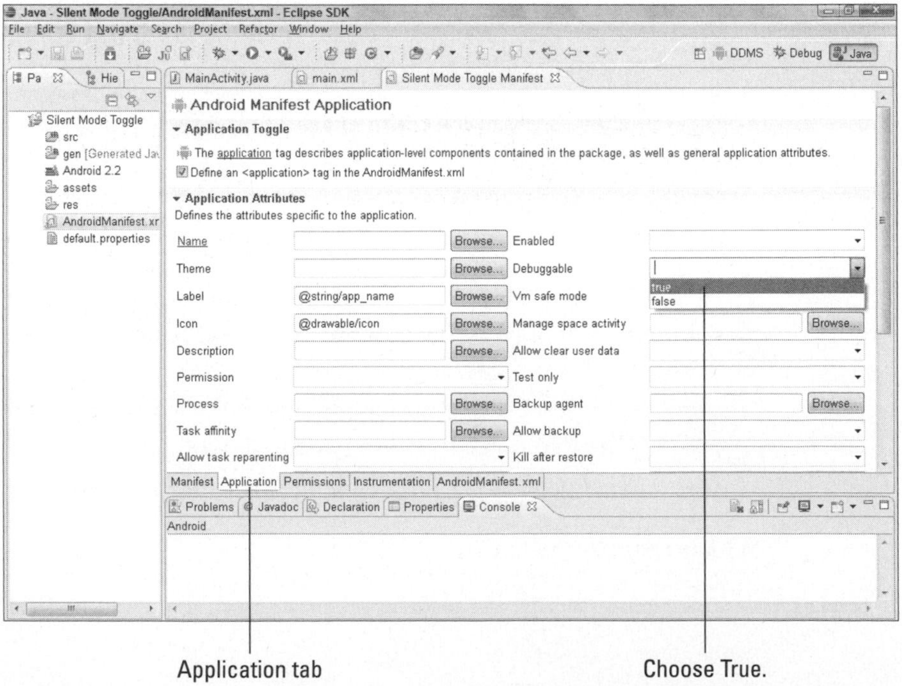

Figure 5-16:
Setting up
the appli-
cation as
debuggable.

Application tab

Choose True.

Failing to set the debuggable property to `true` ensures that you never get to debug your application. Your application won't even attempt to connect to the debugger. If you ever have problems with debugging, check to see whether this property is set to `true`.

Follow these steps to debug your code:

1. **Choose Run⇨Debug or press F11.**

   The ADT and Eclipse install the application on the emulator (or device) and then attach the debugger to it.

2. **Open your emulator.**

   The application installs, and you see the screen shown in Figure 5-17. It notifies you that the ADT and the emulator are trying to make a connection behind the scenes.

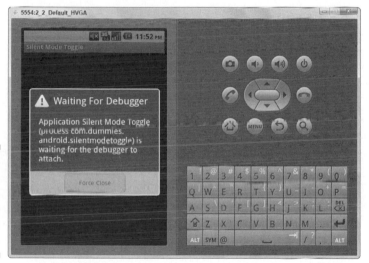

Figure 5-17: The emulator waits for the debugger to attach.

The emulator might sit for a moment while the debugger attaches. Then the emulator runs your application code and stops when it finds its first breakpoint.

You then see a dialog box asking whether the Debug perspective can be opened.

3. **Click Yes to open the Debug perspective.**

   You're now at a breakpoint, as shown in Figure 5-18. You can hover the cursor over variables to see their values.

4. **Hover the cursor over the** `mAudioManager` **variable.**

   The variable is null because you had commented out the code, as shown in Figure 5-18.

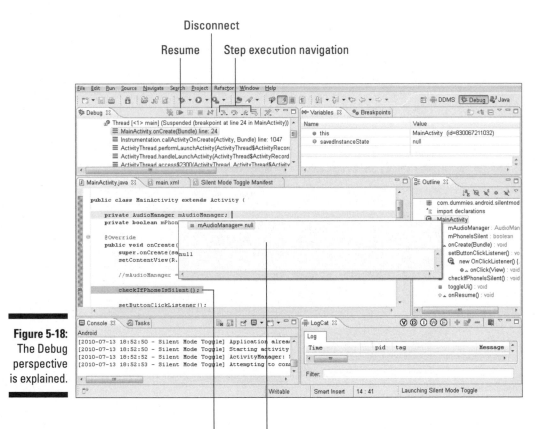

Figure 5-18:
The Debug
perspective
is explained.

You can also step through the execution of the code by operating the debug navigation, as shown in Figure 5-18. If you click the Continue button (or press F8), you can see the Debug perspective change and eventually say `source not found`. Open the emulator, and you can see that your application has crashed, as shown in Figure 5-19. In the Google Play Store, users have come to know this screen as the force-close (or FC) screen. A force-close occurs when a runtime exception isn't handled inside your code.

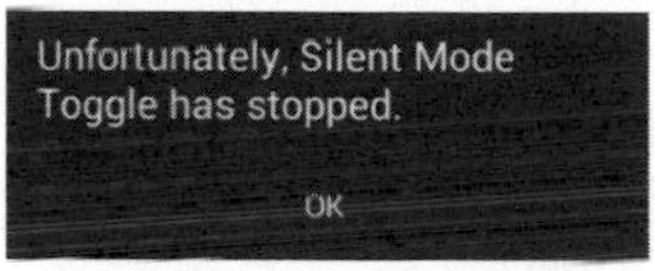

Figure 5-19:
The force-close dialog box opens after a runtime exception.

> Unfortunately, Silent Mode Toggle has stopped.
>
> OK

5. **To disconnect the debugger, click the Disconnect button.**

Return to the Java perspective, and uncomment line 3 from Listing 5-7 in the `MainActivity.java` file to ensure that the application builds successfully.

Checking logic errors

Computers do exactly what you tell them to do, and this little smartphone isn't smart enough to understand what's right or wrong in literal logic. An example of an error in literal logic is demonstrated in Listing 5-8.

Listing 5-8:   Code That Doesn't Check the Phone for Silent Mode

```
/**
 * Toggles the UI images from silent
 * to normal and vice versa.
 */
private void toggleUi() {

    ImageView imageView =
        (ImageView) findViewById(R.id.phone_icon);
            Drawable newPhoneImage;
```

(continued)

Listing 5-8 *(continued)*

```
        if (mPhoneIsSilent) {                                    →11
                newPhoneImage =
                    getResources().getDrawable(R.drawable.phone_silent);

        } else {
            newPhoneImage =
                getResources().getDrawable(R.drawable.phone_on);
        }

        imageView.setImageDrawable(newPhoneImage);
    }

@Override
protected void onResume() {
    super.onResume();
    //checkIfPhoneIsSilent();                                    →26
    toggleUi();
};
```

Listing 5-8 works this way:

→11   This line checks to see whether the phone is in Silent mode.

→26   For the `toggleUi()` method to properly display the correct user interface to the user, the application has to know what state the ringer is in. This line comments out the `checkIfPhoneIs Silent()` method, which updates the class-level `mPhoneIs SilentVariable`.

Because this occurs in the `onResume()` method, the user can leave the app, change its ringer state via the phone's Settings app, then return to the app — and the app would be in an incorrect state simply because of a logic error.

Using a debugger, you can attach a breakpoint on the first line of the `toggleUi()` method to inspect the various variables that help make the logic calls. Then you would notice that `mPhone- IsSilent` isn't being set.

Thinking Beyond the Application Boundaries

At times, the device may perform extraneous work that can affect your application, such as downloading a large file in the background while playing music from an online radio application. Will these heavy network-bound activities affect the application in any way? It depends. If your app needs a connection to the Internet and for some reason cannot connect, will it crash? What will happen? Knowing the answers to these questions means that you're thinking beyond your application boundaries.

Not all apps are created equal — some good ones are out there, along with some *bad* ones. Before building or releasing your first Android application, ensure that you know the ins and outs of your application and anything that can affect it. Be sure that the app doesn't crash when users perform routine tap events and screen navigation.

Building applications on embedded devices is much different from building them on a PC or Mac, and the reason is simple: The resources (memory and processor, for example) are limited. If the Android device happens to be a phone, its main purpose is to perform phone-like duties, such as recognizing an incoming call, maintaining a signal, and sending and receiving text messages.

If a phone call is in progress, the Android system treats that process as vital, whereas a downloading file in the background is considered nonvital. If the phone starts to run out of resources, Android kills all nonvital processes to keep the vital ones alive. A file can be downloaded again, but when a call is lost, it's lost forever — you have to make that call again, which would only frustrate the user if the main purpose for purchasing the device was to have a phone. Your app might download a file in the background and the process gets killed — this is a scenario that you need to test. It can also happen if your phone encounters an area with a poor or non-existent wireless signal. If the connection gets dropped, your file isn't downloaded.

Test for all possible solutions and have a safety guard for them. Otherwise, your app will be prone to runtime exceptions, which can lead to poor reviews from users at the Google Play Store.

What about automated testing?

With the rise of agile methodologies over the past decade, it's only a matter of time before you start to wonder how to perform automated testing in Android. The SDK installs Android unit-testing tools that you can use to test not only Java classes but also Android-based classes and user interface interactions. You can read more about unit testing in the Android documentation at `http://d.android.com/guide/topics/testing/testing_android.html`.

Here are the tools at your disposal:

- ✔ **jUnit:** The SDK installs jUnit integration with the ADT. You can use jUnit, a popular unit-testing framework that's used in Java, to perform unit testing or interaction testing, and you can find more information about jUnit at `www.junit.org`. To make your development life easier, Eclipse has built-in tools to help facilitate testing in jUnit through Eclipse.

- ✔ **Monkey:** The user interface and application exerciser known as Monkey runs on your emulator or device and generates pseudorandom streams of user events, including taps, gestures, touches, clicks, and a number of system events. Monkey, which is installed with the Android SDK, is a helpful way to stress-test an application.

Interacting with your application

To ensure that your app works, fire it up and play with its features. While your app is running, start another app, such as the browser. Visit a few sites, and then return to your app. Click any buttons related to your app to see what happens. Try all kinds of things to see whether you find outcomes that you didn't consider. What happens if a user is interacting with your app and receives a phone call? Are you saving the necessary state in `onPause()` and restoring it in `onResume()`?

Android handles the difficult task management for you, but it's ultimately your responsibility to manage the state of your application.

Testing whether your application works

In the emulator, open the Silent Mode Toggle application from the launcher. You've already performed the first step in the testing process — making sure that the app starts!

After the app is open, check to see whether the phone is in Silent mode by looking for the small phone icon on the notification bar (refer to Figure 5-5).

Click the Toggle Silent Mode button to toggle the ringer mode. Did the application's image change from the green phone to the silent phone (or vice versa)? Try various actions to ensure that your application works as expected. If you find a flaw, use the debugging tools featured in this chapter to help identify the issue.

Chapter 6

Understanding Android Resources

- -

In This Chapter

▶ Knowing why resources are important in Android

▶ Extracting resources

▶ Working with image resources

- -

Resources are mentioned in detail throughout this book, so you might wonder why an entire chapter is devoted to them. Discussing resources and their use in Chapters 3 and 4 is necessary to help you understand the basic structure of the resource directory and the use of resources to build a simple application. One compelling reason to use resources in your application, globalization, is covered in this chapter.

Understanding Resources

Resources are the additional static content and files that are an intrinsic part of your application but aren't part of your Java code. Resources can take these forms:

- ✓ Layout
- ✓ String
- ✓ Image
- ✓ Dimension
- ✓ Style
- ✓ Theme
- ✓ Value
- ✓ Menu
- ✓ Color

Earlier chapters in this book introduce you to layouts, strings, and images because they're the most common types of resources that you use in every-day Android application development. The remaining resources may be muddy, so the following few sections clear them up.

Dimensions

In an Android resource, a *dimension* is a number followed by a unit of measurement, such as 10px, 2in, or 5sp. You use a dimension when specifying any property in Android that requires a numeric unit of measure. For example, you may want the padding of a layout to be 10px. The following units of measure are supported by Android:

✔ **density-independent pixel (dp):** This abstract unit is based on the physical density of the screen. These units are relative to a screen measuring 160 dots per inch (dpi); therefore, 1 dp is equivalent to 1 pixel on a 160 dpi screen. The ratio of dp to pixels changes with screen density, but not necessarily in proportion. This unit of measure is the one that most developers use when developing layouts.

The dp concept is complex; if you plan to actively support multiple screen densities, the Supporting Multiple Screen Sizes article at `http://developer.android.com/guide/practices/screens_support.html` is a must read.

✔ **scale-independent pixel (sp):** This unit resembles the dp unit but is scaled according to the user's font-size preference. Use sp dimensions when specifying font sizes in your application.

✔ **pixel (px):** A pixel corresponds to a pixel on the screen. This unit of measure isn't recommended. Your app may look great on a medium-density device but look distorted and out of place on a high-density screen (and vice versa) because the dpi differs.

✔ **point (pt):** A point is ½ inch, based on the physical size of the screen. Like px, pt is not recommended.

✔ **millimeter (mm):** This unit is based on the size of the screen. Like px, mm is not recommended.

✔ **inch (in):** This unit is based on the physical size of the screen. Like px, in is not recommended.

Styles

Styles in Android are similar to Cascading Style Sheets (CSS) in the web development realm: You use styles to (you guessed it) style an application. A *style* is officially a collection of properties that can be applied to an individual view (within the layout file) or to an activity or to your entire application (from within the manifest file). Styles support inheritance, so you can provide a basic style and then modify it for each particular use case in your application. Style property examples include font size, font color, and screen background.

Themes

A *theme* is a style applied to an entire activity or application, rather than an individual view. When a style is applied as a theme, every view in the activity and/or application inherits the style settings. For example, you can set all `TextView` views to a particular font, and all views in the themed activity or application then display their text in that font.

Values

The value resource can contain many different types of value type resources for your application, including

- ✔ **Bool:** A Boolean value defined in XML whose value is stored in an arbitrary filename in the `res/values/<filename>.xml` file, where *<filename>* is the name of the file. An example is `bools.xml`.

- ✔ **Integer:** An integer value defined in XML whose value is stored with an arbitrary filename in the `res/values/<filename>.xml` file. An example is `integers.xml`.

- ✔ **Integer array:** An array of integers defined in XML whose set of values is stored with an arbitrary name in the `res/values/<filename>.xml` file, where *<filename>* is the name of the file. An example is `integers.xml`. You can reference and use these integers in your code to help define loops, lengths, and other elements.

- ✔ **Typed array:** A *typed array* is used to create an array of resources, such as `drawables`. You can create arrays of mixed types. Therefore, the arrays aren't required to be homogeneous — however, you must be aware of the data type so that you can appropriately cast it. As with other resources, the filename is arbitrary in the `res/values/<filename>.xml` file. An example is `types.xml`.

Menus

Whether your app is using the action bar or a menu, Android treats them both the same and you'll define them the same way. A menu can be defined via either code or XML. The preferred way to define one is via XML; therefore, the various menus you create should be placed into the menu/ directory. Each menu has its own .xml file.

Colors

The colors file, located in the values/colors.xml file, lets you name colors, such as login_screen_font_color. This might depict the color of the font you're using on the logon page, for example. Each color is defined as a hexadecimal value.

Working with Resources

You may have worked with resources a few times in this book, and at this point you're likely familiar with using the R class to access resources from within your application. If you're rusty on resources and the generated R file, see Chapter 3.

Moving strings into resources

As you become an experienced programmer, you may start to take shortcuts to get your project built and working. Say that initially you forget to move strings into resources, and you have to come back at a later time to do it. You can extract a string into a resource using the built-in tools.

The long way

Here's one way to extract a string into a resource:

1. **Create a new string resource.**

2. **Copy its name.**

3. **Replace the string value in your layout with the resource identifier.**

This task may not be a huge pain, but it takes time, possibly 30 to 45 seconds for the average developer.

The fast way

You can cut the time to create a string resource to fewer than 15 seconds. If you do this 30 times a day (which is feasible in an 8-hour day), you can save 15 minutes of just copying and pasting. That's five hours a month doing the copy-and-paste dance!

Follow these steps:

1. **In Eclipse, open the** `main.xml` **file in the** `layouts` **directory.**

2. **Find the following chunk of code in the file:**

```
<Button
        android:id="@+id/toggleButton"
        android:layout_width="wrap_content"
        android:layout_height="wrap_content"
        android:layout_gravity="center_horizontal"
        android:text="Toggle Silent Mode"
/>
```

3. **Select the boldface line** `"Toggle Silent Mode"`.

4. **Press Ctrl+1 on Windows or ⌘+1 on a Mac.**

   A menu opens with three options.

5. **Choose the Extract Android String option.**

   The Extract Android String dialog box opens, as shown in Figure 6-1, and you can set various options for the resource.

6. **Leave the defaults alone, and click OK.**

   You can now see that the layout file has been modified. The text `"Toggle Silent Mode"` has been replaced with `"@string/toggle_silent_mode"`.

   If you open the `strings.xml` file in the `res/values` folder, you can see a new string resource with that name and the value `"Toggle Silent Mode"`.

That's pretty cool! You can see that doing this 20 or 30 times a day can add up and save you a lot of time.

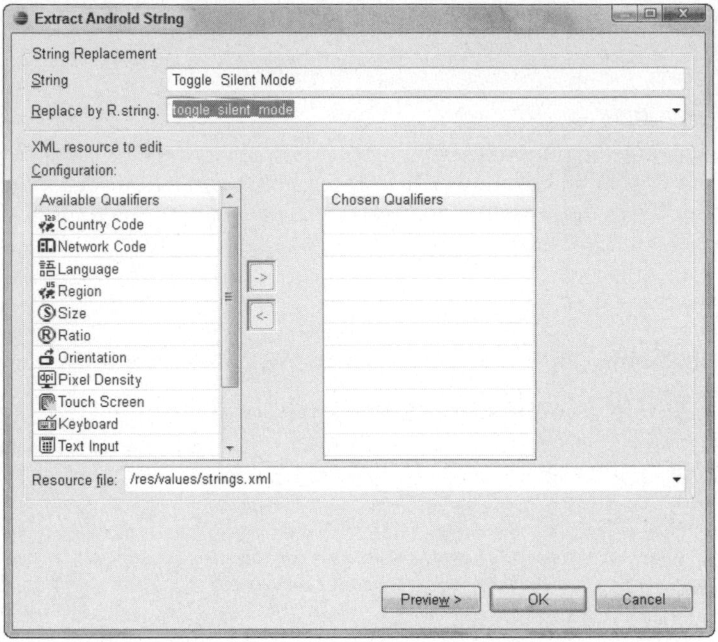

Figure 6-1:
The Extract
Android
String dialog
box.

Wrestling the image beast

One of the most difficult parts about resources can be images. They might look great on medium-density devices but look like garbage on high-density devices. This is where multiple-density folders come into play. These density-specific drawable folders are explained in Chapter 3.

Battling pixelation and compression

The issue you'll most likely encounter is pixelation and compression/expansion (moving from higher- to lower-density devices and vice versa). To work around this issue, design your graphics at a high resolution, such as 300dpi in large-size format. For example, if you're building the launcher icon, build it at 250px high and 250px wide. Although the `xhdpi` folder might need an image of only 96px high by 96px wide (the largest in use), it doesn't mean that in two or three months a higher resolution device won't be released.

This situation can be painful because working with large image files in image editing programs can be difficult if you don't have a computer with decent capabilities. But you have to trust us on this one: Having a large raw-image file that's high density is much easier to mold and shape into the correct densities you'll need.

Downsizing a high-density image doesn't distort its quality (other than losing its fine edges and detail), but upscaling distorts it because it creates pixelation and distortion. Starting with a large file reduces the chance that you'll ever have to upscale, which means that your app graphics will always look crisp.

Using layers

If you're creating graphics in an image editing tool that supports layers, place each item in your graphic on a different layer. The reasons are many, but here are the key factors:

- **Changes:** At some point, you will need to change something in your graphic — its background, font, or logo, for example. If you have all these items in different layers, you can make the change without affecting the rest of the graphic.

- **Localization:** An example from an earlier section in this chapter talks about various strings in different languages, and graphics are no different. Many times as you develop applications, you will encounter graphics with stylized text in the graphic itself. If your application is being translated into Japanese and your graphics contain stylized English text, you can create a Japanese version of those graphics and place them in a Japanese drawable region folder, such as res/drawable-ja. The Android platform recognizes which region it's in (in this case, Japan). If the region's resource folders (res/drawable-ja, res/values-ja, and so on) are available, Android uses them in the application. That being said, it's always easier to keep your text in text resources and your images in image resources. Translating text resources is easier than making new copies of your images for every new language.

Making your apps global with resources

The Android platform surpassed the Apple iPhone in U.S. market share in the first quarter of 2010. Now carriers around the world are developing Android-based smartphones, which simply means more potential users for your apps.

What this statement means to you as a developer is that Android is a huge market with tons of opportunity waiting to be tapped. Though this opportunity is exciting, taking the greatest advantage of it requires that you understand resources and how they affect the usability of your apps. For example, if a user in the United States uses your app and it was written for an English-speaking audience (using resources or not), the user would be able to use it. However, if you hard-code all your string values into your views and activities and then need to release a Chinese version, you have to rewrite your application to use resources. When you use resources, you can have a linguist translate your strings and drawables into the region you're targeting — such as China.

Resources allow you to extract human-readable strings, images, and viewable layouts into resources that you can reference. Various resource folders can be created to handle screens of various sizes, different languages (strings and drawables), and layout options such as landscape and portrait. Landscape and portrait views come into play when a user rotates the device 90 degrees in either direction.

If you want your apps to be viewable on as many Android devices as possible around the world, you should use resources at all times. Always put all strings into the `strings.xml` file because, someday, someone from another country will want your application in another language. To transport your application to another language, you simply need to have a linguist translate your `strings.xml` file into her language, and then you can create various `values` folders to hold the appropriate region's values. Android takes care of the hard work. For example, if the user is in China and his phone is set to the Chinese character set, Android looks for the values folder named `values-cn`, which is where Chinese values are stored — including the Chinese version of the `strings.xml` file. If Android cannot find such a folder, the platform defaults to the default `values` folder, which contains the English version of the `strings.xml` file. (For more on strings, see the section "Moving strings into resources," earlier in this chapter.)

When it comes down to it, having a linguist update your strings and creating a new folder with the new `strings.xml` file located within are simple tasks. Expand this concept to other languages and tablets and televisions and you can see the potential. You're no longer looking at mobile users as your target audience. You're looking at *Android* users, and with the options being released, you could be looking at *billions* of users. Using resources correctly can make your expansion into foreign markets that much easier.

While nothing beats having a person to translate your app strings for you, finding a native speaker for every language you want to support can be tough. There is a simple shortcut you can take to have Google do the translation for you. Visit `http://translate.google.com/toolkit` and upload your `strings.xml` file to have it automatically translated by a computer. The results may sound a little clumsy to a native speaker, but it will at least give you a head start.

Designing your application for various regions is a big topic. You can find more in-depth information in the "Localization" article of the SDK documentation at `http://developer.android.com/guide/topics/resources/localization.html`.

Although designing an application to be ready for various regions sounds compelling, it also helps to know that the Google Play Store allows you to specify the targeted region of your device. You're not forced into releasing your application to all regions. Therefore, if you have written an application for the Berlin bus route system in Germany, it probably doesn't make sense to have a Chinese version, unless you want to cater to Chinese tourists as well as to German residents.

Chapter 7

Turning Your Application into a Home Screen Widget

*U*sability is the name of the game in regard to all disciples of application development: If your application isn't usable, users simply won't use it.

If you've followed the first six chapters of this book to build the Silent Mode Toggle application, it undoubtedly works well and is highly usable. Unfortunately, if the application were published at the Google Play Store, it likely wouldn't be popular yet because a user would have to open the app and then tap a button to silence the phone. If the user hasn't created a Home screen shortcut to the application, and the app is buried in the application launcher with other applications, a few extra steps are required: Unlock the phone, open the launcher, locate the app, open the app, and then tap the Silent button. At this point, the user might as well press the Volume Up and Volume Down keys to silence the phone. To make this application more usable and feasible, simply turn it into a Home screen widget.

In this chapter, you build a Home screen widget for your application. An app widget normally is a small icon or tiny view on the Home screen. Users can interact with your application by simply tapping its icon — the Home screen widget. Then the core functionality kicks in and toggles Silent mode. This chapter introduces you to these classes:

> ✔ Intent
> ✔ BroadcastReceiver
> ✔ AppWidgetProvider
> ✔ IntentService

Each of these classes plays a vital role in Android as well as in the app widget framework.

Working with App Widgets in Android

A *Home screen widget* (or *app widget*) in Android is a special kind of view that can be embedded on your device's Home screen. An app widget can accept user input via click events, and it can update itself regularly. A user can add an app widget to the Home screen by tapping the Applications button and then selecting Widgets. The result is shown in Figure 7-1.

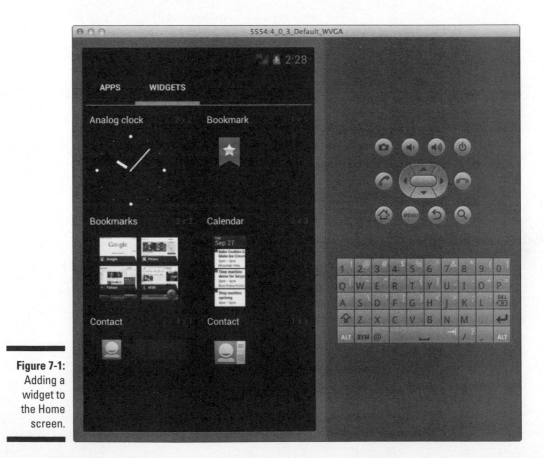

Figure 7-1:
Adding a
widget to
the Home
screen.

To make the Silent Mode Toggle application more usable, build a Home screen widget for it so that users can add the widget to the Home screen. Tapping the widget changes the phone's ringer mode automatically without having to open the application. The widget also updates its layout to indicate what state the phone is in, as shown in Figure 7-2.

Silent mode is enabled.   Phone is in regular mode.

Figure 7-2:
The two
states of the
app widget.

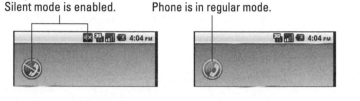

Working with remote views

When you develop apps in Android, remember that it's based on the Linux 2.6 kernel. Linux comes supplied with its own idioms (or "dialect") about security, and the Android platform inherits them. For example, the Android security model is heavily based around the Linux user, file, and process security model.

Because every Android application is (usually) associated with its own unique user, Android prevents applications from modifying the files of other applications. This prevents developers from attempting to inject malicious code into other apps.

Because the Home screen is its own application and thus has its own unique user, developers such as yourself aren't allowed to directly run your application code on the Home screen for safety reasons. To provide a way to access the Home screen and modify the contents of a particular area on it from an application, the Android developers implemented the RemoteViews architecture: It lets you run code inside your application, in a separate process from the Home screen application, but it still allows a widget's view to be updated on the Home screen. The result is that you can still have your widget but no arbitrary code needs to be run inside the Home screen application — all your app widget code runs within your application.

Suppose that a user taps the Home screen app widget (in this case, an icon she added to the Home screen). This action sends a request — addressed to *your* application — to change the ringer mode. Android routes the request to your application, and the application processes the request, instructing the Android platform to change the ringer mode and update the app widget on the Home screen with a new image. None of this code is run in the Home screen application — it's all run remotely in your application, with Android messaging routing the message to the appropriate application.

A *remote view* combines a little magic with innovative engineering. Known as the RemoteViews class on the Android platform, it allows your application to programmatically supply a remote user interface to the Home screen in another process. The app widget code isn't an actual activity (as in earlier chapters), but is an implementation of an AppWidgetProvider. When Android routes a message (as described in the preceding paragraph) to your application from the Home screen, the message is handled in your implementation of the AppWidgetProvider class.

Using AppWidgetProviders

The AppWidgetProvider class allows the developer to programmatically interact with the app widget on the Home screen. When this interaction takes place, messages are sent from the Home screen app widget to your application via broadcast events. Using these broadcast events, you can respond when the app widget is updated, enabled, disabled, or deleted. You can also update the look and feel of the app widget on the Home screen by providing a new view. Because this view is located on the Home screen and not within your running application, you use RemoteViews to update the Home screen layout. All the logic that determines what should happen is initiated via an implementation of AppWidgetProvider.

Picture the app widget framework as the translator of a conversation between two entities. If you need to speak to someone who knows Italian, but you don't know how to speak Italian, you would find a translator who would accept your input, translate it into Italian, and relay the message to the native Italian speaker. The same process applies to the app widget framework: This framework is your translator.

When the Italian native (the Home screen, in this case) needs to let you know that something has happened (such as a user tapping a button), the translator (the app widget framework in the Android system) translates the action into a message that you can understand (tapping a particular button). At that time, you can respond with the action you want to take (such as change the app widget background color to lime green), and the translator (the app widget framework) relays the message to the native Italian speaker (to the Home screen via the Android system). The Home screen updates the background color of the view.

App widgets can only accept input from tap-type events. When you're working within an app widget, you have no access to other basic input views, such as an editable text box or drop-down lists.

Working with Pending Intents

When the user needs to interact with your application, she communicates by tapping the app widget using the Android messaging architecture (as described earlier), and you aren't immediately notified. However, this doesn't mean you *can't* be notified about a click event on your app widget — it's just done a little differently than regular views.

App widget click events contain instructions for what to do when a click event happens via the PendingIntent class in the Android framework. A *pending intent* is an implementation of the Intent class in Android, as explained in the following section.

Understanding the Android intent system

An Intent object in Android is a message telling Android to make something happen. When you turn on a light using a wall switch, the action of your intent is to turn on the light, so you flip the switch to the On position. In Android, this action correlates to creating an instance of the Intent class with an action in it specifying that the light is to be turned on:

```
Intent turnLightOn = new Intent("TURN_LIGHT_ON");
```

This intent is fired off into the Android messaging system (as described in Chapter 1), and the appropriate activity handles the Intent. (If multiple activities respond, Android lets the user choose one to do the work.) However, in the physical world, an electrical connection is made by positioning the switch to the On position, resulting in illuminating the light. In Android, you have to provide code, in the form of an activity, to make this happen. This activity (that can be named TurnLightOnActivity) responds to the turnLightOn intent. If you're working with an app widget, you must handle the intent in a BroadcastReceiver rather than in an activity. An AppWidgetProvider is an instance of a BroadcastReceiver with a few extra bells and whistles that configure a lot of the app widget framework for you. The BroadcastReceiver object is responsible for receiving broadcast messages.

The `AppWidgetProvider` handles the intent from the Home screen and responds with the appropriate result that you determined, using your code, inside your custom `AppWidgetProvider`. It doesn't work with any intent, though. If you want to receive input from your app widget, use `PendingIntent`.

To understand what a `PendingIntent` class is, you need to fully grasp the concept of the basic `Intent` class. A `PendingIntent` contains a child `Intent` object. At a high level, a pending intent acts like a regular intent. An *intent* is a message that can carry a wide variety of data describing an operation that needs to be performed. An intent can be addressed to a specific activity or broadcast to a generic category of receivers known as `BroadcastReceivers` (which includes `AppWidgetProvider`). The `Intent`, `Activity`, and `BroadcastReceiver` system is reminiscent of the message bus architecture, where a message is placed on a message bus and any of the endpoints on the bus respond to the message if (and only if) they know how. If no endpoint knows how to respond to the message, or if the message wasn't addressed to the endpoint, the message is ignored.

An intent can be launched into the message bus system in a couple of ways:

- ✔ **Start another activity:** Use the `startActivity()` call, which accepts an `Intent` object as a parameter.
- ✔ **Notify any interested** `BroadcastReceiver` **components:** Use the `sendBroadcast()` call, which also takes an intent as a parameter.
- ✔ **Communicate with a background service:** Use the `startService()` or `bindService()` call, which both accept intents as parameters.

An activity is the glue that binds various components of the application because it provides a late-binding mechanism that allows inter-application and intra-application communication.

Understanding intent data

An intent's data consists of these elements:

- ✔ **Action:** The general action to be performed. A few common actions include `ACTION_VIEW`, `ACTION_EDIT`, and `ACTION_MAIN`. You can also provide your own custom action.
- ✔ **Data:** The data to operate on, such as a record in a database or a uniform resource identifier that should be opened, such as a URL.

Table 7-1 demonstrates a few action and data parameters for Intent objects and their simple data structure.

Table 7-1	Intent Data Examples	
Action	**Data**	**Result**
ACTION_ VIEW	tel:123	Display the dialer with the given number (123) filled in.
ACTION_ DIAL	content://contacts/ people/1	Display the dialer showing the phone number from the contact with the ID of 1.
ACTION_ EDIT	content://contacts/ people/1	Edit the information about the person whose given identifier is 1.
ACTION_ VIEW	http://www.example. org	Display the web page of the given intent.
ACTION_ VIEW	content://contacts/ people	Display a list of all people in the Contacts system.

Intents can also carry an array of other data that include these elements:

- ✔ **category:** Gives additional information about the action to execute. As an example, if CATEGORY_LAUNCHER is present, the application should show up in the application launcher as a top-level application. Another option, CATEGORY_ALTERNATIVE, can provide alternative actions that the user can perform on a piece of data.

- ✔ **type:** Specifies a particular type (MIME type) of intent data. For example, when you're setting the type to audio/mpeg, the Android system recognizes that you're working with an MP3 file. Normally, the type is inferred by the data itself. By setting the type, you override the inferred type by explicitly setting the type in the intent.

- ✔ **component:** Specifies an explicit component name of the class on which to execute the intent. Normally, the component is inferred by inspection of other information in the intent (action, data/type, and categories), and matching components can handle it. If this attribute is set, none of that evaluation takes place, and this component is used exactly as specified (likely the most common use case in your applications). You can provide another activity as the component — this addresses Android to interact with that specific class.

✔ **extras:** A bundle of additional, key-based information that's used to provide extra information to the receiving component. For example, if you need to send an e-mail address, you use the extras bundle to supply the body and subject and other components of the e-mail.

Evaluating intents

Intents are evaluated in the Android system in one of two ways:

✔ **Explicitly:** The intent has specified an explicit component or the exact class that will execute the data in the intent. (Again, this is likely the most common way to address intents.) This type of intent often contains no other data because it's a means to start other activities within an application. You find out later in this chapter how to use an explicit intent in an application.

✔ **Implicitly:** The intent hasn't specified a component or class. Instead, the intent must provide enough information about the action that needs to be performed with the given data for the Android system to determine which available components can handle the intent — sometimes referred to as an *address* and a *payload*.

An example is setting up an e-mail intent that contains e-mail fields (To, CC, Subject, and Body) and an e-mail MIME type. Android interprets it as an e-mail and gives the user of the device the opportunity to choose which application should handle the intent. Possibilities include Gmail or Exchange or a POP e-mail account. The user determines which e-mail program to use. The Android capability to identify possible matches for the given intent is known as *intent resolution*.

Using pending intents

A `PendingIntent` is an intent at its core, but with a slight paradigm shift in regard to functionality: It's created by your application and given to another, completely different application. By giving another application a `PendingIntent`, you're granting the other application the right to perform the operation you have specified as though the application were your application. In layman's terms, you're giving information about how to call your application to perform work on another application's behalf. When the other application deems that the given work needs to take place, it executes the `PendingIntent`, which instructs the Android messaging system to inform your application to perform the necessary work.

Avoiding the dreaded Application Not Responding (ANR) error

Because all the work that happens in the `AppWidgetProvider` takes place on the main thread of the user interface, you must complete all your work as quickly as possible. If your `AppWidgetProvider` takes too long to respond, your code holds up the UI thread and causes your application to display an Application Not Responding (ANR) dialog box because the Android system believes that the application is frozen and not responding. An example is network communication to download status updates from a service such as Twitter. If downloading the statuses takes too long (which can be much shorter than you might expect), Android shows the ANR dialog box letting the user know that the app widget isn't responding; at that point, the user can force-close the application.

One way to avoid the ANR error is to implement a service inside `AppWidgetProvider` that performs its work in a background thread. The `IntentService` that you implement in the following sections helps you avoid ANR errors and allows the widget to remain very fast.

For the purpose of the Silent Mode Toggle application, you use the `PendingIntent.getBroadcast()` call to obtain a pending intent instance. This call returns a `PendingIntent` that's used for broadcasts throughout the system. The call takes these four parameters:

- ✔ `Context`: The context in which this `PendingIntent` should perform the broadcast.

- ✔ `RequestCode`: The private request code for the sender. Not currently used; therefore, a zero is passed in.

- ✔ `Intent`: The intent to be broadcast.

- ✔ `Flags`: A set of controls used to control the intent when it's started. Not currently used in the Silent Mode Toggle application; therefore, a zero is passed in.

Wait a second — this code uses an `Intent` as well as a `PendingIntent`. Why? The `Intent` object is wrapped inside a `PendingIntent` because a `PendingIntent` is used for cross-process communication. When the `PendingIntent` is fired off, the real work that needs to be done is wrapped up in the child `Intent` object.

That's a lot of information! Now that you understand the basics of the Android intent system, it's time to implement the guts of the application inside this app widget.

Creating the Home Screen Widget

The process of sending messages between the Home screen app widget and your application is handled via the Android messaging system, the `PendingIntent` class, and the `AppWidgetProvider`. In this section, you build each component to get your first app widget up and running on the Home screen.

Implementing the AppWidgetProvider

Implementing the `AppWidgetProvider` is fairly straightforward: Open Eclipse and open the Silent Mode Toggle application.

To add a new class to the `com.dummies.android.silentmodetoggle` package and provide a name, such as `AppWidget.java`, follow these steps:

1. **Right-click** `com.dummies.android.silentmodetoggle` **in the src/ folder and choose New⇨Class.**

   The New Java Class dialog box opens, as shown in Figure 7-3.

2. **Provide the name of the class and set its superclass to** `android.app widget.AppWidgetProvider`.

3. **Click Finish when you're done.**

   The new class is added to the selected package.

The `AppWidgetProvider` does all the work of responding to events from the `RemoteViews`, but how so? If you look at the `AppWidgetProvider` Android documentation, you can see that it's a direct subclass of `BroadcastReceiver`. At a high level, a `BroadcastReceiver` is a component that can receive broadcast messages from the Android system. When a user taps a clickable view in the `RemoteViews` on the Home screen (such as a button), the Android system broadcasts a message informing the receiver that the view was clicked. After the message is broadcast, the `AppWidgetProvider` can handle that message.

Note that because these messages are *broadcast,* they're sent system-wide. If the payload of the message and the destination address information are vague enough, various `BroadcastReceiver` objects might handle the message. The `AppWidgetProvider` you build in this section is addressed to a single destination, similar to walking into a room full of building contractors and asking whether any of them can do some work for you — everyone would respond. You have a vague message address and payload. However, if you ask the same group for a small electronics electrician contractor by the name of Bob Smith, only one might respond. You have a specifically addressed message with a detailed address and payload information.

Communicating with the app widget

The `AppWidgetProvider` class has no code in it at first — it's an empty shell. To make your `AppWidgetProvider` able to do something, you add a code to respond to the intent (the message) that was sent to your `AppWidgetProvider`. In the code file you just created, type the code shown in Listing 7-1 into the editor. (***Note:*** The class is named `AppWidget`, so if yours is different, change that line.)

Listing 7-1: The Initial Setup of the App Widget

```
public class AppWidget extends AppWidgetProvider {                    →1
    @Override
    public void onReceive(Context ctxt, Intent intent) {             →4
            if (intent.getAction()==null) {                          →5
             // Do Something
            } else {
                super.onReceive(ctxt, intent);                      →10
            }
        }


        @Override
        public void onUpdate(Context context, AppWidgetManager
        appWidgetManager, int[] appWidgetIds) {                     →15
         // Do Something
        }
}
```

This list briefly describes the numbered lines:

→1   This line of code informs Android that this class is an
      `AppWidgetProvider` because the class is inheriting from
      `AppWidgetProvider`.

→4   This line overrides the `onReceive()` method to be able to detect
      when a new intent is received from the `RemoteViews`. This intent
      could have been initiated by a user tapping a view to perform an
      action such as a button click. The `Intent` object is contained
      within the `PendingIntent`, which initiated the request.

→5   `Intent` objects can contain various pieces of data. One such slice
      of data is the action. This line of code checks whether the intent
      has an action. If it doesn't have an action, the intent is fired off.
      This process may sound backward, but you can find out more in
      later sections.

→10   This line delegates the work to the superclass because you don't
      need to do anything with the intent. (This intent isn't what you
      were expecting; the intent had an action, and you're expecting an
      intent without an action.) This would happen if the app widget
      automatically updated itself regularly, as you define it in the
      widget metadata. (Metadata is explained in the "Working with
      the app widget's metadata" section, later in this chapter.) Doing
      so would call one of the many built-in methods for enabling, dis-
      abling, starting, stopping, or updating the app widget, as on line 15.

→**15**   The `onUpdate()` method is called by the Android framework on a
timed basis that you can set in the widget metadata. This method
is called because the Android framework first realizes that time
has elapsed and then wants you to have the opportunity to update
the view proactively, without interaction from the user, such as
a news application widget updating itself every 30 minutes with
the latest headlines. It would require no user interaction because
it would occur on a timed basis. This method ensures that your
widget is set up correctly.

Building the app widget's layout

The app widget needs to have a particular layout for Android to determine
how to display the widget on the Home screen. The widget layout file defines
what the widget will look like while on the Home screen. Earlier in this chapter, Figure 7-2 shows the app widget running in the emulator. The icon on the
Home screen is defined by the widget layout file. If you were to change the
background color of the layout file to lime green, the background color of the
widget on the Home screen would be lime green instead of transparent.

The lime green box also identifies the available screen space for the app
widget. Your app widget can occupy one Home screen cell or many cells.
This app widget is occupying only one.

To create the widget layout, create an XML layout file in the `res/layouts`
directory. Create one now and name it `widget.xml`.

The contents of `widget.xml` are shown in Listing 7-2.

Listing 7-2:   The Contents of widget.xml

```
<?xml version="1.0" encoding="utf-8"?>
<RelativeLayout xmlns:android="http://schemas.android.com/apk/res/android"
    android:layout_width="fill_parent"
    android:layout_height="fill_parent">
    <ImageView android:id="@+id/phoneState"
        android:layout_height="wrap_content"
        android:layout_width="wrap_content"
        android:layout_centerInParent="true"
        android:src="@drawable/ic_launcher"
        android:clickable="true" />                              →9
</RelativeLayout>
```

This layout should be nothing new. It's a `RelativeLayout` that has one child view: a clickable `ImageView`. You can click it by setting the clickable property to `true` on line 9 in Listing 7-2.

Note the `src` property of the `ImageView`, set to the icon of the application. It may seem odd to you, but when you build the layout, you haven't yet created the phone-state buttons that represented silent and normal states. You need to preview the view in the layout designer while designing the layout. Therefore, this code uses `@drawable/ic_launcher` as the value of the `ImageView` to glean a vision of how the view will look. Don't be concerned about using the application icon — when the app widget loads, the `ToggleService` switches the icon value to either the Silent or Normal mode state icon, as shown later in this chapter.

These icons help the user of the application identify the current state of the application. The `phone_state_normal` icon signifies when the phone is in Normal ringer mode. The `phone_state_silent` icon signifies when the phone is in Silent ringer mode.

Doing work inside an AppWidgetProvider

After the pending intent has started your `AppWidgetProvider`, you perform some work on behalf of the calling application (in this case, the Home screen application). In the following sections, you perform time-sensitive work on behalf of the caller.

Before you delve into the code, you should understand how `AppWidget Provider` works. Due to the nature and resource intensity of remote processes, all nontrivial work should be done inside a background service, such as changing the ringer mode via a background service.

Understanding the IntentService

This section explains why you use a background service for a trivial task, such as changing the phone ringer mode.

Any code that executes for too long without responding to the Android system is subject to the Application Not Responding (ANR) error. App widgets are especially vulnerable to ANR errors because they're executing code in a remote process and because app widgets execute across process boundaries that can take time to set up, execute, and tear down — the entire process is quite CPU-, memory-, and battery-intensive. The Android system watches app widgets to ensure that they don't take too long to execute. When they do, the calling application (the Home screen) locks up and the device is unusable. Therefore, the Android platform wants to ensure that you're never capable of making the device unresponsive for more than a couple of seconds.

Because app widgets are expensive in regard to CPU and memory, judging whether an app widget will cause an ANR error is difficult. If the device isn't doing any other expensive tasks, the app widget would probably work just fine. However, if the device is in the middle of expensive CPU or IO operations, the app widget can take too long to respond — causing an ANR error. To work around this problem, move any CPU- or IO-intensive work of the app widget into an `IntentService` that can take as long as it needs to complete — which in turn doesn't affect the Home screen application.

Unlike most background services, which are long-running, an `Intent Service` uses the work queue processor pattern, which handles each intent in turn using a worker thread, and it stops when it runs out of work. In layman's terms, the `IntentService` simply runs the work given to it as a background service, and then stops the background service when no more work needs to be done.

Implementing the AppWidgetProvider and IntentService

In the `AppWidgetProvider` class, type the code in Listing 7-3 into your code editor.

Listing 7-3: The Full AppWidget Implementation

```
public class AppWidget extends AppWidgetProvider {
        @Override
        public void onReceive(Context context, Intent intent) {
            if (intent.getAction()==null) {
                context.startService(new Intent(context,
                                      ToggleService.class));        →6
            } else {
                super.onReceive(context, intent);
             }
        }

        @Override
        public void onUpdate(Context context, AppWidgetManager
             appWidgetManager, int[] appWidgetIds) {
        context.startService(new Intent(context,
                                  ToggleService.class));            →16
        }

        public static class ToggleService extends IntentService {   →19

        public ToggleService() {
           super(ToggleService.class.getName());                    →22
        }
```

(continued)

Listing 7-3 *(continued)*

```
    @Override
    protected void onHandleIntent(Intent intent) {              →26
        ComponentName me=new ComponentName(this, AppWidget.class);  →27
        AppWidgetManager mgr=AppWidgetManager.getInstance(this);    →28
        mgr.updateAppWidget(me, buildUpdate(this));                 →29
    }
    private RemoteViews buildUpdate(Context context) {          →30
        RemoteViews updateViews=new
        RemoteViews(context.getPackageName(),R.layout.widget);  →32
        AudioManager audioManager =
(AudioManager)context.getSystemService(Activity.AUDIO_SERVICE); →34

        if(audioManager.getRingerMode() ==
            AudioManager.RINGER_MODE_SILENT) {

            updateViews.setImageViewResource(R.id.phoneState,
                R.drawable.phone_state_normal);                 →40

        audioManager.setRingerMode(AudioManager.RINGER_MODE_NORMAL);
        } else {
            updateViews.setImageViewResource(R.id.phoneState,
            R.drawable.phone_state_silent);                     →45

        audioManager.setRingerMode(AudioManager.RINGER_MODE_SILENT);
        }
        Intent i=new Intent(this, AppWidget.class);             →49

        PendingIntent pi
            = PendingIntent.getBroadcast(context, 0, i,0);

        updateViews.setOnClickPendingIntent(R.id.phoneState,pi); →54

        return updateViews;                                     →56
    }
  }
}
```

The following list briefly explains the purpose of the major sections of code:

→6   This line of code starts a new instance of `ToggleService`. The `context` object refers to the Android `Context` object, which is an interface to global information about the application. The context is passed into the `onReceive()` and `onUpdate()` method calls. A new intent is created to let the Android system know what should happen. This method is initiated by the user when the user taps the app widget on the Home screen.

→**16**   This line performs the same actions as in line 6.

→**19**   This implementation of an `IntentService` handles the same logic as the `MainActivity` for handling phone-mode switching but in regard to the app widget infrastructure. It's an implementation of a background service in the Android platform. This class is a nested static class within the app widget.

→**22**   This method calls the superclass with the name `"com.dummies.android.silentmodetoggle.AppWidget$ToggleService"`. This method call is taking place to help with debugging for the thread name. If you omit this line of code, a compiler error informs you that you must explicitly invoke the superclass constructor.

→**26**   The `onHandleIntent()` method is responsible for handling the Intent that was passed to the service. In this case, it would be the intent that was created on lines 6 and 16. Because the intent you created was an explicit intent (you specified a class name to execute), no extra data was provided, and by the time you get to line 26, you no longer need to use the intent. (You can provide extra information to the `Intent` object to be extracted from this method parameter. In this case, the `Intent` object was merely a courier to instruct the `ToggleService` to start its processing.)

→**27**   Creates a `ComponentName` object. This object is used with the `AppWidgetManager` (explained next) as the provider of the new content that will be sent to the app widget via the `RemoteViews` instance.

→**28**   Obtains an instance of `AppWidgetManager` from the static `AppWidgetManager.getInstance()` call. The `AppWidgetManager` class is responsible for updating the state of the app widget and provides other information about the installed app widget. You use it to update the app widget state.

→**29**   Updates the app widget with a call to `updateAppWidget()`. This call needs two components: the Android `ComponentName` that's doing the update and the `RemoteViews` object used to update the app widget. The `ComponentName` is created on line 27. The `RemoteViews` object used to update the state of the app widget on the Home screen is a little more complicated (as explained next).

→**30**   This method definition for the `buildUpdate()` method returns a new `RemoteViews` object that's used on line 29. The logic for what should happen and the actions needed to proceed are included in this method.

→**32**   This line builds a RemoteViews object with the current package name as well as the layout that will be returned from this method. The layout, R.layout.widget, is shown in Listing 7-3.

→**34**   This line obtains an instance of the AudioManager, and then, directly afterward, checks the state of the ringer. If the ringer is silent, the user has tapped the app widget to change its state, indicating that she wants the phone's ringer to be normal now.

→**40**   This line updates the RemoteViews object. The RemoteViews object is changing the R.id.phoneState ImageView drawable to the R.drawable.phone_state_normal drawable. (Refer to the icon on the right side of Figure 7-2.)

→**45**   The else statement located above this line flows through to update the image in the ImageView to R.drawable.phone_state_silent because the ringer mode wasn't in Silent mode previously. (The user wants to now silence the phone.)

→**49**   Creates an Intent object that starts the AppWidget class when initiated.

App widgets cannot communicate with vanilla intents; they require the use of a PendingIntent. Remember that because app widgets use cross-process communication, PendingIntent objects are needed for communication. On this line, the PendingIntent instructs the app widget of its next action via the child intent.

→**52**   Builds the PendingIntent built that instructs the app widget what to do when someone clicks or taps the view.

→**54**   Sets the click listener for the ImageView in the app widget. Because you're working with a RemoteViews, you have to rebuild the entire event hierarchy in the view, because the app widget framework replaces the entire RemoteViews with a brand-new one that you supply via this method. Therefore, you have one remaining task: Tell the RemoteViews what to do when it's tapped or clicked from the Home screen. The setOnClick PendingIntent() sets up the PendingIntent. This method accepts two parameters: the ID of the view that was clicked (in this case, an image), and the pi argument, which is the PendingIntent.

→**56**   Returns the newly created RemoteViews object so that the updateAppWidget() call on line 29 can update the app widget.

Working with the app widget's metadata

After you've written the code to handle the updating of the app widget, you might wonder how to list the app widget on the Widgets menu. This fairly simple process requires you to add a single XML file to your project. This XML file describes basic metadata about the app widget so that the Android platform can determine how to lay out the app widget on the Home screen. Follow these steps:

1. **In your project, right-click the** `res` **directory and choose New⇨New Folder.**

2. **Name the folder** xml **and click Finish.**

3. **Right-click the new** `res/xml` **folder, and choose New⇨Android XML File.**

4. **In the New Android XML File Wizard, type** widget_provider.xml **for the filename.**

5. **Select** `AppWidgetProvider` **from the drop-down list and then click Finish.**

6. **After the file opens, open the XML editor and type the following code into the** `widget_provider.xml` **file:**

```xml
<?xml version="1.0" encoding="utf-8"?>
<appwidget-provider xmlns:android="http://schemas.android.com/apk/res/
        android"
        android:minWidth="79px"
        android:minHeight="79px"
        android:updatePeriodMillis="1800000"
        android:initialLayout="@layout/widget"
/>
```

The minWidth and minHeight properties are used for setting the minimum amount of space that the view needs on the Home screen. These values can be larger, if you want, but for a phone app, all you really need is 79x79 to fit the indicator icon that the widget will display.

The updatePeriodMillis property defines how often the app widget should attempt to update itself. In the case of the Silent Mode Toggle application, you rarely, if ever, need for this to happen. Therefore, this value is set to 1800000 milliseconds — 30 minutes. Every 30 minutes, the app attempts to update itself by sending an intent that executes the onUpdate() method call in the AppWidgetProvider.

The initialLayout property identifies what the app widget looks like when the app widget is first added to the Home screen, before any work takes place. The app widget may take a few seconds to initialize and update your app widget's RemoteViews object by calling the onReceive() method.

An example of a longer delay is an app widget that checks Twitter for status updates. The initialLayout is shown until updates are received from Twitter. Inform the user in the initialLayout that information is loading to keep him aware of what's happening when the app widget is initially loaded on the Home screen. You can do this by providing a `TextView` with the contents of `"Loading . . ."` while the `AppWidgetProvider` does its work.

Registering your new components with the manifest

Anytime you add an activity, a service, or a broadcast receiver (or certain other items) to your application, you need to register them with the application manifest file. The application manifest presents vital information to the Android platform — namely, the components of the application. The system doesn't recognize the `Activity`, `Service`, and `BroadcastReceiver` objects that aren't registered in the application manifest. Therefore, if you added the app widget to the Home screen, it would crash because your `AppWidgetProvider` is a `BroadcastReceiver`, and the code in the receiver is using a service that isn't registered in the manifest.

To add your `AppWidgetProvider` and `IntentService` to your application manifest file, open the `AndroidManifest.xml` file and type the code shown in Listing 7-4 into the already existing file. Bolded lines are newly added lines for the new components.

Listing 7-4:   An Updated AndroidManifest.xml File with New Components Registered

```
<?xml version="1.0" encoding="utf-8"?>
<manifest xmlns:android="http://schemas.android.com/apk/res/android"
     package="com.dummies.android.silentmodetoggle"
     android:versionCode="1"
     android:versionName="1.0">
   <application android:icon="@drawable/ic_launcher"
      android:label="@string/app_name"
      android:debuggable="true">
      <activity android:name=".MainActivity"
             android:label="@string/app_name">
          <intent-filter>
              <action android:name="android.intent.action.MAIN" />
              <category android:name="android.intent.category.LAUNCHER" />
          </intent-filter>
      </activity>
      <receiver android:name=".AppWidget"
             android:label="@string/app_name"
             android:icon="@drawable/ic_launcher">             →18
          <intent-filter>
              <action
             android:name="android.appwidget.action.APPWIDGET_UPDATE" />  →21
```

```
            </intent-filter>
            <meta-data
                                        android:name="android.appwidget.
        provider"
                android:resource="@xml/widget_provider" />              →25
        </receiver>
        <service android:name=".AppWidget$ToggleService" />             →27
    </application>
    <uses-sdk android:minSdkVersion="4" />
</manifest>
```

The following list briefly describes each section:

→18   The opening element registers a BroadcastReceiver as part
        of this application. The name property identifies the name of the
        receiver — in this case, .AppWidget, which correlates to the
        AppWidget.java file in the application. The name and label help
        identify the receiver.

→21   Identifies what kind of intent (based on the action of the intent in
        the intent filter) the app widget automatically responds to when
        the particular intent is broadcast. Known as an IntentFilter,
        it helps the Android system understand what kind of events your
        app should be notified of. In this case, your application is con-
        cerned about the APPWIDGET_UPDATE action of the broadcast
        intent. This event fires after the updatePeriodMillis property
        has elapsed, which is defined in the widget_provider.xml file.
        Other actions include enabled, deleted, and disabled.

→25   Identifies the location of the metadata that you recently built into
        your application. Android uses the metadata to help determine
        defaults and to lay out parameters for your app widget.

→27   The <service> element registers the AppWidget$ToggleService
        IntentService with your application. This is the background
        service that does most of the work for your widget.

At this point, your application is ready to be installed and tested. To install
the application, choose Run➪Run or press Ctrl+F11. It should show up on the
emulator. Return to the Home screen by pressing the Home key. You can now
add to the Home screen the app widget that you recently created.

Placing Your Widget on the Home Screen

The usability experts on the Android development team did a great job of
allowing application widgets to be easily added to the Home screen. Adding
one is easy — follow these steps:

1. **Open the application list on the Home screen of the emulator.**

2. **When the list of applications is visible, select Widgets.**

3. **Choose Silent Mode Toggle, as shown in Figure 7-4.**

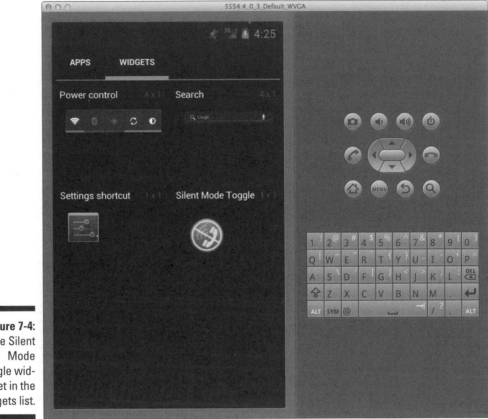

Figure 7-4:
The Silent Mode Toggle widget in the Widgets list.

You have now added the Silent Mode Toggle widget to the Home screen, as shown in Figure 7-5. You can tap the icon to change the ringer mode, and the background changes accordingly. (Refer to Figure 7-2.)

Figure 7-5:
The app widget, added to the Home screen.

Chapter 8

Publishing Your App to the Google Play Store

The Google Play Store is the official application distribution mechanism behind Android. Publishing your application to the store enables your application to be downloaded, installed, and used by millions of users across the world. Users can also rate your application and leave comments about it, which helps you identify possible use trends and problematic areas that users might be encountering.

The Google Play Store also provides a set of valuable statistics that you can use to track the success of your application.

In this chapter, you publish your application to the Google Play Store. You find out how to provide a couple of screen shots, a promotional screen shot, and a short description of your application.

Creating a Distributable File

So you have a great idea, and it has led you to develop the next hit application or game for the Android platform. Now you're ready to put the application into the hands of users. The first thing you need to do is package your application so that it can be placed on their devices. To do so, you create an Android package file, or *APK* file.

In the following sections, you create an APK file.

Revisiting the manifest file

Before you jump in and create the distributable APK file, you should take great care to ensure that your application is available to as many users as possible, by familiarizing yourself with the uses-sdk element in the AndroidManifest.xml file. Your AndroidManifest.xml file now has a uses-sdk entry (see Chapter 4):

```
<uses-sdk android:minSdkVersion="4" />
```

The minSdkVersion property identifies which versions of the Android platform can install this application — in this instance, level 4. The Silent Mode Toggle application was developed by setting the target software development kit (SDK) to version 15.

The Android platform is, for the most part, backward compatible. Most features from version 3 are also in version 4. Small changes and sometimes new, large components are released in each new version, but everything else in the platform remains basically backward compatible. Therefore, stating that this application needs a minimum of SDK version 4 signifies that any Android operating system of version 4 or later can run the application.

Using the minSdkVersion information, the Google Play Store can determine which applications to show the user of a specific device. If you were to release the application now with the minSdkVersion value set to 4 and you open the Google Play Store on an Android device running version 3 (Android 1.5) or earlier, you wouldn't find your application — Google Play Store filters it out because you, the developer, have specified that this app can run only on devices of API Level 4 or greater. If you were to open the Google Play Store on a device running API Level 4 or higher, you could find and install your application.

If you don't provide a minSdkVersion value in the uses-sdk element of the application's manifest, the Google Play Store defaults the minSdkVersion to 1, which means that this application is compatible with all versions of Android. If your application happens to use a component that's unavailable in older versions of the platform (such as the Account Manager introduced in Android 2.0) and a user installs your application, the app will crash.

Always set the `minSdkVersion` to the lowest version of the SDK on which you tested your application, and set the `targetSdkVersion` to the highest tested version.

Choosing your tools

You can build an Android APK file in numerous ways:

- ✔ Android Development Tools (ADT) inside Eclipse
- ✔ Automated build process, such as a continuous integration server
- ✔ Command line with Ant
- ✔ Maven or Gradle build systems

You use the ADT within Eclipse to create an APK file. The ADT provides an array of tools that compiles, digitally signs, and packages your Android application into an APK file. Here, the digital signature process takes place, as discussed in the next section.

Other options, such as Ant and continuous integration, are possible but are used in more advanced scenarios. You can find more information about setting up an Ant build process in the Android documentation at `http://d.android.com/tools/publishing/app-signing.html`.

Digitally signing your application

The Android system requires all installed applications to be digitally signed with a certificate that contains a public/private key pair. The private key is held by the developer. The certificate that's used to digitally sign the application identifies developer and establishes the trust relationships between applications.

You need to know some key information about signing Android applications:

- ✔ All Android applications *must be signed*. The system won't install applications that aren't signed.
- ✔ You can use self-signed certificates to sign your applications; a certificate authority isn't needed.
- ✔ When you're ready to release your application to the store, you must sign it with a private key. You cannot publish the application with the debug key that signs the APK file when debugging the application during development.

✔ The certificate has an expiration date, and it's verified only at install time. If the certificate expires after the application has been installed, the application continues to operate normally.

✔ If you don't want to use the ADT tools to generate the certificate, you can use standard tools such as Keytool or Jarsigner to generate and sign your APK files.

You can create modular applications that can communicate with each other if the applications were signed with the same certificate. This arrangement allows applications to run within the same process, and the system can, if requested, treat them as a single application. Using this methodology, you can create your application in modules, and users can update each module as they see fit — for example, to create a game and then release update packs to upgrade it. Users can decide to purchase only the updates they want.

The certificate process is outlined in detail in the Android documentation at `http://d.android.com/tools/publishing/app-signing.html`.

Creating a keystore

A *keystore* in Android (and in Java) is a container in which your personal certificates reside. You can use a couple of tools in Android to create a keystore file:

✔ **ADT Export Wizard:** Installed with the ADT, it lets you export a self-signed APK file that can digitally sign the application as well as create the certificate and keystore (if needed) in a wizard-like process. You create a keystore when you create your APK file in the upcoming section.

✔ **Keytool application:** It lets you create a self-signed keystore via the command line. Keytool, located in the Java bin directory, provides many options via the command line.

Safeguarding your keystore

The keystore file contains your private certificate, which Android uses to identify your application in the Google Play Store. Back up your keystore in a safe location because if you happen to lose it, you cannot sign the application with the same private key. Neither can you upgrade your application because the Google Play Store platform recognizes that the application isn't signed by the same key and restricts you from upgrading it — the store sees the file as a new Android application. This also happens if you change the package name of the app; Android doesn't recognize it as a valid update because the package and/or certificate are not the same.

Creating the APK file

To create your first APK file, follow these steps:

1. **Open Eclipse, if it isn't already open.**

2. **Right-click the Silent Mode Toggle app, choose Android Tools, and then choose Export Signed Application Package.**

   The Export Android Application Wizard, shown in Figure 8-1, opens with the current project name filled in.

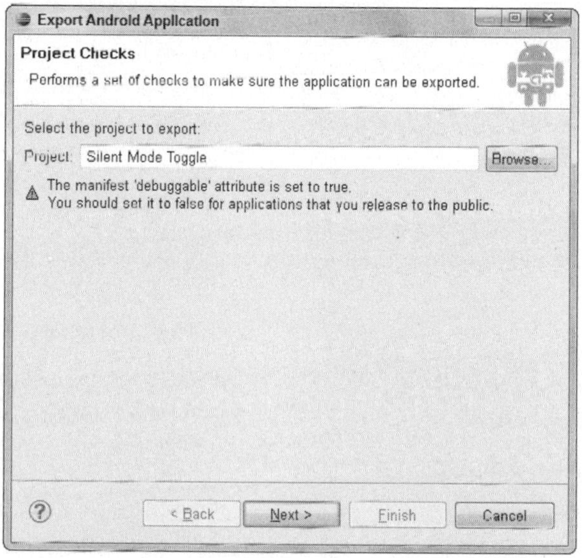

Figure 8-1:
The Export
Android
Application
Wizard.

3. **Click the Next button.**

   The Keystore Selection screen opens, as shown in Figure 8-2.

4. **Select the Create New Keystore radio button.**

   If you already have a keystore, choose the Use Existing Keystore option instead.

5. **Choose the location of your keystore.**

   In the `c:\android` path, choose a location for the keystore, which should end with the `.keystore` extension. For example

   ```
   c:\android\dummies.keystore
   ```

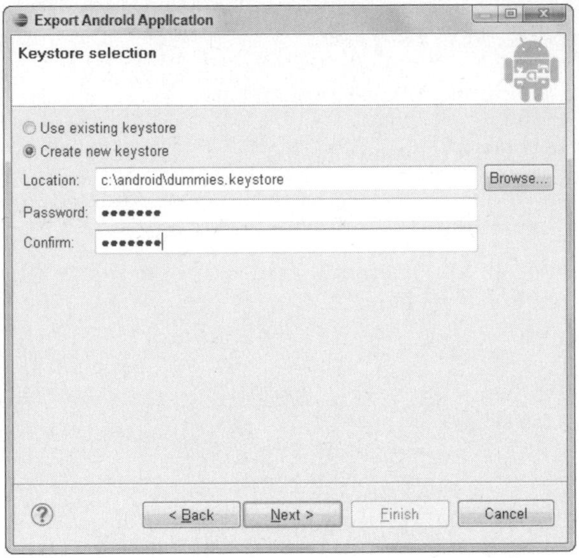

Figure 8-2:
The
Keystore
Selection
screen.

6. **Enter a password that you'll remember, and reenter it in the Confirm field.**

   If using an existing keystore, you won't need to confirm your password.

   Your keystore file has been created, but now you need to create a key.

7. **Click the Next button.**

   The Key Creation screen appears, as shown in Figure 8-3.

Figure 8-3:
The Key
Creation
screen.

8. **Fill out the following fields:**

    • *Alias:* The alias that you use to identify the key.

    • *Password and Confirm:* The password that will be used for the key.

    • *Validity:* Indicates how long this key will be valid. Your key must expire after October 22, 2033.

9. **Complete the certificate issuer section, filling out at least one of these fields:**

    • First and Last Name

    • Organization Unit

    • Organization

    • City or Locality

    • State or Province

    • Country Code (XX)

10. **Click the Next button.**

    The final screen is the Destination and Key/Certificate Checks screen, shown in Figure 8-4.

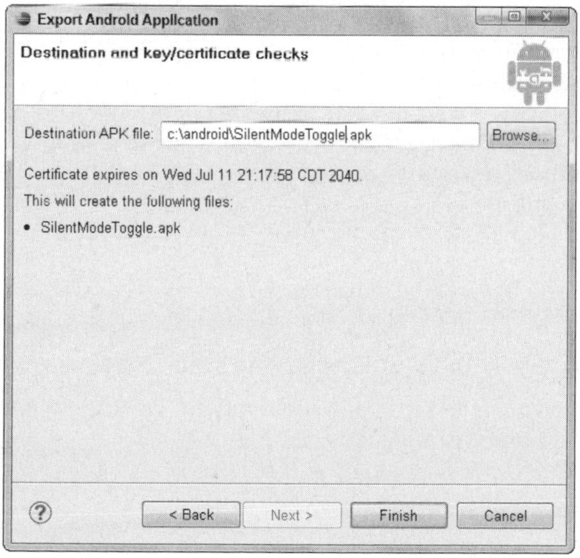

Figure 8-4:
Choosing a name and destination for your first APK file.

11. **Enter the location for where you want to save the APK file containing your signed application.**

12. **Click the Finish button.**

    The `.apk` file is created in your chosen location as well as a keystore in the location you chose in Step 5. Open these locations, and you can see a `.keystore` file as well as an `.apk` file, as shown in Figure 8-5.

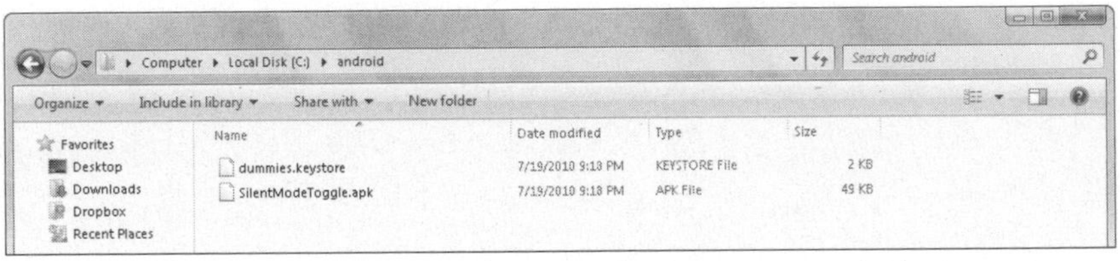

Figure 8-5:
Providing a
destination
for the APK
file.

You have created a distributable APK file and a reusable keystore for future updates.

Creating a Google Play Developer Profile

After you have created an APK file, you can release the application on the Google Play Store. To do so, you create a Google Play developer profile. To create this profile, you first need a Google account. Any Google-based account, such as a Gmail account, works. If you have no Google account, you can open a free one by navigating to `www.google.com/accounts`.

To create the Google Play developer profile, follow these steps:

1. **Open your web browser and navigate to** `http://play.google.com/apps/publish`.

2. **On the right side of the screen, sign into your Google account.**

    If you're already signed into your account, you go straight to Step 3 to fill in your developer profile.

3. **Fill out the following fields to complete your developer profile, as shown in Figure 8-6:**

   - *Developer Name:* The name that appears as the developer of the applications you release, such as your company name or your personal name. You can change it later, after you've created your developer profile.

   - *E-mail Address:* The e-mail address to which users can send e-mail with questions or comments about your application.

   - *Web Site URL:* The URL of your website. If you don't have one, try a free blog from `www.tumblr.com`.

   - *Phone Number:* A valid phone number at which to contact you to discuss problems with your published content.

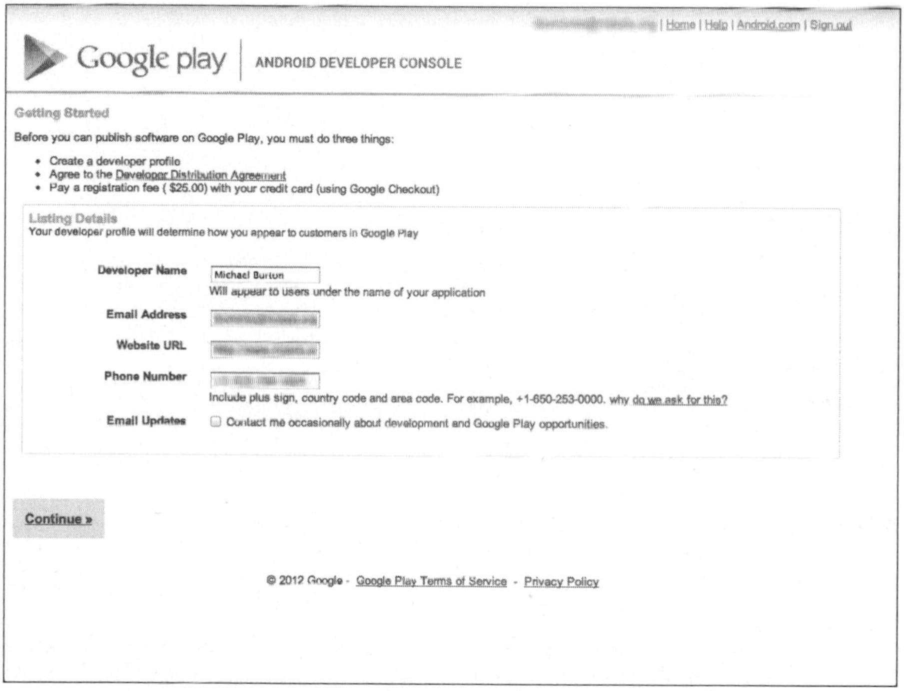

Figure 8-6: Developer listing details.

4. **Click the Continue button.**

   The Android Developer Agreement page opens.

5. **Read the terms, and then click the I Agree, Continue link to pay the developer fee via Google Checkout.**

   If you don't pay the developer fee, you cannot publish applications.

6. **On the Secure Checkout page, fill in your credit card details and billing information; then click the Agree and Continue button.**

   If you already have a credit card on file with Google, you may not see this page. If you already have a card set up, select one and continue.

7. **On the order confirmation page, click the Place Your Order Now button.**

   Depending on the speed of your Internet connection — and your order — you may not see the loading screen.

   When the process is complete, you see a message confirming that you're an Android developer. (See Figure 8-7.)

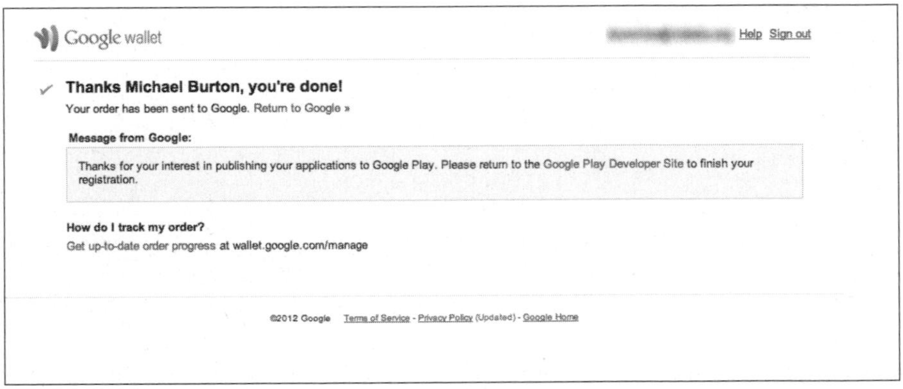

Figure 8-7:
Confirmation of your registration.

8. **Click the Google Play Store Developer Site link.**

   The Android developer home page opens, as shown in Figure 8-8, where you can upload your application or set up a merchant account (which you need, if you'll be charging a fee for your apps). See the nearby "Google Checkout merchant accounts" sidebar.

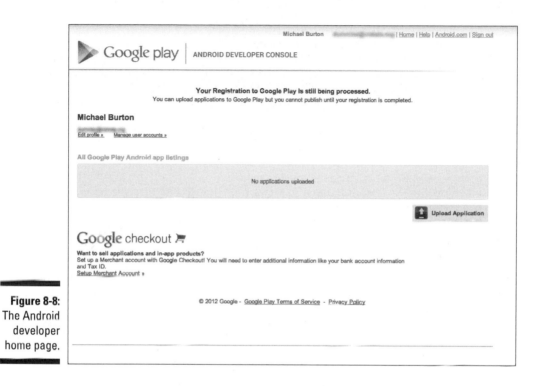

Pricing Your Application

So you have created an APK file and you're a registered Android developer. Now you're ready to put your app into users' hands. (Finally!) But you must answer one last question — is your app a free app or a paid app?

Google Checkout merchant accounts

To have a paid application on the Google Play Store, you must set up a Google Checkout merchant account. To set it up, choose Setup Merchant Account from the Android developer home page (refer to Figure 8-8) and provide these types of information:

✔ Personal and business name

✔ Tax identity (personal or corporation)

✔ Expected monthly revenue ($1 billion, right?)

After you have set up a Google Checkout merchant account, you can sell your applications.

Make this decision before you release your app, because its price has psychological consequences for potential customers or users and monetary consequences for you. If yours is a paid application, you have to determine your price point. Only you can make this decision, so inspect similar applications in the Play Store, and their price points, to determine your pricing strategy. Because the majority of apps are priced between $0.99 and $9.99, you rarely see one priced beyond the $10 threshold. Keeping the pricing of your app competitive with your product is a game of economics that you have to play to determine what works for your application.

The paid-versus-free discussion is an evergreen debate, and both sides are profitable. You only have to figure out what works best for your application, given your situation.

Choosing the paid model

If you choose the paid model for your app, you generally start seeing money in your pocket within 24 hours of the first sale (barring holidays and weekends). However, your paid application probably won't receive many active installs.

Users who download your app from the Google Play Store get a free, 15-minute trial period to try out your paid application. During the trial period, users can experiment with the fully functional application, and if they don't like it, simply uninstall it for a full refund. The trial period is extremely useful because users aren't penalized for taking your app for a brief test-drive.

Choosing the free model

If you choose to take the free route, users can install the application for free. Between 50 and 80 percent of the users who install your free app will keep the application on the device; the others will uninstall it. The elephant in the room now is the question of how to make money by creating free apps.

As the age-old saying goes, nothing in life is free, and the saying applies to making money on free apps. You have two basic options:

✔ **In-app purchases:** You identify different "upgrades" that users can buy when using your app, which are then managed via the Google Play Store.

✔ **Advertising:** Various mobile advertising agencies provide third-party libraries to display ads on your mobile application.

The top mobile advertising companies are Google AdSense (www.google.com/adsense) and AdMob (www.admob.com). Obtaining a free account from one of these companies is fairly straightforward. They offer useful SDKs and walk you through the steps to run ads on your native Android applications. Most of them pay on a net-60-day cycle, so you may have to wait a few months to receive your first check.

Getting Screen Shots for Your Application

Screen shots are a vital part of the Google Play Store ecosystem because they allow users to preview an application before installing it. Allowing users to view a couple of screen shots of your application can be the determining factor in installing your application. If you've spent weeks (or months) creating detailed graphics for a game that you want users to play, you want potential users and buyers to see them so that they can see the overall look of your app.

To grab real-time shots of your application, you use an emulator or a physical Android device. To grab screen shots with an emulator, follow these steps:

1. **Open the emulator and place the widget on the Home screen.**

2. **In Eclipse, open the DDMS Perspective.**

   Visit Chapter 5 for a refresher on how to use DDMS.

3. **Choose the emulator in the Devices panel, as shown in Figure 8-9.**

4. **Click the Screen Shot button to capture a screen shot.**

   After the screen shot is taken, save the file somewhere on your computer.

Choose the emulator.

Click for screen shot.   Screen shot

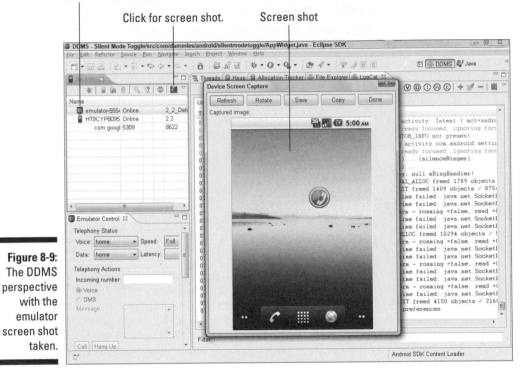

Figure 8-9:
The DDMS
perspective
with the
emulator
screen shot
taken.

Uploading Your Application to the Google Play Store

You've finally reached the apex of Android application development: You're ready to publish the application. To publish your app, you'll need to collect the following information:

- The signed application APK
- Your application screenshots
- A description and promotional text for your application
- An optional promotional image used to advertise your app if it's featured in the Google Play Store

Publishing an application is easy — follow these steps:

1. **On the Android developer's home page (refer to Figure 8-8), click the Upload Application button.**

   The Upload an Application page opens, as shown in Figure 8-10.

Your Registration to the Android Market is approved!
You can now upload and publish software to the Android Market.

Upload an Application

Upload assets

Application .apk file   com.dummies.android.silentmodetoggle (40k)   [Upload Upgrade]
                         Silent Mode Toggle
                         Version: 1.0
                         Localized to: default

                         This apk requests 0 permissions that users will be warned about

Screenshots   Screenshots:
0 or 2   320w x 480h or 480w x 854h
                         24 bit PNG or JPEG (no alpha)
                         Full bleed, no border in art
                         Landscape thumbnails are cropped

                         Replace this image | delete

                         Replace this image | delete

Promotional Graphic   Promo Graphic:
optional   180w x 120h
                         24 bit PNG or JPEG (no alpha)
                         Full bleed, no border in art

                         Replace this image | delete

Figure 8-10:
The upload
page.

---

2. **For the Application APK file, choose the `.apk` file that you create earlier in this chapter, and then click Upload.**

   No two applications can have the same package name in the Google Play Store. (Google uses the Java package name as the identifier.) Therefore, if you try to upload the Silent Mode Toggle application at this point, you see this error message:

```
The package name of your apk (com.dummies.android.silentmodetoggle) is the
          same as the package name of another developer's application.
Choose a new package name.
```

When you upload an application that you've created, you don't see this message.

3. In the Screenshots section, add two screen shots from your application.

Apps with screen shots have higher install rates than apps without them. These screen shots allow users to preview your application in a running state without having to install your application.

4. Add a promotional shot.

The promo shot is not a screen shot but rather is an advertisement used for random promotions that Android chooses to showcase. A promo shot isn't required to publish the app.

5. Set the title of your application.

Choose a title that fits your application. This text is indexed for the Google Play Store search engine.

6. Set the description for your application.

Users see this description when they inspect your application to determine whether to install it. All this text is indexed for the Google Play Store search engine.

7. Set the promotional text of your application.

Promotional text is used when your application is featured or promoted in the Google Play Store. Getting your application featured is likely based on the popularity of your application. If it's chosen to be featured in the promotional area of the Google Play Store (usually in the upper area of the screen of each category), the promo text shows up as the promotional component for it.

8. Set the application type.

This app falls into the Applications type; if you have a game app, choose the Games type.

9. Set the category for the app.

The category is based on your application type.

10. Turn off copy protection.

Copy protection prevents your application from being illegally copied to other devices. To avoid that, use the Google Play Licensing service instead at `http://d.android.com/guide/google/play/licensing/index.html`.

11. Select the list of locations where the application should be visible.

For example, if your application is meant for an Italian audience, deselect All Locations and select Italy as the destination location, to ensure
that only devices in the Italy region can see it in the store. If you leave
All Locations enabled, all locations can (you guessed it) see your app in
the store.

12. Fill out the Web Site and E-Mail fields (and Phone, if you want).

These fields are used to contact you for various reasons, including app
feature requests and bug reports. If you fill in the Phone field, remember
that users can call to speak with you. If you're writing an app for one company and publishing it under your developer account, you can change the
Web Site, E-Mail, and Phone fields so that users can't contact you.

**13. Verify that your application meets the Android content guidelines and
that you have complied with applicable laws by selecting the pertinent check boxes.**

14. Choose one of these options:

- *Publish:* Saves and publishes the app to the store in real time. The
  Upload an Application page opens. (Refer to Figure 8-10.)

- *Save:* Saves changes, but doesn't publish the app. Your app is
  shown as saved on the Android developer's home page, as shown
  in Figure 8-11. When you're ready to publish your app, select the
  title and click the Upload Application button.

You can also choose Delete at this time, but you probably don't want to.
You'll delete all your work.

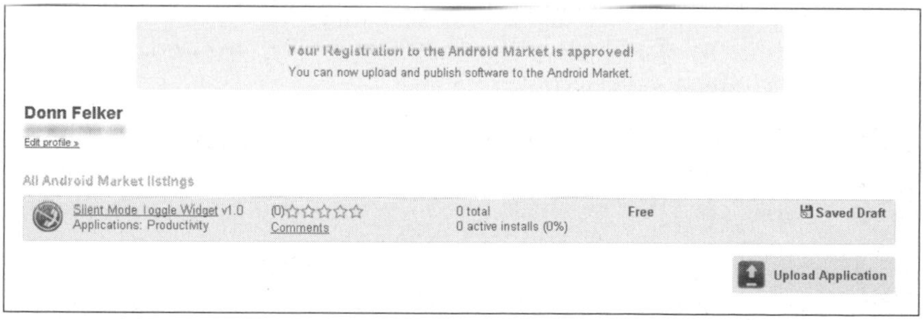

Figure 8-11:
The saved
app on your
Android
developer's
Home
screen.

Your Registration to the Android Market is approved!
You can now upload and publish software to the Android Market.

Donn Felker

Edit profile »

All Android Market listings

Silent Mode Toggle Widget v1.0   (0)☆☆☆☆☆   0 total   Free   📰 Saved Draft
Applications: Productivity   Comments   0 active installs (0%)

⬆ Upload Application

15. Scroll to the bottom of the page and click the Publish button.

Your application is published to the Google Play Store.

Figure 8-12 shows an application in the Google Play Store on a Nexus One device.

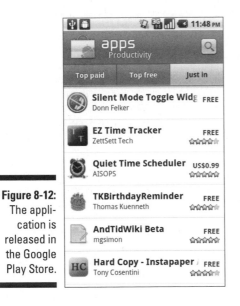

Figure 8-12:
The appli-
cation is
released in
the Google
Play Store.

You've probably noticed a certain highlight in this process: It has no app-approval process (like a certain other platform does). You can create an app now and publish it, and users can install it right away. You can then complete a quick release cycle and get new features out the door as quickly as you finish them — very cool.

If you ever need to remove your application from the Google Play Store, select the app title from the Android developer's home screen, scroll to the bottom, and clicked the Unpublish button.

Watching the Number of Installs Soar

You've finally published your first application. Now it's time to watch those millions start rolling in, right? Kind of. You might be an independent developer who's releasing the next standout first-person shooter game, or you might be a corporate developer who's pushing out your company's Android application. Regardless, to be aware of the user experience on various devices, you can identify how your application is doing in various ways:

✔ **Five-star rating system:** The higher average rating your app receives, the better.

✔ **Comments:** Give people the courtesy of reading the comments they leave. You might be surprised at the outstanding ideas people provide to you for free. Users get excited about new features and return to the store to update their comments with a much more positive ratings boost.

✔ **Error reports:** Users who were gracious enough to submit error reports want to let you know that the app experienced a runtime exception for an unknown reason. Open these reports, examine the error, review the stack trace, and fix the problem. An app that's reported to force-close frequently can quickly receive lots of bad reviews. Stack traces are available only for devices that are running Android 2.2 and later.

✔ **Installs versus active installs:** Though this comparison isn't the best metric for identifying user satisfaction, it's an unscientific way to determine whether users who install your app will tend to keep it on their devices. Users who keep your app obviously like it.

✔ **Direct e-mail:** Users will return to the Google Play Store to find your e-mail address or website address and ask questions about features or send comments about their user experience. They may also send you ideas about how to improve your app or ask you to create another app that does something they cannot find at the Google Play Store. Reply if you have the time! Though maintaining an active dialogue with users is difficult if your app has a million active users, it makes users happy to know that they can contact you about issues with your app.

Staying in touch with your user base is a large task in itself, but doing so can reap the reward of dedicated, happy customers who refer their friends and family to your application.

Like the Google Play Store, the Amazon App Store for Android (one of the largest non-Google app stores for Android devices) offers applications for users to buy and install. Developers can sell their applications and receive a competitive rate for their apps from Amazon, or post free apps. Amazon also provides great sales metrics for developers and marketers. Find out more at `http://developer.amazon.com`. You can find out how to port your app to the Amazon App Store in Chapter 18.

Part III
Creating a Feature-Rich Application

The 5th Wave   By Rich Tennant

HORNER BROS.
MAKERS OF PREMIUM
BELLS & WHISTLES

"As an application developer, I never thought
I'd say this, but your app needs more
bells and whistles."

In this part . . .

Part III expands on the knowledge that you acquire in Part II by demonstrating how you can build a feature-rich application. There are also a few advanced topics that can help bridge the gap between beginner and advanced Android developer.

In this part, you create certain features to enhance users' experiences with your application. At the end of Part III, you have a fully functioning advanced application that interacts with a local database and custom preferences.

Chapter 9

Designing the Task Reminder Application

. . . .

In This Chapter

▶ Listing the application's requirements

▶ Developing multiple screens

▶ Building a list activity

▶ Working with intents

. . . .

*B*uilding Android applications is fun, but building truly in-depth applications is exciting because you dive into the guts of the Android platform. This chapter introduces you to the Task Reminder application, which you build in the next few chapters.

The Task Reminder application lets users create a list of items that have a reminder time associated with every individual item.

Reviewing the Basic Requirements

The Task Reminder application has a few basic requirements so that it can fulfill what's expected of it:

✔ The app must be able to accept user input. (Having a personalized task application that doesn't allow user input would be silly!)

✔ Tasks must be easy to manage.

✔ Every task must have a reminder date and time when the user will be reminded of the task.

- ✔ The user must be notified of the task when the reminder time has arrived.
- ✔ Users must be able to delete tasks.
- ✔ Users must be able to not only add tasks but also edit them.

This application invites lots of interaction between the user and the Android system. The following sections delve into the features that you need to build into the application to give users all the functionality they need.

Scheduling a reminder script (That's alarming!)

For the Task Reminder application to work well, you need to implement a reminder-based system. The first thing that comes to mind is a scheduled task, or cron job. In the Windows operating system, you create a scheduled task to handle the execution of code and scripts at a given time. In the world of Unix and Linux, you use cron (short for the Greek word *chronos,* which means *time*) to schedule scripts or applications.

Because Android is running the Linux kernel, you might assume that Android uses cron to schedule tasks. Unfortunately, Android doesn't have cron; however, Android has the AlarmManager class, which accomplishes the same task. The AlarmManager class lets you specify when your application should start. An alarm can be set as a single-use alarm or repeating. The Task Reminder application uses AlarmManager to remind users of pending tasks.

Storing data

All the activities, task data, and alarms needed to make the Task Reminder app work are stored in these locations:

- ✔ **Activities and broadcast receivers:** In a single Java package
- ✔ **Task data:** In a ContentProvider backed by a SQLite database
- ✔ **Alarm info:** In the AlarmManager via the intent system after being pulled from the ContentProvider

Distracting the user (nicely)

After an alarm fires, the app has to notify the user of the alarm. The Android platform provides mechanisms to bring your activity to the foreground when the alarm fires, but that isn't an optimal notification method because it steals focus from whatever the user is already doing. Imagine if the user is dialing a phone number or answering a phone call and an alarm fires that brings an activity to the foreground. The user is likely to be confused because an activity started that he didn't initiate manually.

You have two ways to grab the user's attention without stealing the main focus away from the current activity:

- ✔ **Toast:** A small view that contains a brief message for the user. The message doesn't persist because it's usually available for only a few seconds — a toast never receives focus. The Task Reminder app uses a toast not for *reminding* the user but uses it instead for notifying the user when her activity has been saved.

- ✔ **Notification Manager:** The NotificationManager class notifies a user that events have taken place. They can appear on the status bar at the top of the screen. Notification items can contain various views and are identified by icons you provide. The user can slide down the notification list to view notifications. The Task Reminder application uses the NotificationManager class to handle alarms. (See Chapter 1 if you're unsure how the notification area works.)

You can grab a user's attention by displaying a dialog box that immediately steals the focus from the already running app. Despite its effectiveness, the user may become irritated because your app is stealing the focus (possibly continually, for numerous reminders) from the current action in another application.

Creating the Application's Screens

The Task Reminder application needs two different screens to perform all its basic functions: create, read, update, and delete (CRUD) tasks:

- ✔ One view lists all current tasks in the application. This view also allows the user to delete a task by long-pressing the item.

- ✔ A view to allow the user to view (read), add (create), or edit (update) a task.

Each screen eventually interacts with a database for changes to be persisted over the long-term use of the application.

Each screen consists of a single code fragment that contains most of the user interface for the screen, and that fragment is contained in an activity.

You can reuse fragments if — or *when* — you build tablet support into your app. See Part IV for tablet development.

Starting the new project

To get started, open Eclipse and create a new Android project with a valid name, package, and activity. Table 9-1 shows the Eclipse settings for the Task Reminder app. (If you're unfamiliar with how to create an Android project, see Chapter 3.)

If you download the source code from this book's website, you can also open the Chapter 9 Android project example.

Table 9-1	New Project Settings
Property	*Value*
Project Name	Task Reminder
Build Target	Android 4.0.3 (API Level 15)
Application Name	Task Reminder
Package Name	com.dummies.android.taskreminder
Create Activity	ReminderListActivity
Min SDK Version	4

Note the Create Activity property value — `ReminderListActivity`. Normally, you give the first activity in an application the name of `MainActivity`; however, the first screen the user sees in the Task Reminder app is a list of current tasks. Therefore, this activity is an instance of a `ListActivity`; hence the name `ReminderListActivity`.

The Task Reminder app uses features from the Android Support Library to support devices running Android 2.x and earlier. Add the library to your Eclipse project by following these steps:

1. **Copy the** `android-support-v13.jar` **file to your project's libs directory.**

   It's in `ANDROID_SDK/extras/android/support/v13`.

   If you can't find the `android-support-v13.jar` file in your Android SDK directory, you may not have installed the support library yet. Open the Android SDK Manager and click Extras to install the support library from there.

2. **Choose Project⇨Clean from the Eclipse menu.**

   Once the project finishes rebuilding, your Android Dependencies listing should look like the one shown in Figure 9-1.

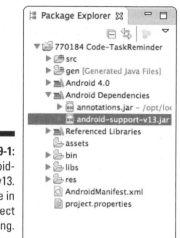

Figure 9-1:
The android-
support-v13.
jar file in
your project
listing.

Creating the ReminderListActivity

The `ReminderListActivity` class that Eclipse generated for you is practi-
cally empty so you'll want to make some changes to it. Do the following:

- **Rename the** `activity_main.xml` **file to** `reminder_list.xml`.
  Eclipse starts your project with the `activity_main.xml` file, located
  in the `res/layout` directory. To make it easy to find your layout file
  when you open the directory, rename it to something more informative. To rename the `activity_main.xml` file, right-click it and choose
  Refactor⇨Rename or select the file and press Shift+Alt+R.

- **Update the Java file.** After you change the filename, you need to
  update the name of the file in the `setContentView()` call inside
  the `ReminderListActivity.java` file. Open the file and replace
  `R.layout.activity_main` with `R.layout.reminder_list`.

- **Change the inheritance.** Because the `ReminderListActivity` contains fragments, it needs to inherit from the `FragmentActivity` class
  instead of the regular base activity. Make that change, too.

Your new `ReminderListActivity` class now looks like Listing 9-1.

Listing 9-1: The ReminderListActivity Class

```
public class ReminderListActivity extends FragmentActivity {
    /** Called when the activity is first created. */
    @Override
    public void onCreate(Bundle savedInstanceState) {
        super.onCreate(savedInstanceState);
        setContentView(R.layout.reminder_list);
    }
}
```

setContentView() uses the reminder_list layout file, but you haven't defined that yet. Open the res/layout/reminder_list.xml file and update it to look like Listing 9-2.

Listing 9-2: The reminder_list.xml Contents

```
<?xml version="1.0" encoding="utf-8"?>
<fragment
    xmlns:android="http://schemas.android.com/apk/res/android"
    android:name="com.dummies.android.taskreminder.ReminderListFragment"
    android:layout_width="fill_parent"
    android:layout_height="fill_parent" />
```

The layout file for your activity has only a single element in it, the ReminderListFragment, which takes up the full height and width of the screen. The ReminderListFragment does all the hard work to display the list of tasks to the user.

Creating the ReminderListFragment

Fragments are the parts of your activities that are meant to be re-used throughout your application. Most activities have one or two fragments. The list activity needs a fragment to display the list of tasks, so create a new file named ReminderListFragment and copy the code in Listing 9-3.

Listing 9-3: The ReminderList Fragment

```
package com.dummies.android.taskreminder;

import android.os.Bundle;
import android.support.v4.app.ListFragment;                              →4
import android.view.View;

public class ReminderListFragment extends ListFragment {

    @Override
    public void onActivityCreated(Bundle savedInstanceState) {           →10
        super.onActivityCreated(savedInstanceState);
        setEmptyText(getResources().getString(R.string.no_reminders));   →12
    }

}
```

Knowing when to use activities or fragments

Both activities and fragments are central parts of your user interface (UI) code. So how then do you decide whether to put certain functionality into a fragment or an activity?

If activities are the lunchbox of UI code, fragments are its Tupperware. You can insert your UI code directly into your lunchbox, but it would be a bit of a mess and make the lunchbox code hard to reuse. Put your UI code into your fragment Tupperware instead, where you can shift it from lunchbox to lunchbox as you need to use it again.

If you're absolutely certain that the code you're writing is specific to a given activity, put it directly into an activity. But if you're unsure, put your UI code in a fragment. In most applications, fragments contain all your UI code, and your activities contain only the glue that binds the fragments together.

Here's a brief explanation of the code in Listing 9-3:

→4   This line ensures that you're using the `android.support.` `v4.app.*` imports and not their equivalents from `android.app`.

Import `android.support.v4.app.Fragment` and `android.` `support.v4.app.FragmentTransaction`, and not their equivalents from `android.app`. Using the `android.support.v4.*` classes from the Android Support Library ensures that your application works on devices with Android versions going back to v4 (Android 1.6). If you don't care about versions of Android before 3.x, feel free to skip the support library.

→10   The activity's (not the fragment's) `onCreate()` method returns and calls the `onActivityCreated()` callback.

If you need to do anything with your fragment's views, `onActivity` `Created()` is a great place to do it because your fragment's views are guaranteed to be fully constructed at that point.

→12   The `ListFragment` supports showing a message when the list is empty. The call uses a value of `setEmptyText()`, and the message uses a value of `R.string.no_reminders`.

Add `<string name="no_reminders">No Reminders Yet</` `string>` to your `strings.xml` file. See Chapter 6 for more information about adding strings to your `strings.xml` file.

Using an activity to create and edit reminders

The Task Reminder application needs an additional screen that allows the user to edit a task and its information. This new activity and fragment will allow users to create, read, and update tasks.

In Eclipse, follow these steps:

1. **Create a new activity that can handle the create, read, and update roles.**

   Right-click the package name in the src folder and choose New⇨Class, or press Shift+Alt+N and then choose Class. Name it ReminderEditActivity.

2. **In the new Java class window, set the superclass to** android. support.v4.app.FragmentActivity **and click Finish.**

   A new activity class file opens.

3. **Replace the contents of the activity class file with Listing 9-4.**

   This code creates the activity, sets its content view, and then sets up the fragment for the activity.

Listing 9-4:   ReminderEditActivity

```
package com.dummies.android.taskreminder;

import android.os.Bundle;
import android.support.v4.app.Fragment;                                    →3
import android.support.v4.app.FragmentActivity;
import android.support.v4.app.FragmentTransaction;

public class ReminderEditActivity extends FragmentActivity {
    @Override
    public void onCreate(Bundle savedInstanceState) {
        super.onCreate(savedInstanceState);
        setContentView(R.layout.reminder_edit_activity);                   →11

        Fragment fragment = getSupportFragmentManager().findFragmentByTag(
                ReminderEditFragment.DEFAULT_EDIT_FRAGMENT_TAG);           →15

        if (fragment == null) {                                            →17
            fragment = new ReminderEditFragment();
            Bundle args = new Bundle();
            args.putExtra(ReminderProvider.COLUMN_ROWID, getIntent()
```

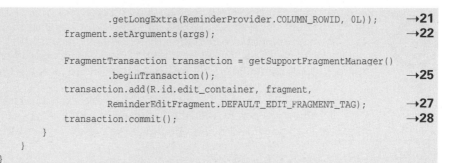

```
                .getLongExtra(ReminderProvider.COLUMN_ROWID, 0L));    →21
        fragment.setArguments(args);                                 →22

        FragmentTransaction transaction = getSupportFragmentManager()
                .beginTransaction();                                 →25
        transaction.add(R.id.edit_container, fragment,
                ReminderEditFragment.DEFAULT_EDIT_FRAGMENT_TAG);     →27
        transaction.commit();                                        →28
    }
  }
}
```

Here's a brief explanation of the code in Listing 9-4:

→**3**   This line ensures you're using the `android.support.v4.app.*` imports and not their equivalents from `android.app`.

→**11** This line sets the layout for this fragment. Listing 9-5 shows the code for the `R.layout.reminder_edit_activity`.

→**15** Before a fragment is added for the first time, this line checks to see whether one is already there.

   If an activity was re-created from another activity — say, after a screen rotation — the previous fragment would have also been re-created, and that one is used instead of creating one from scratch.

→**17** If the activity couldn't find a previous fragment, this line creates a new fragment.

→**21** Intents can have extras, which allow activities to pass information from one to another. In line 21, the intent uses `getLongExtra()` to retrieve the `long` named `COLUMN_ROWID` if it's there. If it's not, the intent uses the value `0L` (or 0 as a `long`).

→**22** Fragments need arguments. Unlike with normal Java classes, you can't pass arguments to a fragment via a constructor. Instead, line 22 uses a bundle named `Fragment.setArguments()`.

→**25** Any time you want to interact with a fragment, you must use a `FragmentTransaction`. This line calls `FragmentActivity.getSupportFragmentManager()` to get the `FragmentManager`, and from there calls `FragmentManager.beginTransaction()` to start a transaction. All fragments operate between the `FragmentTransaction.beginTransaction()` and `FragmentTransaction.commit()` calls.

→**27** This line adds the fragment to the activity. It places the fragment in a `FrameLayout` placeholder named `R.id.edit_container` (which you define in Listing 9-5) and names it `DEFAULT_EDIT_FRAGMENT_TAG` so that the app can find it again by that name.

→**28** This line finishes the transaction.

You may notice that the fragment is set up differently in this class than for the `ReminderListActivity` class. In `ReminderListActivity`, the `<fragment>` element is added directly to the XML because the fragment needed no parameters. The `ReminderEditFragment` activity needs the fragment to be manually added by using Java code to pass the reminder ID.

The `reminder_edit_activity.xml` layout file shown in Listing 9-5 consists of a single full-screen placeholder element called `edit_container` that the Java code in Listing 9-1 uses to attach the `ReminderListFragment`.

Listing 9-5:   R.layout.reminder_edit_activity

```xml
<?xml version="1.0" encoding="utf-8"?>
<LinearLayout xmlns:android="http://schemas.android.com/apk/res/android"
      android:layout_width="fill_parent"
      android:layout_height="fill_parent">

    <FrameLayout
            android:id="@+id/edit_container"
            android:layout_width="fill_parent"
            android:layout_height="fill_parent"
        />

</LinearLayout>
```

The `ReminderEditActivity` uses a constant in a class called `ReminderProvider` which doesn't exist yet, so create that class now and edit it to look like the following:

```java
package com.dummies.android.taskreminder;

public class ReminderProvider {
    public static final String COLUMN_ROWID = "_id";
}
```

You also need to inform the Android platform about the existence of the `ReminderEditActivity` by adding it to the Android Manifest. You can do so by adding it to the `Application` element of the `AndroidManifest.xml` file, as shown here in bold:

```xml
<application android:icon="@drawable/ic_launcher" android:label="@string/
        app_name">
    <activity android:name=".ReminderListActivity"
            android:label="@string/app_name">
        <intent-filter>
            <action android:name="android.intent.action.MAIN" />
            <category android:name="android.intent.category.LAUNCHER" />
        </intent-filter>
    </activity>
    <activity android:name=".ReminderEditActivity"
            android:label="@string/app_name" />
</application>
```

If you don't add the activity to the `AndroidManifest.xml` file, you receive a runtime exception informing you that Android cannot find the class (the activity).

Adding a fragment to the activity

After you've created an activity to hold the `ReminderEditFragment`, it's time to create the fragment. Create a new Java class, name it **ReminderEditFragment**, and copy the following code into the file:

```
package com.dummies.android.taskreminder;

import android.os.Bundle;
import android.support.v4.app.Fragment;                              →4
import android.view.LayoutInflater;
import android.view.View;
import android.view.ViewGroup;
import android.widget.Button;
import android.widget.EditText;

public class ReminderEditFragment extends Fragment {
    public static final String DEFAULT_EDIT_FRAGMENT_TAG = "editFragmentTag";  →12

    private EditText mTitleText;
    private EditText mBodyText;
    private Button mDateButton;
    private Button mTimeButton;
    private Button mConfirmButton;
    private long mRowId;                                             ·19

    @Override
    public void onCreate(Bundle savedInstanceState) {               →22
        super.onCreate(savedInstanceState);

        Bundle arguments = getArguments();                          →25
        if (arguments != null) {
            mRowId = arguments.getLong(ReminderProvider.COLUMN_ROWID);
        }
    }

    @Override
    public View onCreateView(LayoutInflater inflater, ViewGroup container,
            Bundle savedInstanceState) {                            →33

        View v = inflater.inflate(R.layout.reminder_edit, container, false);  →35

        mTitleText = (EditText) v.findViewById(R.id.title);
```

```
        mBodyText = (EditText) v.findViewById(R.id.body);
        mDateButton = (Button) v.findViewById(R.id.reminder_date);
        mTimeButton = (Button) v.findViewById(R.id.reminder_time);
        mConfirmButton = (Button) v.findViewById(R.id.confirm);


        return v;
    }
}
```

Here's how the code works:

→**4**   Make sure you're using the `android.support.v4.app.*`
         imports and not their equivalents from `android.app`.

→**12**   Activities need a tag or an ID to refer to when they work with frag-
         ments. This line gives the `ReminderEditFragment` a tag so it
         can be found again later using the same tag.

→**19**   Every instance of `ReminderEditFragment` has an ID for the
         reminder. The Row ID corresponds to a row in the database.
         When editing existing reminders, `mRowId` is the ID of the row in
         the database for that reminder. New reminders get a `mRowId` of 0.

→**22**   Fragments have `onCreate()` methods, just as activities do.
         `onCreate()` is called when the fragment is created, and you gen-
         erally do most of the fragment initialization in `onCreate`.

         Unlike with activities, though, you don't do initialization related
         to views in `onCreate`. Those have to wait until `onCreateView()`
         on line 33.

→**25**   The fragment finds out which reminder the user is editing or cre-
         ating by calling `getArguments()`.

         Arguments come from the bundle that's returned by `get`
         `Arguments()`, not from the bundle that's passed into `on`
         `Create()` (an easy mistake to make).

→**33**   Unlike with activities, you inflate your XML layouts in `Fragment.`
         `onCreateView()` instead of using `Activity.setContent`
         `View()`. This line inflates `R.layout.reminder_edit` layout,
         and then calls `findViewById()` to set up the `View` objects,
         much like you would do when initializing an activity.

         You could set up the `View` objects in `onActivityCreated()`,
         but it's convenient to do so in `onCreateView()` in this case
         because you're not manipulating views. See the sidebar "The
         fragment lifecycle" for more information about `onActivity`
         `Created()` versus `onCreateView()`.

→**35**   This line calls `inflate()` with `attachToRoot` set to `false`,
         because the fragment attaches the view.

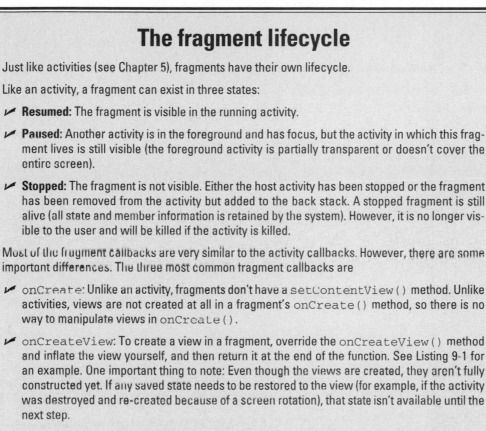

The fragment lifecycle

Just like activities (see Chapter 5), fragments have their own lifecycle.

Like an activity, a fragment can exist in three states:

✔ **Resumed:** The fragment is visible in the running activity.

✔ **Paused:** Another activity is in the foreground and has focus, but the activity in which this fragment lives is still visible (the foreground activity is partially transparent or doesn't cover the entire screen).

✔ **Stopped:** The fragment is not visible. Either the host activity has been stopped or the fragment has been removed from the activity but added to the back stack. A stopped fragment is still alive (all state and member information is retained by the system). However, it is no longer visible to the user and will be killed if the activity is killed.

Most of the fragment callbacks are very similar to the activity callbacks. However, there are some important differences. The three most common fragment callbacks are

✔ onCreate: Unlike an activity, fragments don't have a setContentView() method. Unlike activities, views are not created at all in a fragment's onCreate() method, so there is no way to manipulate views in onCreate().

✔ onCreateView: To create a view in a fragment, override the onCreateView() method and inflate the view yourself, and then return it at the end of the function. See Listing 9-1 for an example. One important thing to note: Even though the views are created, they aren't fully constructed yet. If any saved state needs to be restored to the view (for example, if the activity was destroyed and re-created because of a screen rotation), that state isn't available until the next step.

✔ onActivityCreated: onActivityCreated() is the final step called before your fragment is fully created. At this point, your fragment is fully set up. Because of this, it's usually best to put most of the code involving views or saved state in onActivityCreated().

Creating the adding/editing fragment layout

The layout for adding and editing is fairly simple because the form contains only a few fields:

✔ **Title:** The title of the task as it will show in list view

✔ **Body:** The body of the task, where the user would type details

✔ **Reminder Date:** The date on which the user should be reminded of the task

✔ **Reminder Time:** The time at which the user should be reminded on the reminder date

When the app is complete and running on a device or an emulator, the screen looks like Figure 9-2.

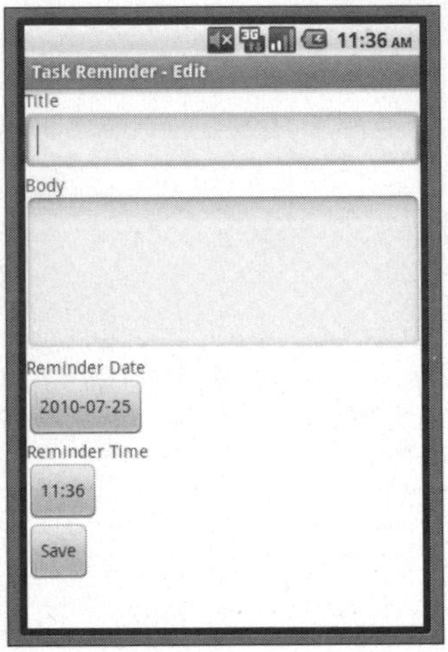

Figure 9-2:
The Add/
Edit Task
Reminder
screen.

To create this layout, create a layout file in the `res/layout` directory with an appropriate name; for example, `reminder_edit.xml`. To create this file, follow these steps:

1. **Right-click the** `res/layout` **directory and choose New⇨Android XML File.**

2. **Provide the name in the File field.**

3. **Leave the default type of resource selected — Layout.**

4. **Leave the folder set to** `res/layout`.

5. **Set the root element to** `ScrollView`.

6. **Click the Finish button.**

You now need to provide all view definitions to build the screen. (Refer to Figure 9-2.) To do this, type the code shown in Listing 9-6.

Listing 9-6:   The reminder_edit.xml File

```
<?xml version="1.0" encoding="utf-8"?>
<ScrollView
        xmlns:android="http://schemas.android.com/apk/res/android"
        android:layout_width="fill_parent"
        android:layout_height="fill_parent">
```
→**5**

```
<LinearLayout                                                        →6
    android:orientation="vertical"                                   →7
    android:layout_width="fill_parent"
    android:layout_height="fill_parent">
    <TextView android:layout_width="wrap_content"
              android:layout_height="wrap_content"
              android:text="@string/title" />                        →12
    <EditText android:id="@+id/title"
              android:layout_width="fill_parent"
              android:layout_height="wrap_content" />                →15
    <TextView android:layout_width="wrap_content"
              android:layout_height="wrap_content"
              android:text="@string/body" />                         →18
    <EditText android:id="@+id/body"
              android:layout_width="fill_parent"
              android:layout_height="wrap_content"
              android:minLines="5"
              android:scrollbars="vertical"
              android:gravity="top" />                               →24
    <TextView android:layout_width="wrap_content"
              android:layout_height="wrap_content"
              android:text="@string/date" />                         →27
    <Button
              android:id="@+id/reminder_date"
              android:layout_height="wrap_content"
              android:layout_width="wrap_content"/>                  →31
    <TextView android:layout_width="wrap_content"
              android:layout_height="wrap_content"
              android:text="@string/time" />                         →34
    <Button
              android:id="@+id/reminder_time"
              android:layout_height="wrap_content"
              android:layout_width="wrap_content" />                 →38
    <Button   android:id="@+id/confirm"
              android:text="@string/confirm"
              android:layout_width="wrap_content"
              android:layout_height="wrap_content" />                →42
</LinearLayout>
</ScrollView>
```

Here's brief explanation of the code in Listing 9-6:

→5   The parent view is ScrollView, which creates a scroll bar and
      allows the view to be scrolled when the contents of the view are
      too large to fit onscreen. The screen shown in Figure 9-2 is shown
      in Portrait mode. However, if the device is rotated 90 degrees, the
      view flips and more than half is cut off. The parent ScrollView
      allows the remaining contents of the screen to be scrollable.
      Therefore, the user can flick a finger upward on the screen to
      scroll the contents and see the remainder of the view.

→**6**   A `ScrollView` can have only one child — in this case, the main `LinearLayout` that houses the rest of the layout.

→**7**   The orientation of the linear layout is set to vertical to signify that the views inside this layout should be stacked on top of one another.

→**12**   This is the label for the `Title` field.

→**15**   The `EditText` that allows the user to provide a title for the task. You add `<string name="title">Title</string>` to `strings.xml`.

→**18**   The label for the `Body` field and add the `<string name="body">Body</string>` to the `strings.xml`.

→**24**   The `EditText` that defines the `Body` field. The `EditText` view has set the `minLines` property to `5` and the `gravity` property to `top` to inform the Android platform that the `EditText` is at least five lines tall and that when the user starts typing, the text should be bound to the top of the view (the gravity).

→**27**   The reminder date label also uses a string resource. You need to add a string resource with the name of `"date"` and a value of `"Reminder Date"`.

→**31**   When this reminder date button is tapped, a `DatePickerDialog` is launched. The user can choose a date with a built-in Android date picker. When the date is set via the `DatePicker`, the value of the date is set as the button text.

→**34**   This reminder time label uses a string resource. You need to add a string resource with the name of `"time"` and a value of `"Time"`.

→**38**   When this time reminder button is clicked, a `TimePicker` is launched. The user can choose a time with a built-in Android time picker. When the time is set via the `TimePickerDialog`, the value of the time is set as the button text.

→**42**   This confirmation button saves the values of the form when clicked. Add `<string name="confirm">Save</string>` to the `strings.xml`.

Completing Your List Fragment

The `ListFragment` class displays a list of items by binding to a data source such as an array or a cursor, and it exposes callback methods when the user selects an item. However, to build a list of items to display in a list, you need to add a layout that defines what each row will look like.

A cursor provides random read and write access to the result set that's returned by a database query.

Add a new layout to the res/layout directory with a root element of TextView, and give it a proper name for a row type of item; for example, reminder_row.xml. Inside this view, type the following code:

```xml
<?xml version="1.0" encoding="utf-8"?>
<TextView
    xmlns:android="http://schemas.android.com/apk/res/android"
    android:id="@+id/text1"                                          ▸4
    android:layout_width="fill_parent"
    android:layout_height="fill_parent"
    android:padding="10dip"/>
```

This code simply defines a row in which text values can be placed with a padding of ten density-independent pixels. Line 4 defines the ID of the view that you need when loading the list with data.

The view you added is provided out of the box in the Android system. If you look at the Android documentation under Android.R.layout under simple_list_item_1 and inspect it via the Android source control repository, you can see virtually the same XML definition. The source can be found at

```
https://github.com/android/platform_frameworks_base/blob/
        master/core/res/res/layout/simple_list_item_1.
        xml
```

The ListFragment requires that an adapter fill the contents of the list view. Various adapters are available, but because you don't yet have a data store (built with an SQLite database in Chapter 12), you can temporarily create fake data so that you can see the list in action. In the following section, you add fake data, so you can set the ListFragment's adapter with a call to setListAdapter().

Getting stubby with fake data

Add the following field and method to your ReminderListFragment class:

```
private ListAdapter mAdapter;

@Override
public void onCreate(Bundle savedInstanceState) {
    super.onCreate(savedInstanceState);

    String[] items = new String[] { "Foo", "Bar", "Fizz", "Bin" };      →7

    mAdapter = new ArrayAdapter<String>(getActivity(),                  →9
            R.layout.reminder_row, R.id.text1, items);
    setListAdapter(mAdapter);                                           →11
}
```

Here's a brief explanation of the code:

→7   An array of string items that will eventually be displayed in the list.

→9   The creation of a new `ArrayAdapter` of string types. An `ArrayAdapter` manages a `ListView` backed by an arbitrary number of arbitrary objects — in this case, a simple string array. This code is using Java generics, which allow you to specify the type of object that the `ArrayAdapter` will work with. The constructor of the `ArrayAdapter` contains these elements:

- `getActivity()`: The current context. (Because the activity is an implementation of the `Context` class, you can use the current instance as the context.)

- `R.layout.reminder_row`: The row layout that should be used for each row in the `ListView`.

- `R.id.text1`: The ID of the `TextView` inside `R.layout.reminder_row` in which to place the values from the array.

- `items`: The array of strings to load into the `ListView`.

→11   The call to `setListAdapter()` that informs the `ListFragment` how to fill the `ListView`. In this case, you're using the `ArrayAdapter`, created on line 4, to load the `ListView`.

Start the Android application by choosing Run⇨Run or by pressing Ctrl+F11. The screen you see should look similar to Figure 9-3.

The previous code and example illustrate how to use a static data source for the `ListFragment`. In Chapter 12, you replace this code with code that will load the data from an SQLite database.

Figure 9-3:
The Task
Reminder
running with
fake data.

Handling user click events

The items in the list expose click events that allow the user to interact with each item. Android View objects have two main types of click events:

- ✔ **Click:** The user briefly taps a view, such as a button.
- ✔ **Long-click:** The user taps on a button and holds it for an extra moment.

Every view and activity can intercept these events via various methods. In the following sections, you respond to each type of event in a List Fragment. In Chapter 11, you set up the app to respond to Button click events.

Short clicks

The ListFragment in Android does a lot of the event-handling heavy lifting for you (which is good because programming shouldn't be a physical exercise).

After the onCreate() method in ReminderListFragment, type this method:

```
@Override
public void onListItemClick(ListView l, View v, int position, long id) {
    super.onListItemClick(l, v, position, id);
}
```

This code overrides the default implementation of `onListItemClick()` that's provided by the `ListFragment`. When a list item is clicked, this method is called, and the following parameters are passed into the call:

- ✔ l: The `ListView` where the click happened
- ✔ v: The item that was clicked with the `ListView`
- ✔ position: The position of the clicked item in the list
- ✔ id: The row ID of the item that was clicked

Using these variables, you can determine which item was clicked and then perform an action based on that information. When an item is clicked in this list, an intent opens the `ReminderEditActivity` to allow the user to edit the item, as shown in the section "Starting new activities with intents," later in this chapter.

Long clicks

A *long-click* (or *long-press*) occurs whenever a user presses a view for an extended period. To handle the list item's long-click event in a `ListFragment`, add the following line of code at the end of the `onViewCreated()` method in `ReminderListFragment`:

```
registerForContextMenu(getListView());
```

The outer method, `registerForContextMenu()`, is responsible for registering a context menu to be shown for a given view. Multiple views can show a context menu; it isn't limited to a single view. Every list item is therefore eligible to create a context menu. The `registerForContextMenu()` accepts a `View` object as a parameter that the `ListFragment` should register as eligible for the context menu creation. The inner method, `getListView()`, returns a `ListView` object that's used for the registration. The call, `getListView()`, is a member of the `ListFragment` class.

Now that you've registered the `ListView` to be eligible to create a context menu, you need to respond to the long-click event on any given item. When an item is long-clicked in the `ListView`, the `registerForContextMenu()` recognizes it and calls the `onCreateContextMenu()` method when the context menu is ready to be created. In this method, you set up your context menu.

At the end of the `ReminderListFragment` class file, type the following method:

```
@Override
public void onCreateContextMenu(ContextMenu menu, View v, ContextMenuInfo
            menuInfo) {
    super.onCreateContextMenu(menu, v, menuInfo);
}
```

This method is called with the following parameters:

- ✔ menu: The context menu that's being built.
- ✔ v: The view for which the context is being built (the view that the user long-clicked).
- ✔ menuInfo: Extra information about the item for which the context menu should be shown. (It can vary depending on the type of view in the v parameter.)

Inside this method, you can modify the menu that's presented to the user. For example, when a user long-presses an item in the task list, she should be allowed to delete it. Therefore, present her with the Delete option on a context menu (as described in Chapter 10).

Identifying Your Intent

Even applications that have only two screens (such as the Task Reminder application) have a great deal happening behind the scenes. One notable interaction that happens between the application and the user is the introduction of new screens as the user tries various features of the application. As with any application that has a rich feature set, the user can interact with each screen independently. The big question that arises is, "How does a user open another screen?"

Screen interaction is handled via the Android intent system. In the following sections, you set up intents that allow the user to navigate from one screen to the next. Thankfully, it's a simple process. (Turn to Chapter 7 to find out more about the intent system.)

Starting new activities with intents

Activities are initiated via the Android intent framework. An Intent is a class that represents a message that's placed in the Android intent system (similar to a message-bus type of architecture), and whoever can respond to the intent lets the Android platform know, resulting in either an activity starting or a list of applications to choose from. (This chooser concept is explained in the later section "Creating a chooser.") You can think of an intent as an abstract description of an operation.

Starting a particular activity is easy. In your ReminderListFragment, type the following code into the onListItemClick() method:

```
@Override
public void onListItemClick(ListView l, View v, int position, long id) {
    super.onListItemClick(l, v, position, id);
    Intent i = new Intent(getActivity(), ReminderEditActivity.class);      →4
    i.putExtra(ReminderProvider.COLUMN_ROWID, id);                          →5
    startActivity(i);                                                       →6
}
```

Here's a brief explanation of each line:

→4   This line creates a new intent using the `Intent` constructor that
      accepts the current context, which is the current running activity,
      as well as a class that the intent system should attempt to start —
      the `ReminderEdit` activity.

→5   This line places extra data into the `Intent` object. This intent
      includes a key/value pair. The key is `RowId`, and the value is the
      ID of the view that was clicked. This value is placed into the intent
      so that the receiving activity (the `ReminderEditActivity`) can
      pull this data from the `Intent` object and use it to load the infor-
      mation about the intent. In Chapter 12, you can see data flowing
      into the `ReminderEditFragment`.

→6   This line starts the activity from within the current activity. This
      call places the intent message into the Android intent system and
      allows Android to decide how to open that screen for the user.

Creating a chooser

At some point, you may run into a particular instance where you need to provide the user with a list of applications that can handle a particular intent. A
common example is sharing data with a friend via a common networking tool,
such as e-mail, SMS, Twitter, Facebook, or Google Latitude.

The Android intent system was built to handle these types of situations.
Though it isn't used in the Task Reminder application, it can come in handy.
The code to display various available options to the user is shown in Listing
9-7.

Listing 9-7:   Creating an Intent Chooser

```
Intent i = new Intent(Intent.ACTION_SEND);                                 →1
i.setType("text/plain");                                                    →2
i.putExtra(Intent.EXTRA_TEXT, "Hey Everybody!");                            →3
i.putExtra(Intent.EXTRA_SUBJECT, "My Subject");                            →4
Intent chooser = Intent.createChooser(i, "Who Should Handle this?");        →5
startActivity(chooser);                                                     →6
```

Here's a brief explanation of each line in Listing 9-7:

→1   The creation of a new intent that informs the intent system that the user wants to send, or mail, something.

→2   The content type of the message. It can be set to any explicit MIME type. MIME types are case-sensitive, unlike RFC MIME types, so always type them in lowercase letters to specify the type of the intent. Only applications that can respond to this type of intent will then show up in the chooser.

→3   Placing extra data into the intent. It's the body of the message that the application will use. If an e-mail client is chosen, this line comprises the e-mail body. If Twitter is chosen, the message of the tweet is the body. Every application that responds to the intent can handle the extra data in its own, special manner. Don't expect the data to be handled as you might believe it should be, in the destination application. The developer of this type of application determines how the application should handle the extra data.

→4   Similar to line 3, but with a subject extra provided. If an e-mail client responds, this line normally comprises the subject of the e-mail.

→5   Creates the chooser. (The `Intent` object has a static helper method that helps you.) The chooser is itself an intent. You simply provide the target intent (the action that you want to happen) as well as a title for the pop-up chooser that is shown.

→6   Starts the intent. It creates the chooser from which you choose an application.

The chooser that's created from Listing 9-7 is shown in Figure 9-4.

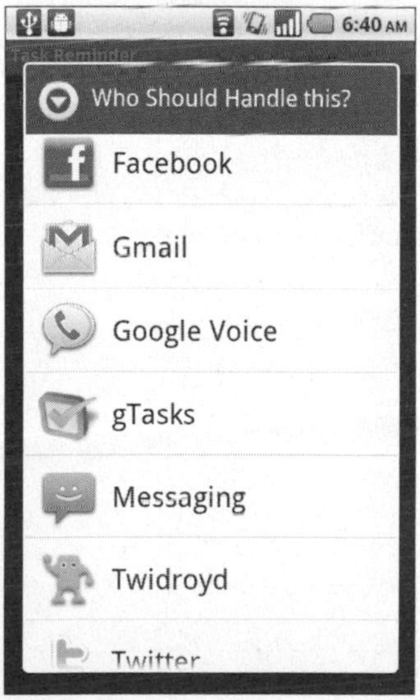

Figure 9-4:
The new chooser that was created.

If the intent system can find no valid applications to handle the intent, the chooser is created with a message informing the user that no applications can perform the action, as shown in Figure 9-5.

Figure 9-5:
The chooser informs the user that Android cannot find a matching application to handle the intent.

The chooser is a helpful way to increase the interoperability of an application. However, if you simply call `startActivity()` with your intent without creating a chooser, your application might crash because Android is giving you full reign and assumes that you know what you're doing. By not including a chooser, you're assuming that the destination device has at least one application to handle the intent. If it doesn't, Android throws an exception (visible via DDMS) to inform you that no class can handle the intent. To the user, your app has crashed.

To provide a satisfactory user experience, always provide an intent chooser when firing off intents that are intended for interoperability with other applications. The chooser provides a smooth and consistent usability model that the rest of Android already provides.

Chapter 10

Going a la Carte with Your Menu

. . . .

. . . .

*E*very good Android application includes menus. If you have an Android device and you've downloaded a few applications from the Google Play Store, you've probably encountered a few good and bad menu implementations.

A bad menu provides very little (if any) helpful text in the menu description and provides no icon. A few common menu faux pas include

✔ A poor menu title

✔ A menu without an icon

✔ No menu

A good menu should have a visual as well as textual appeal to the end user. The appearance of a menu icon shows that the developer actually thought through the process of creating the menu and decided which icon best suits the application.

Activities and fragments can both have menus, in which case they'll both be combined into one. In this chapter, you add option and context menus to the fragments in the Task Reminder app, but you could just as easily add them to an activity, too.

Understanding Options and Context Menus

Android provides a simple mechanism for you to add menus to your applications. You find the following types of menus:

- ✓ **Options menu or action bar menu:** This is, most likely, the most common type of menu that you'll work with. It's the primary menu for an activity or fragment.

  On Android 3.x and later, the Options menu is in the action bar at the top of the screen (read more about the action bar in Chapter 1). On Android 2.x and earlier, the Options menu is presented to the user with the press of the Menu key on the device. Figure 10-1 shows the same menus on two different devices.

  Within the options menu are two groups:

  - *Icon:* These menu options are available at the bottom of the screen. The device supports up to six menu items, and they're the only menu items that support the use of icons. They don't support check boxes or radio buttons.

  - *Expanded:* The expanded menu is a list of menu items that goes beyond the six menu items on the Icon menu. This menu is presented by the More menu icon that is automatically placed onscreen when the app developer has more items than will fit on the Icon menu.

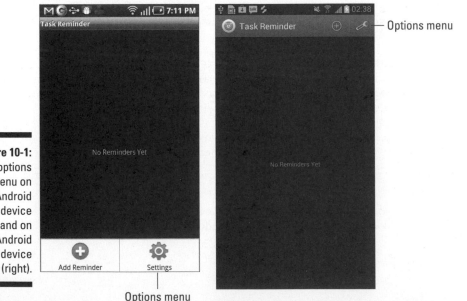

Figure 10-1:
The options menu on an Android 2.x device (left), and on an Android 4.x device (right).

✔ **Context menu:** A floating list of menu items that's presented when a user long-presses a view.

✔ **Submenu:** A floating list of menu items that the user opens by tapping a menu item on the Options menu or on a context menu. A submenu item can't support nested submenus.

Creating Your First Menu

You can create a menu through code or through an XML file that's provided in the res/menu directory. The preferred method of creating a menu is to define it through XML and then inflate it into a programmable object that you can interact with. This helps separate the menu definition from the actual application code.

Defining the XML file

To define an XML menu, follow these steps:

1. **Create a** menu **folder in the** res **directory.**

2. **Add a file by the name of** list_menu.xml **to the menu directory.**

3. **Type the following code into the** list_menu.xml **file.**

```xml
<?xml version="1.0" encoding="utf-8"?>
<menu
    xmlns:android="http://schemas.android.com/apk/res/android">
    <item android:id="@+id/menu_insert"
            android:icon="@android:drawable/ic_menu_add"
            android:title="@string/menu_insert" />
</menu>
```

Notice that a new string resource is included (shown in bold). You'll create that in Step 4. The android:icon value is a built-in Android icon. The ldpi, mdpi, hdpi and xhdi versions of this icon are all built into the Android platform, so you don't have to provide this bitmap in your drawable resources. To view other resources available, view the android.R.drawable documentation at

```
http://developer.android.com/reference/android/R.
        drawable.html
```

All resources in the android.R class give your application a common user interface and user experience with the Android platform.

4. **Create a new string resource with the name** menu_insert **with the value of** Add Reminder **in the** strings.xml **resource file.**

5. **Open the** ReminderListFragment **class and make sure the bold lines are in your** onViewCreated():

```
@Override
public void onViewCreated(View view, Bundle savedInstanceState) {
    super.onViewCreated(view, savedInstanceState);
    setEmptyText(getResources().getString(string.no_reminders));
    registerForContextMenu(getListView());
    setHasOptionsMenu(true);
}
```

registerForContextMenu() tells Android that the ListView wants to contribute to the context menu (the one that shows up when a user long-presses the view). setHasOptionsMenu() tells Android 2.x to show the menu when the user presses the Menu button, and Android 3.x or later to show the menu in the action bar. Turn to Chapter 9 for more information about registerForContextMenu() and setHas OptionsMenu().

6. **Add the** onCreateOptionsMenu() **method to your class:**

```
@Override
public void onCreateOptionsMenu(Menu menu, MenuInflater inflater) {
    super.onCreateOptionsMenu(menu,inflater);
    inflater.inflate(R.menu.list_menu, menu);
}
```

The MenuInflater inflates the XML menu layout created earlier and adds it to the menu that was passed as an argument in the method call.

7. **Install the application in the emulator, and click the Menu button.**

Figure 10-2 shows the Add Reminder menu icon that you just created.

Figure 10-2:
The Add
Reminder
menu icon.

Handling user actions

After you've created the menu, you then have to add what happens when a user clicks it. To do this, type the following code at the end of the class file:

```
@Override
public boolean onOptionsItemSelected(MenuItem item) {          →2
    switch (item.getItemId()) {                                →3
    case R.id.menu_insert:                                     →4
        editReminder(0);                                       →5
        return true;                                           →6
    }

    return super.onOptionsItemSelected(item);                  →9
}
```

The lines of code are explained in detail here:

→**2**   This is the method that's called when a menu item is selected. The `item` parameter identifies which menu item the user tapped.

→**3**   To determine which item you're working with, compare the ID of the menu items with the known menu items you have. Therefore, a `switch` statement is used to check each possible valid case. You obtain the menu's ID through the `MenuItem` method `getItemId()`.

→**4**   The ID of the Add Reminder menu item checks whether the user selected that menu item.

→**5**   If the user selected the Add Reminder menu item, the application is instructed to create a reminder through the `editReminder()` method (defined in the next section). By convention, calling `edit Reminder()` with an ID of 0 means the app should create a new reminder.

→**6**   This line returns true to inform the `onMenuItemSelected()` method that a menu selection was handled.

→**9**   If the menu selection and return isn't handled earlier, the parent class tries to handle the menu item.

You may receive compilation errors at this time, but don't worry! You finish the application in the following section.

Creating a reminder task

The `editReminder()` method allows the user to navigate to the `Reminder EditActivity` to edit or create a new task with a reminder. Type the following method at the bottom of your `ReminderListFragment` class file:

```
public void editReminder(long id) {
    Intent i = new Intent(getActivity(), ReminderEditActivity.class);
    i.putExtra(ReminderProvider.COLUMN_ROWID, id);
    startActivity(i);
}
```

This code creates a new intent that starts the ReminderEditActivity, then calls startActivity() to, you guessed it, start the activity.

Creating a Context Menu

A context menu appears when a user long-presses a view. The context menu is a floating menu that hovers above the current screen and allows users to choose from various options related to the view they long-pressed.

Thankfully, creating a context menu is quite similar to creating an option menu. You can define the menu in XML and inflate it using the same mechanism that you used when you created the options menu. All you need to do is call registerForContextMenu() with a view as the target. (See Chapter 9 to find out how to create a view as the target.) After you create that, you need to override the onCreateContextMenu() call — also demonstrated in Chapter 9.

The Task Reminder application needs a mechanism in which to delete a task when it's no longer needed. Users can long-press the task in the list, and a context menu pops up that allows them to delete the task by selecting an item from the menu.

Creating the menu XML file

To create this menu, create a new XML file in the res/menu directory. Name it list_menu_item_longpress.xml. Type the following into the XML file:

```xml
<?xml version="1.0" encoding="utf-8"?>
<menu xmlns:android="http://schemas.android.com/apk/res/android">
    <item android:id="@+id/menu_delete"
          android:title="@string/menu_delete" />
</menu>
```

Notice that the title property uses a new string resource menu_delete. You need to create a new string resource with the name of menu_delete and the value of Delete Reminder. Also note that you don't need an icon associated with this menu.

A context menu doesn't support icons; it's simply a list of menu options that floats above the current activity.

Loading the menu

To load the menu XML and display it to the user, type the following code into the `onCreateContextMenu()` method:

```
@Override
public void onCreateContextMenu(ContextMenu menu, View v,
        ContextMenuInfo menuInfo) {
    super.onCreateContextMenu(menu, v, menuInfo);
    MenuInflater mi = getActivity().getMenuInflater();
    mi.inflate(R.menu.list_menu_item_longpress, menu);
}
```

This code performs the same function as the `onCreateOptionsMenu()` call, but this time you're inflating the menu for the context menu — and you're loading the context menu. Now, if a user long-presses a list item in the list view, he receives a context menu, as shown in Figure 10-3.

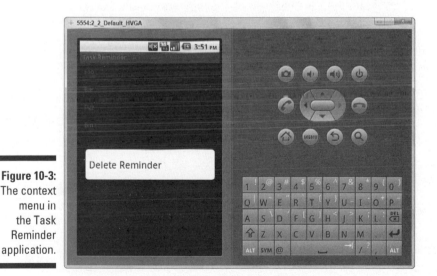

Figure 10-3: The context menu in the Task Reminder application.

Handling user selections

Handling the selection of the context menu items is very similar to handling that with an option menu. Type the following code into the bottom of your class file:

```
@Override
public boolean onContextItemSelected(MenuItem item) {          →2
    switch(item.getItemId()) {                                 →3
        case R.id.menu_delete:                                 →4
            // Delete the task
            return true;
    }
    return super.onContextItemSelected(item);
}
```

The code lines are explained here:

→**2**   This is the method that's called when a context menu item is
            selected. The item parameter is the item that was selected in the
            context menu.

→**3**   A switch statement determines which item was selected, based on
            the ID as defined in the list_menu_item_longpress.xml file.

→**4**   This is the ID for the menu_delete button in the list_menu_
            item_longpress.xml file. If this menu option is selected, the
            following code would perform some action based on that determi-
            nation. Nothing is happening in the code block in this chapter, but
            that changes in Chapter 12, where you delete the task from the
            SQLite database.

You can add many different context menu items to the list_menu_item_
longpress.xml file and switch between them in the onContextMenuItem
Selected() method call — each performing a different action.

Chapter 11

Handling User Input

* *

In This Chapter

▶ Working with `EditText` views

▶ Creating date pickers and time pickers

▶ Setting up alert dialog boxes

▶ Validating user input

* *

Rarely does an application not allow users to interact with it. Whether they use text, a date or time picker, a radio button, a check box, or any other input mechanism, users need to interact with your application in one way or another. The generalization of input also refers to buttons, screen dragging, menus, long-pressing, and various other options. This chapter focuses solely on user input in the form of alerts, free-form text, and dates and times.

Creating the User Input Interface

The most common input type is the `EditText` view, used for free-form text entry. Using an `EditText` view, you can provide an onscreen keyboard or let the user choose the physical keyboard (if the device provides one) to enter input.

In case you're familiar with other programming platforms, a text box performs the same function as an `EditText` view.

Creating an EditText view

In Chapter 9, you created a view layout XML file, named `reminder_edit.xml`, that contained these lines of code:

```
<EditText android:id="@+id/title"
    android:layout_width="fill_parent"
    android:layout_height="wrap_content" />
```

The snippet creates an input mechanism on the screen where the user can type a task title. The `EditText` view spans the width of the screen and occupies only as much height as it needs. When the view is selected, Android automatically opens the onscreen keyboard to allow user input.

The previous example takes a minimalistic approach, compared to the following `EditText` example, which is also present in the `reminder_edit.xml` layout file:

```
<EditText android:id="@+id/body" android:layout_width="fill_parent"
    android:layout_height="wrap_content"
    android:minLines="5"
    android:scrollbars="vertical"
    android:gravity="top" />
```

This code creates the body description text of the task. The layout width and height are the same as in the `EditText` view in the previous example, and the `EditText` view spans the width of the screen. These three properties outline the differences in this `EditText` definition:

- ✔ `minLines`: Specifies the height of the `EditText` view. Because the `EditText` view is a subclass of the `TextView` object, they share this property. This code specifies a minimum of five lines for the `EditText` object onscreen so that the view resembles a text input mechanism for long messages.

  Compare this view to the body portion of any e-mail client, and you can see that they're much the same — the body is much larger than the subject. In this case, the body is much larger than the title.

- ✔ `scrollbars`: Defines which scroll bars should be present when the text overflows the available input area; specifies vertical scroll bars on the side of the `EditText` view.

- ✔ `gravity`: Aligns text (by default) to the middle of the view when the user places focus into an `EditText` field (as shown on the left in Figure 11-1), though it isn't what users would expect when they work with a multiline input mechanism. To position the cursor at the top of the `EditText` view, as users would reasonably expect, you must set the gravity of the `EditText` view to `top`, to force the text to gravitate to the top of the `EditText` input as shown on the right in Figure 11-1.

Default cursor   Cursor set at top

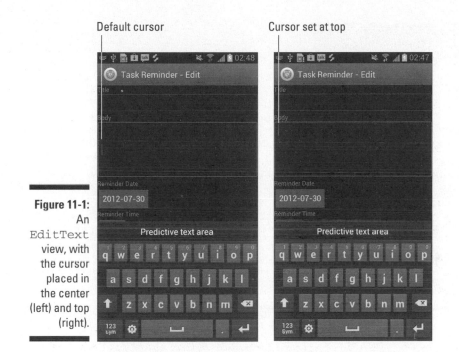

Figure 11-1:
An
`EditText`
view, with
the cursor
placed in
the center
(left) and top
(right).

Displaying an onscreen keyboard

The `EditText` view is responsible for the onscreen keyboard display. Because some devices have no physical keyboard, an onscreen keyboard must be present for interaction with the input mechanisms. One property that the `EditText` view provides is a way to manipulate the visual aspect of the onscreen keyboard.

You adjust the onscreen keyboard because different `EditText` input types might need different keys. For example, if the `EditText` is a phone number, the onscreen keyboard should display only numbers. If the `EditText` value is an e-mail address, however, the onscreen keyboard should display common e-mail style attributes — such as the at (@) symbol.

Configuring the onscreen keyboard properly can increase the usability of your application.

You can configure the way the onscreen keyboard looks by using the `inputType` property on the `EditText` view. For example, if you set `android:inputType="number"` on the body `EditText`, the keyboard displays number keys instead of letter keys, as shown in Figure 11-2.

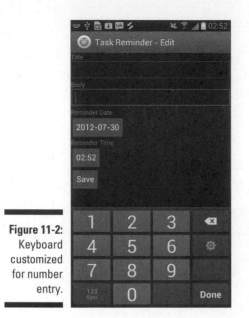

Figure 11-2:
Keyboard
customized
for number
entry.

The inputType property has too many options to cover in this book, but you can examine the full list at http://developer.android.com/reference/android/widget/TextView.html#attr_android:inputType.

Getting Choosy with Dates and Times

A Task Reminder application without a way to set the date and time is a poor Task Reminder application — it would only be a simple task list application.

If you've programmed dates and times in another programming language, you realize that building a mechanism for a user to enter the date and time can be a painstaking process. The Android platform comes to your rescue by providing two classes to assist you: DatePicker and TimePicker. These pickers also provide built-in classes for opening a dialog box where the user selects a date and time. Therefore, you can either embed the DatePicker or TimePicker into your application's views or use the DialogFragment classes.

Creating picker buttons

The reminder_edit.xml file contains mechanisms to help show the DatePicker and TimePicker (under the EditText definitions described earlier). These two buttons have labels above them, as shown in Listing 11-1.

Listing 11-1: **The Date and Time Buttons with Their Corresponding TextView Labels**

```
<TextView android:layout_width="wrap_content"                        →1
    android:layout_height="wrap_content"
    android:text="@string/date" />
<Button                                                              →4
    android:id="@+id/reminder_date"
    android:layout_height="wrap_content"
    android:layout_width="wrap_content"
    />
<TextView android:layout_width="wrap_content"                        →9
    android:layout_height="wrap_content"
    android:text="@string/time" />
<Button                                                              ▸12
    android:id="@+id/reminder_time"
    android:layout_height="wrap_content"
    android:layout_width="wrap_content"
    />
```

The code lines are explained in this list:

→1   The `TextView` label for the Date button; displays the value of `"Reminder Date"` according to the string resource

→4   Defines a button that the user clicks to open the `DatePicker DialogFragment` (as explained in the following section)

→9   The `TextView` label for the Time button; displays the value of `"Reminder Time"` according to the string resource

→12   Defines a button that the user clicks to open the `TimePickerDialogFragment` (explained in the section, "Creating the time picker")

Creating the date picker

A user who clicks the Date button should be able to edit the date, as described in the following several sections.

Setting up the Date button click listener

To set up the Date button click listener, open the activity where your code will be placed. For the Task Reminder application, open the `ReminderEditFragment.java` file.

Add the code lines shown in bold in Listing 11-2 to the `onCreateView()` method.

Listing 11-2:   **Implementing the Date Button Click Listener**

```
@Override
public View onCreateView(LayoutInflater inflater, ViewGroup container,
        Bundle savedInstanceState) {

    View v = inflater.inflate(R.layout.reminder_edit, container, false);

    mTitleText = (EditText) v.findViewById(R.id.title);
    mBodyText = (EditText) v.findViewById(R.id.body);
    mDateButton = (Button) v.findViewById(R.id.reminder_date);
    mTimeButton = (Button) v.findViewById(R.id.reminder_time);
    mConfirmButton = (Button) v.findViewById(R.id.confirm);

    mDateButton.setOnClickListener(new View.OnClickListener() {      →13
        @Override
        public void onClick(View v) {                                →15
            showDatePicker();                                        →16
        }
    });

    return v;
}
```

The numbered lines are described in this list:

→13   Sets the `onClickListener()` for the `mDateButton`. The `onClickListener()` executes when the button is clicked. The action that takes place on the button click is shown on line 16.

→15   Overrides the default click behavior of the button so that you can provide your own set of actions to perform. The `View v` parameter is the view that was clicked.

→16   Defines what you want to happen when the button is clicked; calls a method on the `showDatePicker()` fragment, as explained in the later section "Creating the `showDatePicker()` method."

Creating the DatePickerDialogFragment

The Android operating system comes supplied with a built-in `Date PickerDialog` that lets users select (rather than type) a date. It doesn't come wrapped neatly in a fragment, so you have to do it yourself.

The old `dialog` objects were designed to be called from activities, not from fragments. When opening a dialog box from a fragment, you have to use a subclass of the `DialogFragment` class if you want the dialog box to behave properly.

Create a new file, name it `DatePickerDialogFragment`, and add the following code:

```
package com.dummies.android.taskreminder;

import android.app.DatePickerDialog;
import android.app.Dialog;
import android.os.Bundle;
import android.support.v4.app.DialogFragment;                              →6

public class DatePickerDialogFragment extends DialogFragment {
    @Override
    public Dialog onCreateDialog(Bundle savedInstanceState) {              →10
        Bundle args = getArguments();                                     →11
        Fragment editFragment = getFragmentManager()                      →12
                .findFragmentByTag(
                        ReminderEditFragment.DEFAULT_EDIT_FRAGMENT_TAG);
        OnDateSetListener listener = (OnDateSetListener) editFragment;    →15

        return new DatePickerDialog(getActivity(), listener,              →17
                args.getInt(ReminderEditFragment.YEAR),
                args.getInt(ReminderEditFragment.MONTH),
                args.getInt(ReminderEditFragment.DAY));
    }
}
```

Here's how the code works:

→**6**   Be sure to use the `android.support.v4.app.*` imports and not their equivalents from `android.app`.

→**10**   The method that's called when Android wishes to display the `DatePicker` dialog box. This method creates it and returns it.

Sometimes you may need to use `savedInstanceState` to restore the state from previous instances. However, in this case, the dialog box already does it for you, so you can safely ignore `savedInstanceState` in this method.

→**11**   Constructor-like arguments for a fragment are passed via `setArguments()`, not via the fragment's constructor, so this line retrieves those arguments using `getArguments()`, which you need on line 17.

→**12**   Asks the `FragmentManager` to find the fragment named `DEFAULT_EDIT_FRAGMENT_TAG`, which is the `ReminderEditFragment`.

→**15**   Casts the `editFragment` to an `OnDateSetListener`. The dialog box created by the `onCreateDialog` needs the `OnDateSetListener` object to inform the `ReminderEditFragment` when the user has picked a date.

→**17** This line calls the `DatePickerDialog` constructor and passes `getActivity()`, the current context listener obtained on line 12, and `args.getInt(ReminderEditFragment.YEAR)`, `args.getInt(ReminderEditFragment.MONTH)`, `args.getInt(ReminderEditFragment.DAY)`, the year, month, and day, as specified in the arguments to this fragment.

Creating the showDatePicker() method

After you have a `DatePickerDialogFragment` class, you can create an instance of it and show it to the user. The date button's `onClickListener` called `showDatePicker`, so you can implement `showDatePicker()` now. Add the following code to the `ReminderEditFragment` class after your `onCreateView()`:

```
//
// Dialog Constants
//
static final String YEAR = "year";
static final String MONTH = "month";
static final String DAY = "day";
static final String HOUR = "hour";
static final String MINS = "mins";
static final String CALENDAR = "calendar";
private void showDatePicker() {
    FragmentTransaction ft = getFragmentManager().beginTransaction();   →11
    DialogFragment newFragment = new DatePickerDialogFragment();        →12
    Bundle args = new Bundle();                                         →13
    args.putInt(YEAR, mCalendar.get(Calendar.YEAR));                    →14
    args.putInt(MONTH, mCalendar.get(Calendar.MONTH));
    args.putInt(DAY, mCalendar.get(Calendar.DAY_OF_MONTH));
    newFragment.setArguments(args);                                     →17
    newFragment.show(ft, "datePicker");                                 →18
}
```

This is how the code works:

→**11** Implements a fragment transaction for the new fragment.

→**12** Creates a `DatePickerDialogFragment` instance.

→**13** Creates the fragment constructor arguments in a bundle.

→**14** Sets the year, month, and day of the dialog box fragment to the year, month, and day set in the `mCalendar` object.

→**17** Sets the fragment's arguments to the values in the bundle created in line 4.

→**18**   Shows the `DatePicker` dialog box fragment, which allows the
dialog box to open onscreen. Because `show()` calls `commit()`,
you don't need to call it explicitly.

Creating the time picker

The `TimePickerDialogFragment` allows users to select a time to be
reminded of a pending task.

Setting up the Time button click listener

Setting up a `TimePickerDialogFragment` is almost identical to setting up a
`DatePickerDialogFragment`. You first declare the `onClickListener()`
for the Time button. In `ReminderEditFragment.onCreateView()`, add
the following code snippet right before the return at the end:

```
mTimeButton.setOnClickListener(new View.OnClickListener() {
    @Override
    public void onClick(View v) {
        showTimePicker();
    }
});
```

This method is the same as the Date button's `onClickListener()`, except
that you're calling `showTimePicker()` instead of `showDatePicker()`.

Creating the showTimePicker() method

To help you create the `showTimePicker()` method, the full method definition, with code, is shown in Listing 11-3.

Listing 11-3:   The showTimePicker() Method

```
private void showTimePicker() {
    FragmentTransaction ft = getFragmentManager().beginTransaction();
    DialogFragment newFragment = new TimePickerDialogFragment();          →3
    Bundle args = new Bundle();
    args.putInt(HOUR, mCalendar.get(Calendar.HOUR_OF_DAY));                →5
    args.putInt(MINS, mCalendar.get(Calendar.MINUTE));
    newFragment.setArguments(args);
    newFragment.show(ft, "timePicker");                                    →8
}
```

The code in Listing 11-3 is fairly straightforward because it's almost identical
to that of the `showDatePicker()` method. However, you can see differences
on these lines:

→**3**   Creates a new instance of `TimePickerDialogFragment`.

→**5**   Sets the arguments for the `TimePickerDialogFragment` to be the calendar's hour and minute components.

→**8**   Shows the fragment using the tag `"timePicker"`, which isn't visible to the user.

Creating the TimePickerDialogFragment

The Android operating system comes supplied with a built-in `TimePicker Dialog` that lets users select (rather than type) a time. Like the `Date PickerDialog`, the `TimePickerDialog` doesn't come wrapped neatly in a fragment, so you have to do it yourself.

The code for the `TimePickerDialogFragment` is nearly identical to the `DatePickerDialogFragment` except that it wraps a `TimePickerDialog` instead of a `DatePickerDialog`:

```
package com.dummies.android.taskreminder;

import android.app.Dialog;
import android.app.TimePickerDialog;
import android.app.TimePickerDialog.OnTimeSetListener;
import android.os.Bundle;
import android.support.v4.app.DialogFragment;

public class TimePickerDialogFragment extends DialogFragment {
    @Override
    public Dialog onCreateDialog(Bundle savedInstanceState) {
        Bundle args = getArguments();
        OnTimeSetListener listener = (OnTimeSetListener) getFragmentManager()
                .findFragmentByTag(
                        ReminderEditFragment.DEFAULT_EDIT_FRAGMENT_TAG);
        return new TimePickerDialog(getActivity(), listener,
                args.getInt(ReminderEditFragment.HOUR),
                args.getInt(ReminderEditFragment.MINS), false);
    }
}
```

Adding the fragment to handle date picker and time picker callbacks

The remaining step in getting your date and time pickers working is to implement the `OnDateSetListener` and `OnTimeSetListener` so that the dialog box stores the new date and time when the user chooses a date or time. You store that value in a `Calendar` object. It requires three steps:

1. Add the `OnDateSetListener` and `OnTimeSetListener` interfaces to the `ReminderEditFragment`.

2. Add a `Calendar` object called `mCalender` to store the values that the user sets.

3. Set the `mCalendar` object when the user picks a date or time, and then update the date and time buttons on the user interface with the new values.

From Listing 11-4, add the code in bold to the `ReminderEditFragment` class to get your date and time pickers working.

Listing 11-4:   Adding the OnDateSetListener and OnTimeSetListener interfaces to the ReminderEditFragment class

```
public class ReminderEditFragment extends Fragment implements
        OnDateSetListener, OnTimeSetListener {                         →2

    private static final String DATE_FORMAT = "yyyy-MM-dd";
    private static final String TIME_FORMAT = "kk:mm";

    private Calendar mCalendar;                                        →7

    @Override
    public void onDateSet(DatePicker view, int year, int monthOfYear,
            int dayOfMonth) {                                          →11
        mCalendar.set(Calendar.YEAR, year);
        mCalendar.set(Calendar.MONTH, monthOfYear);
        mCalendar.set(Calendar.DAY_OF_MONTH, dayOfMonth);
        updateButtons();                                              →15
    }


    @Override
    public void onTimeSet(TimePicker view, int hour, int minute) {    →19
        mCalendar.set(Calendar.HOUR_OF_DAY, hour);
        mCalendar.set(Calendar.MINUTE, minute);
        updateButtons();
    }

    private void updateButtons() {                                    →25
        // Set the time button text
        SimpleDateFormat timeFormat = new SimpleDateFormat(TIME_FORMAT);
        String timeForButton = timeFormat.format(mCalendar.getTime());
        mTimeButton.setText(timeForButton);

        // Set the date button text
        SimpleDateFormat dateFormat = new SimpleDateFormat(DATE_FORMAT);
        String dateForButton = dateFormat.format(mCalendar.getTime());
        mDateButton.setText(dateForButton);
    }
}
```

Listing 11-4 works this way:

→**2**   Implements the `OnDateSetListener` and `OnTimeSetListener` callback objects.

→**7**   Stores the user's date and time selections with a standard Java `Calendar` object.

→**11**   Implements the `onDateSet()` method of the `OnDateSet Listener`. When the user sets the date in the dialog box, the `Calendar` object is updated to reflect the new date.

→**15**   Updates the user interface buttons to reflect the new date and time.

→**19**   Sets the hour and minutes of the `Calendar` object for the `onTimeSet()` method of the `OnTimeSetListener`.

→**25**   Updates the buttons to reflect the values selected by the user. The `Calendar` object is converted into a couple of text strings — one for the date button and one for the time button — which are then used to set the text on those buttons. The first `Simple DateFormat` uses `TIME_FORMAT` to produce a time string in the format `kk:mm`; the second `SimpleDateFormat` uses `DATE_ FORMAT` to produce a date string in the format `yyyy-MM-dd`.

            Visit `http://docs.oracle.com/javase/6/docs/api/ java/text/SimpleDateFormat.html` for more details about `SimpleDateFormat` date and time formatting.

To add the `mCalendar` object, add the following lines to `onCreate()`:

```
if (savedInstanceState != null
        && savedInstanceState.containsKey(CALENDAR)) {                    →2
    mCalendar = (Calendar) savedInstanceState.getSerializable(CALENDAR); →3
} else {
    mCalendar = Calendar.getInstance();                                  →5
}
```

The code works this way:

→**2**   This line checks a `savedInstanceState` for a `CALENDAR` field indicating that an earlier activity was saved and temporarily destroyed, such as rotating from Landscape mode to Portrait mode.

If you're creating a brand-new instance of this fragment, saved InstanceState is null and the application moves to line 5.

→**3**   If the savedInstanceState includes a CALENDAR field, this line pulls out the associated Calendar object and sets mCalendar to that value.

→**5**   When you're creating a ReminderEditFragment from scratch and you aren't resurrecting a previous instance, this line sets mCalendar to a new Calendar instance (obtained by calling Calendar.getInstance()). New Calendar instances always default to the current date and time.

Now the mCalendar instance is initialized.

Because onCreate() is looking for a calendar instance in savedInstance State on lines 1-2, you have to save your mCalendar object to the saved InstanceState whenever your activity is destroyed. That way, onCreate() can pick up the saved value if the activity is ever re-created. To do so, add the following method to your class:

```
@Override
public void onSaveInstanceState(Bundle outState) {                →2
    super.onSaveInstanceState(outState);

    // Save the calendar instance in case the user changed it      →4
    outState.putSerializable(CALENDAR, mCalendar);
}
```

The code works this way:

→**2**   onSaveInstanceState() is a special method that Android calls whenever it's about to destroy a fragment. You can store any data that you might be using, so if Android ever needs to re-create the same activity, it has all the necessary information.

Most views already know how to store their state and resurrect themselves, and they do it in the call to super.onSaveInstance State().

→**4**   The only task you have to handle manually is the mCalendar field, so this line stores it in the bundle to use later when the activity is re-created.

Calendar objects can be serialized (stored as data), so this line uses the putSerializable() method to save them.

Saving field names in Android

Android activities and fragments aren't like standard Java objects, where you can store information in a field in the object and expect it always to be there. Normally in Java, if a `person` object is set to the name `"Michael"`, you can expect that name to always be `"Michael"`, but surprisingly this isn't always the case in Android.

Unlike in Java, Android can destroy activities and fragments at any time. These elements can also be re-created later — and a re-created activity needs to look indistinguishable from one that was never destroyed and re-created. Android reserves the right to destroy objects when memory is running low, but it retains the

ability to re-create them later, to offer the user a seamless experience.

If you store the string `"Michael"` in a field named `name`, that field isn't saved automatically if the activity or fragment is destroyed and re-created. You have to save the field manually, by storing it in a bundle in `onSaveInstance State()` and restoring it from the `saved InstanceState` bundle in `onCreate()`.

Remember: Anytime you add a field to an activity or a fragment, you must add the appropriate code to the `onSavedInstanceState()` and `onCreate()` methods to save it and restore it — otherwise, your app will behave strangely in some circumstances but not in others.

Find out more information about Java serialization at `http://java.sun.com/developer/technicalArticles/Programming/serialization`.

You can save all kinds of other types into bundles, such as ints, longs, strings, parcelables, and other exotic elements, so check `http://d.android.com/reference/android/os/Bundle.html` to see the full list.

Creating an Alert Dialog Box

From time to time it may be necessary to alert the user to something that has happened. In the Task Reminder app, perhaps you want to display a welcome message and offer instructions on how to create a task. The Android system has a framework, built around dialog boxes that provide you with the implementation you may need.

Various types of dialog boxes are available:

- ✔ **Alert:** Notifies the user of an important occurrence. Also allows you to set the text value of a button and the action to be performed when it's clicked. As a developer, you can provide the `AlertDialog` with a list of items to display, allowing the user to select from a list of items.

✔ **Progress:** Used to display a progress wheel or bar. This type of dialog box is created via the `ProgressDialog` class.

✔ **Custom:** A custom dialog box created and programmed by you, the master Android developer. You create a custom dialog box class by extending the `Dialog` base class or using custom layout XML files.

Seeing why you should work with dialog boxes

If you've never worked with an application that failed to alert you, or warn you appropriately, consider the example of an e-mail client not notifying you that you have new e-mail. How annoying would that be? Alerting users to important issues or choices that need to be made is an integral part of any user experience.

This list gives a few examples of using a dialog box to inform the user of a message or a necessary action:

✔ Something is happening in the background. (The `ProgressDialog` does this.)

✔ The values in an `EditText` view are invalid.

✔ The network has become unavailable.

✔ The user needs to select a date or time (as in the Task Reminder app).

✔ The state of the phone is incompatible with the application. (It might need to have GPS enabled or an SD card added, for example.)

✔ The user needs to choose from a list of items.

Though this list isn't comprehensive, it gives you an inkling into what is possible with dialog boxes.

When you work with any type of blocking process (network communication or long-running tasks, for example), always provide the user with an informative dialog box or progress indicator. A user who doesn't realize that an element of your app needs attention is likely to mistakenly believe that it has stopped responding and could even uninstall it. The Android framework provides various progress indicators, such as the common progress classes `ProgressDialog` and `ProgressBar`.

Though a discussion of the `AsyncTask` class is beyond the scope of this book, you would use this class to manage long-running tasks while updating the user interface. (See the helpful "Painless Threading" tutorial at `http://android-developers.blogspot.com/2009/05/painless-thread-ing.html`.) You can also create a new thread in code — the `AsyncTask` class helps simplify this process.

Choosing the appropriate dialog box for a task

Though you determine which dialog box to use for a given scenario, you can ask a logical series of questions to choose the appropriate one:

1. **Is this task long-running?**

   - *Yes:* Use `ProgressDialog` to let the user know that something is happening in the background and that the app isn't frozen. A great resource that explains how to do this is located here: `http://d.android.com/guide/topics/ui/dialogs.html#ProgressDialog`.

   - *No:* Continue to Step 2.

2. **Does the user need to be able to perform an advanced action in the dialog box?**

   An *advanced action* isn't supported by the `AlertDialog` class.

   - *Yes:* Create a custom `Dialog` class by extending the `Dialog` base class or creating one from a custom layout XML file. You can find more information about custom dialog boxes at `http://d.android.com/guide/topics/ui/dialogs.html#CustomDialog`.

   - *No:* Continue to Step 3.

3. **Does the user need to answer a question such as "Are you sure?" with a Yes or No value?**

   - *Yes:* Create an `AlertDialog` and react to the buttons on the `AlertDialog` by using `onClickListener()` calls.

   - *No:* Continue to Step 4.

4. **Does the user need to make a selection from a simple list of items?**

   - *Yes:* Create an `AlertDialog`.

   - *No:* Continue to Step 5.

5. **Does the user simply need to be alerted?**

   - *Yes:* Create a simple `AlertDialog`.

   - *No:* You may not need a dialog box, if you can notify the user another way.

Creating your own alert dialog box

At times, you need to notify the user of important information by presenting a dialog box. Android makes it quite simple with its introduction of the `AlertDialog.Builder` class, which lets you easily create an `AlertDialog` with various options and buttons. Your app can react to these button clicks via the `onClickListener()` of each button.

You don't need to use the `AlertDialog.Builder` class in a simple application, such as Task Reminder. However, Listing 11-5 shows how to create one when you create more complex applications.

Suppose that the user has tapped the Save button in the Task Reminder application and you want to open a window (similar to the one in Figure 11-3) so that the user can confirm.

In Listing 11-5, you create an `AlertDialog` object using the `AlertDialog.Builder` class and then add an `AlertDialogFragment` (which works similarly to `DatePickerDialogFragment` and `TimePickerDialogFragment`).

Listing 11-5:   Creating an AlertDialogFragment with the AlertDialog. Builder Class

```
public class AlertDialogFragment extends DialogFragment {
    @Override
    public Dialog onCreateDialog(Bundle savedInstanceState) {
        AlertDialog.Builder builder
            = new AlertDialog.Builder(getActivity());                      →5
        builder.setMessage("Are you sure you want to save the task?")      →6
            .setTitle("Are you sure?")                                     →7
            .setCancelable(false)                                          →8
            .setPositiveButton("Yes",                                      →9
            new DialogInterface.OnClickListener() {                        →10
                public void onClick(DialogInterface dialog, int id) {
                        // Perform some action such as saving the item     →12
                }
            })
            .setNegativeButton("No", new DialogInterface.OnClickListener() {→15
                public void onClick(DialogInterface dialog, int id) {
                        dialog.cancel();                                   →17
                }
        });
        return builder.create();                                          →20
    }
}
```

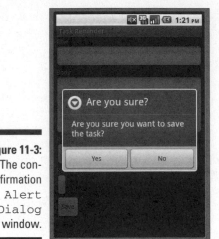

Figure 11-3:
The con-
firmation
`Alert`
`Dialog`
window.

The code is explained in this list:

→**5**   Sets up the `AlertDialog.Builder` class with the context of the `AlertDialog.Builder` as the current running activity.

→**6**   Specifies the message to show in the middle of the `AlertDialog` (as shown in Figure 11-3). The value can be a string or a string resource.

→**7**   Sets the title of the `AlertDialog`. The value can be a string or a string resource.

→**8**   Sets the cancelable attribute to `false`, requiring the user to select a button in the `AlertDialog`. If this flag is set to `false`, the user cannot tap the Back button on the device to exit the `AlertDialog`. Set it to `true` and the user can tap the Back button.

→**9**   Specifies the text on the positive button. The user clicks the Yes button to perform the action indicated on line 10. This value can be a string or a string resource.

→**10**   A block of code (ending on line 12) that defines the `onClick Listener()` for the Yes button. The code on line 12 executes when the button is tapped.

→**15**   Specifies the text on the negative button. This button indicates that the user doesn't want to perform the action being requested via AlertDialog. The text value of this button is set to No. It can be a string or a string resource.

→**17**   Sets the onClickListener() for the negative button. The listener provides a reference to the dialog box that's being shown. It's called the cancel() method on the Dialog object to close the dialog box when the user clicks No on the AlertDialog.

→**20**   Notifies Android to create the AlertDialog via the create() method.

To show the dialog box, you start a fragment transaction in the usual manner:

```
FragmentTransaction ft = getFragmentManager().beginTransaction();
DialogFragment newFragment = new AlertDialogFragment();
newFragment.show(ft, "alertDialog");
```

Creating a dialog box with the AlertDialog.Builder class is easier than having to derive your own Dialog class. If possible, create your dialog box with the AlertDialog.Builder class because it gives your application a consistent user experience that's familiar to most Android users.

When the user taps the Save button (or whatever button the code is attached to), an AlertDialog opens so that the user can confirm saving the task. This data most likely is stored in a database, as covered in Chapter 12.

You can find helpful examples of using other options on the Dialog class at http://d.android.com/guide/topics/ui/dialogs.html.

Validating Input

After you've created your application so that users can enter information, and perhaps you've already created the mechanism to save the content to a database or remote server, what happens when the user enters invalid text or no text? Input validation now enters the picture.

Input validation verifies the input before the save takes place. If a user enters no text for the title or the message and attempts to save, should she be allowed to? Of course not.

The method in which you provide validation to the user is up to you. Here are some common methods:

- ✔ `EditText.setError()`: If you detect that the user has tried to enter invalid text in a field, simply call `setError()` and pass the error message. Android then decorates `EditText` with an error icon and displays an error message. The message stays onscreen until the user changes the value of the field or until you call `setError(null)`.

- ✔ `TextWatcher`: Implement a `TextWatcher` on the `EditText` view. This class provides callbacks to you every time the text changes in the `EditText` view. Therefore, you can inspect the text on each keystroke.

- ✔ `On Save`: When the user attempts to save a form, inspect all the form fields at that time and inform the user of any issues that were found.

- ✔ `onFocusChanged()`: Inspect the values of the form when the `onFocusChanged()` event is called — which is called when the view has focus and when it loses focus. This is usually a good place to set up validation.

The Task Reminder application provides no input validation. However, you can add validation via one of the methods described earlier.

Toasting the user

The most common way to inform the user of a potential problem, such as an error in input value, is to display a `Toast` message. This type of message appears onscreen for only a few seconds by default.

Providing a `Toast` message is as simple as implementing the following code, where you inform the user of the input error:

```
Toast.makeText(getActivity(), "Title must be filled in", Toast.LENGTH_SHORT).
        show();
```

You might show this message when the user fails to enter a title in the title field and then clicks the Save button.

The only problem with a `Toast` message is that it's short-lived by default. A user who happens to glance away at the wrong time will likely miss seeing it. You can configure your `Toast` messages to display longer by using `Toast.LENGTH_LONG` instead of `Toast.LENGTH_SHORT`.

Using other validation techniques

A `Toast` message isn't the only way to inform users of a problem with their input. A few other popular validation techniques are described in this list:

- ✔ `AlertDialog`: Create an instance of an `AlertDialog` that informs the user of errors. This method ensures that the user sees the error message because the alert must be either canceled or accepted.

- ✔ **Input-field highlighting:** If the field is invalid, the background color of the input field (the `EditText` view) can change to indicate that the value is incorrect.

- ✔ **Custom validation:** If you're feeling adventurous, you can create a custom validation library to handle validations of all sorts. It might highlight the field and draw small views with arrows pointing to the error, for example, similar to the Google validation of its sign-in window when you log on to a device for the first time.

You can use these common methods to display input validation information, or you can dream up new ways to inform users of errors. For example, Chapter 14 introduces the notification bar, which you can use to inform users of a problem with a background service.

Chapter 12

Getting Persistent with Data Storage

. . . .

In This Chapter

▶ Discovering data-storage media

▶ Getting user permissions

▶ Creating an SQLite database

▶ Querying your database

. . . .

In certain types of applications, Android requires application developers to use data persistence, where information about a user's preferences, such as favorite background colors or radio stations, is saved on the device for reuse later, after the device is turned off and then on again. For example, the Task Reminder application wouldn't be useful if it didn't save tasks, would it? Thankfully, the Android platform (in combination with Java) provides a robust set of tools that you can use to store user data.

This chapter delves deeply into creating and updating an SQLite database and producing a `ContentProvider` to access it. You need to be familiar with a certain level of database theory to tackle the data storage tasks in this chapter.

If you're unfamiliar with SQL (Structured Query Language) or the SQL database, see the SQLite website at `www.sqlite.org` for more information.

This chapter is code-intensive — if you start feeling lost, you can download the completed application source code from this book's website.

Finding Places to Put Data

Depending on the requirements of your application, you may need to store data in a variety of places. For example, if an application interacts with music files and a user wants to play them in more than one music program, you have to store them in a location where all applications can access them. An application that needs to store sensitive data, such as encrypted usernames and password details, shouldn't share data — placing it in a secure, local storage environment is the best strategy. Regardless of your situation, Android provides various options for storing data.

Viewing your storage options

The Android ecosystem provides various locations where data can be persisted:

✔ **Shared preferences:** Private data stored in key-value pairs. (See Chapter 15 to find out how to handle shared preferences.)

✔ **Internal storage:** A location for saving files on the device. Files stored in internal storage are private to your application by default, and other applications cannot access them. (Neither can the user, except by using your application.) When the application is uninstalled, the private files are deleted as well.

✔ **Local cache:** The internal data directory for caching data rather than storing it persistently. Cached files may be deleted at any time. You use the `getCacheDir()` method, available on the `Activity` or `Context` objects in Android.

If you store data in an internal data directory and the internal storage space begins to run low, Android may delete files to reclaim space. Don't rely on Android to delete your files for you though! You should delete your cache files yourself to stay within a reasonable limit (about 1 MB) of space consumed in the cache directory.

✔ **External storage:** Every Android device supports shared external storage for files — either removable storage, such as a Secure Digital card (SD card) or nonremovable storage. Files saved to external storage are *public* (any person or application can alter them), and no level of security is enforced. Users can modify files by either using a file manager application or connecting the device to a computer via a USB cable and mounting the device as external storage. Before you work with external storage, check the current state of the external storage with the `Environment` object, using a call to `getExternalStorageState()` to check whether the media is available.

In Android 2.2, a new set of methods was introduced to handle external files. The main method is a call on the `Context` object — `getExternal FilesDir()`. This call takes a string parameter as a key to help define the type of media you're saving, such as ringtones, music, or photos. For more information, view the external data storage examples and documents at `http://d.android.com/guide/topics/data/data-storage.html#filesExternal`.

✔ **SQLite database:** A lightweight SQL database implementation that's available across various platforms (including Android, iPhone, Windows, Linux, and Mac) and fully supported by Android. You can create tables and perform SQL queries against the tables accordingly. You implement an SQLite database in this chapter to handle the persistence of the tasks in the Task Reminder application.

✔ **Content provider:** A "wrapper" around another storage mechanism. A content provider is used by an app to read and write application data that can be stored in preferences, files, or SQLite databases, for example.

✔ **Network connection:** (Also known as remote storage.) Any remote data source that you have access to. For example, because Flickr exposes an API that allows you to store images on its servers, your application might work with Flickr to store images. If your application works with a popular tool on the Internet (such as Twitter, Facebook, or Basecamp), your app might send information via HTTP — or any other protocol you deem necessary — to third-party APIs to store the data.

Choosing a storage option

The various data storage locations offer quite the palette of options. However, you have to figure out which one to use, and you may even want to use *multiple* storage mechanisms.

Suppose that your application communicates with a third-party remote API such as Twitter, and network communication is slow and less than 100 percent reliable. You may want to retain on the server a local copy of all data since the last update, to allow the application to remain usable (in some fashion) until the next update. When you store the data in a local copy of an SQLite database and the user initiates an update, the new updates refresh the SQLite database with the new data.

If your application relies solely on network communication for information retrieval and storage, use the SQLite database (or any other storage mechanism) to make the application remain usable when the user cannot connect to a network and must work offline — a common occurrence. If your application doesn't function when a network connection is unavailable, you'll likely receive negative reviews in the Google Play Store — as well as feature requests to make your app work offline. This strategy introduces quite a bit of extra work into the application development process, but it's worth your time tenfold in user experience.

Creating Your Application's SQLite ContentProvider

The best place to store and retrieve a user's tasks in the Task Reminder application is inside an SQLite database. Your application needs to be able to perform CRUD — create, read, update, and delete — tasks from the database using a `ContentProvider`.

Understanding how the SQLite ContentProvider works

The two fragments in the Task Reminder application need to perform various duties to operate. `ReminderEditFragment` needs to complete these steps:

1. Create a new record.

2. Read a record so that it can display the details for editing.

3. Update the existing record.

The `ReminderListFragment` needs to perform these duties:

1. Read all tasks to show them onscreen.

2. Delete a task by responding to the click event from the context menu after a user has long-pressed an item.

To work with an SQLite database, you communicate with the database via a `ContentProvider`. Programmers commonly remove as much of the database communication as possible away from the `Activity` and `Fragment` objects. The database mechanisms are placed into a `ContentProvider` to help separate the application into layers of functionality. Therefore, if you need to alter code that affects the database, you know that you need to change the code in only one location to do so.

Creating a ContentProvider to hold the database code

To create a `ContentProvider` in your Android project that will house the database-centric code, you first name the file `ReminderProvider.java`.

Defining the key elements of a database

Before you create and open a database, you need to define a few key fields.
Replace the code in your `ReminderProvider` class with the code from
Listing 12-1.

Listing 12-1:   The Constants, Fields, and Constructors of the
RemindersDbAdapter Class

```
package com.dummies.android.taskreminder;

import android.content.ContentProvider;
import android.database.sqlite.SQLiteDatabase;

public class ReminderProvider extends ContentProvider {
    // Database Related Constants
    private static final int DATABASE_VERSION = 1;                          →8
    private static final String DATABASE_NAME = "data";                     →9
    private static final String DATABASE_TABLE = "reminders";               →10

    // Database Columns
    public static final String COLUMN_ROWID = "_id";                        →13
    public static final String COLUMN_DATE_TIME = "reminder_date_time";     →14
    public static final String COLUMN_BODY = "body";                        →15
    public static final String COLUMN_TITLE = "title";                      →16

    private static final String DATABASE_CREATE = "create table "           →18
            + DATABASE_TABLE + " (" + COLUMN_ROWID
            + " integer primary key autoincrement, " + COLUMN_TITLE
            + " text not null, " + COLUMN_BODY + " text not null, "
            + COLUMN_DATE_TIME + " integer not null);";

    private SQLiteDatabase mDb;                                             →24

    @Override
    public boolean onCreate() {                                             →27
        mDb = new DatabaseHelper(getContext()).getWritableDatabase();      →28
        return true;
    }

}
```

The numbered lines are explained in this list:

→8   The version of the database. If you were to update the schema
         in your database, you would increment the version and pro-
         vide an implementation of the `onUpgrade()` method of the
         `DatabaseHelper`.

→**9**   The physical name of the database that will exist in the Android file system.

→**10**   The name of the database table that will hold the tasks.

→**13–16** Define the column names of the database table.

→**18**   Defines the create script for the database. Column names from earlier lines are combined into a single SQL statement that will create the database.

→**24**   The class-level instance of the SQLite database object that allows you to create, read, update, and delete records.

→**27**   Creates the `ContentProvider` and calls the `onCreate()`.

→**28**   Calls `getWritableDatabase()` on a `DatabaseHelper` object.

The SQL database is ready to be created!

For information about the database table or components of the script, see the next section "Visualizing the SQL table." For information about the database helper or the database table, see the later section "Creating the database table."

Visualizing the SQL table

The *table object* in SQL is the construct that holds the data you manage. Visualizing a table in SQLite is similar to looking at a spreadsheet: Each row consists of data, and each column represents the data inside the row. Earlier in this chapter, Listing 12-1 defines column names for the database. These column names equate to the header values in a spreadsheet, as shown in Figure 12-1. Each row contains a value for each column, which is how data is stored in SQLite.

Figure 12-1:
Visualizing
data in
the Task
Reminder
application.

_id	title	body	reminder_date_time
1	Order Flight Tickets	Go to travel site and order ti...	2010-11-15 16:15
2	Schedule Time Off	Email manager at work to ...	2010-11-17 15:00
3	Take Vacation	YES! Finally take that much n...	2010-12-10 14:30
4	Pay Bills	Pay the bills through bill pay.	2010-11-10 12:15

Line 18 in Listing 12-1 assembles the database `create` script, which concatenates various constants from within the file to create a database create script. When you run this script in SQLite, SQLite creates a table named `reminders` in a database named `data`. The columns and how they're built in the create script are described in this list:

- ✔ `create table DATABASE_TABLE`: This portion of the script notifies SQLite that you want to create a database table named `reminders`.

- ✔ `COLUMN_ROWID`: This property acts as the identifier for the task. This column has the `integer primary key autoincrement` attributes applied to it. The `integer` attribute specifies that the row is an integer. The `primary key` attribute states that the `COLUMN_ROWID` is the primary identifier for a task. The `autoincrement` attribute notifies SQLite, whenever a new task is inserted, to simply set the row's ID to the next available integer automatically. For example, if rows 1, 2, and 3 exist and you insert another record, the value of the `COLUMN_ROWID` in the next row is 4.

- ✔ `COLUMN_TITLE`: The user provides this task title, such as *Schedule Vacation*. The text attribute informs SQLite that the column is a text column. The `not null` attribute states that the value of this column cannot be null — the user must provide a value.

- ✔ `COLUMN_BODY`: This is the body or description of the task. The attributes for this column are the same as for `COLUMN_TITLE`.

- ✔ `COLUMN_DATE_TIME`: The date and time of the reminder are stored in this field. It stores an integer because SQLite has no storage class associated with storing dates or times, so you convert the `Calendar` object to a Java `long`, which can be represented — problem free — as an SQL integer.

For more information on dates and times in SQLite, visit `www.sqlite.org/datatype3.html#datetime`.

Creating the database table

When you're ready to create the database table, you provide an implementation of `SQLiteOpenHelper`. The `ReminderProvider` class type, shown in Listing 12-2, lets you create a nested Java class inside the `RemindersDbAdapter` class.

Upgrading your database

Suppose that you release your application and 10,000 users install it and are using it — and they love it! Some even send you feature requests, so you implement one that requires a change in the database schema. You then perform SQL ALTER statements inside the onUpgrade() call to update your database.

You could upgrade the database by "dropping" the existing one and then creating a new one. But you don't want to do this — dropping a database *deletes all of the user's data.* Imagine updating your favorite Task Reminder application, only to see that the upgrade has erased all preexisting tasks (a *major* bug).

Listing 12-2:   Creating a Database Table

```
private static class DatabaseHelper extends SQLiteOpenHelper {          →1
    DatabaseHelper(Context context) {
        super(context, DATABASE_NAME, null, DATABASE_VERSION);          →3
    }

    @Override
    public void onCreate(SQLiteDatabase db) {                           →7
        db.execSQL(DATABASE_CREATE);                                    →8
    }

    @Override
    public void onUpgrade(SQLiteDatabase db, int oldVersion,
                int newVersion) {                                       →12
        throw new UnsupportedOperationException();
    }
}
```

The numbered lines are described in this list:

→**1**   The implementation of SQLiteOpenHelper.

→**3**   The call made to the base SQLiteOpenHelper constructor. This call creates, opens, and/or manages a database, which isn't created or opened until getReadableDatabase() or getWriteable Database() is called on the SQLiteOpenHelper instance.

→**7**   The onCreate() method, which is called when the database is created for the first time.

→**8**   Creates your database and database table ("where the magic happens"). The execSQL() method accepts an SQL script string as a parameter. The SQLite database executes the SQL from Listing 12-1 to create the database table.

→**12**   Uses the onUpgrade() method when you need to upgrade an existing database.

Resolving ContentProvider URLs

An Android `ContentProvider` uses URLs to identify data. Typically, you can use a URL to identify a specific piece of data, such as a single reminder, or all reminders in your database. If you store other types of data there, you can use URLs for them, too.

In your application, you use two kinds of URLs — `content://com.dummies.android.taskreminder.ReminderProvider/reminder` to retrieve a list of all reminders in your database or `content://com.dummies.android.taskreminder.ReminderProvider/reminder/9` to retrieve a specific reminder from the database (in this case the reminder with the ID of 9).

These content provider URLs are undoubtedly similar to the URLs you're already familiar with. Their main differences are described in this list:

✔ **content://**: A `ContentProvider` begins with `content://` rather than with `http://`.

✔ **com.dummies.android.taskreminder.ReminderProvider:** The second part of the URL identifies the authority (the `ReminderProvider` `ContentProvider`) of the content. Though this string can be virtually anything, convention dictates using the fully qualified name of your `ContentProvider`.

✔ **reminder:** The third part of the URL identifies the path — in this case, the type of data you're looking up. This string identifies which table in the database to read. If the application stores multiple types in the database (say, a list of users in addition to a list of reminders), a second type of path might be named `user`.

✔ **9:** In the first URL, the path ends with `reminder`. However, in the second URL, the path continues to include the specific ID of the reminder being requested.

Before you can use the `ContentProvider`, ensure that it's listed in the `Android Manifest.xml` file, by adding this code before the `</application>` tag:

```
<provider
    android:name="com.dummies.android.taskreminder.ReminderProvider"
    android:authorities="com.dummies.android.taskreminder.ReminderProvider"
    android:exported="false"
/>
```

It tells Android that a `ContentProvider` named `ReminderProvider` will handle URLs that use the specific authority of `com.dummies.android.taskreminder.ReminderProvider`. It also indicates that the data in the provider is not exported to other apps on the user's phone. In general, you should set `exported="false"` unless you want to make your provider available to other apps.

Now you have to add the code to support these URLs in your `Content Provider`. Open `ReminderProvider` and add the following lines to the class:

```
// Content Provider Uri and Authority
public static String AUTHORITY = "com.dummies.android.taskreminder.
        ReminderProvider";                                          →2
public static final Uri CONTENT_URI = Uri.parse("content://" + AUTHORITY
        + "/reminder");                                             →4

// MIME types used for searching words or looking up a single definition
public static final String REMINDERS_MIME_TYPE = ContentResolver.CURSOR_DIR_
        BASE_TYPE
        + "/vnd.com.dummies.android.taskreminder.reminder";         →8
public static final String REMINDER_MIME_TYPE = ContentResolver.CURSOR_ITEM_
        BASE_TYPE
        + "/vnd.com.dummies.android.taskreminder.reminder";

// UriMatcher stuff
private static final int LIST_REMINDER = 0;                          →13
private static final int ITEM_REMINDER = 1;
private static final UriMatcher sURIMatcher = buildUriMatcher();      →15

/**
 * Builds up a UriMatcher for search suggestion and shortcut refresh
 * queries.
 */
private static UriMatcher buildUriMatcher() {
    UriMatcher matcher = new UriMatcher(UriMatcher.NO_MATCH);         →22
    matcher.addURI(AUTHORITY, "reminder", LIST_REMINDER);            →23
    matcher.addURI(AUTHORITY, "reminder/#", ITEM_REMINDER);         →24
    return matcher;
}

/**
 * This method is required in order to query the supported types. It's also
 * useful in the query() method to determine the type of Uri received.
 */
@Override
public String getType(Uri uri) {                                     →33
    switch (sURIMatcher.match(uri)) {
    case LIST_REMINDER:
        return REMINDERS_MIME_TYPE;
    case ITEM_REMINDER:
        return REMINDER_MIME_TYPE;
    default:
        throw new IllegalArgumentException("Unknown Uri: " + uri);
    }
}
```

This chunk of code may seem intimidating, but it consists mostly of constants with one useful method (getType()). Here's how the numbered lines work:

→**2**   The authority for the ContentProvider — by convention, the same as the fully qualified class name. This value must match the value you added to the AndroidManifest.xml file for the provider authorities.

→**4**   The base URL (or URI) for the ContentProvider. Every time your application asks for data for this URL, Android routes the request to this ContentProvider.

    The ContentProvider supports two types of URLs: one for listing all reminders and one for listing a specific reminder.

    The first type of URL is the CONTENT_URI, and the second one is the CONTENT_URI with the reminder ID appended to the end.

→**8**   Because the ContentProvider supports two types of data, it defines two types (or MIME types) for this data. *MIME types* are simply strings commonly used on the web to identify data types. For example, web HTML content typically has a MIME type of text/html, and audio MP3 files have audio/mpeg3. Because the reminders are of no known standard type, you can make up MIME type strings as long as you follow Android and MIME conventions.

    The List MIME type begins with ContentResolver.CURSOR_ DIR_BASE_TYPE, and the individual Reminder MIME type begins with ContentResolver.CURSOR_ITEM_BASE_TYPE. DIR represents the list, and ITEM represents the item — simple enough.

    This line also checks to see whether the subtype (which follows the /) begins with vnd. The subtype is followed by the fully qualified class name and the type of data — in this case, com.dummies. android.taskreminder and reminder. Visit http:// developer.android.com/reference/android/content/ ContentResolver.html for more information about the Android conventions for MIME types.

→**13**   Uses another constant to identify list types versus item types, which are ints.

→**15**   The UriMatcher is used to determine the URL type: list or item. You build a UriMatcher using the method named build UriMatcher() on line 21.

→**22**   Creates the UriMatcher, which can indicate whether a given URL is the list type or item type. The UriMatcher.NO_MATCH parameter tells the application which default value to return for a match.

→**23**   Defines the list type. Any URL that uses the com.dummies. android.taskreminder.ReminderProvider authority

and has a path named "reminder" returns the value LIST_
REMINDER.

→24   Defines the item type. Any URL that uses the com.dummies.
android.taskreminder.ReminderProvider authority and
has a path that looks like reminder/# (where # is a number)
returns the value ITEM_REMINDER.

→33   Uses the UriMatcher on line 15 to determine which MIME type to
return. If the URL is a list URL, it returns REMINDERS_MIME_TYPE.
If it's an item URL, it returns REMINDER_MIME_TYPE.

Creating and Editing Tasks with SQLite

After you have a ContentProvider, you can create a task for it: Insert a
record, and then list all tasks on the ReminderListFragment. The user can
then tap a task to edit it, or long-press the task to delete it. These user interactions cover the create, read, update, and delete(CRUD) operations needed
to make the Task Reminder application work.

Inserting a task entry

Inserting tasks is simple, after you get the hang of it. To insert your first task
into the SQLite database, build the Save button click listener to:

1. Retrieve values from EditText views.

2. Store the values to the ReminderProvider database using a
ContentResolver.

3. Update the user interface by displaying a toast and closing the edit
activity.

After inserting your first task, you should have enough of a grasp on the
ReminderProvider class interaction to perform more tasks. The next sections introduce you to the entire implementation of ReminderProvider,
which outlines the CRUD operations.

Saving values from the screen to the database

When the user creates a task, it takes place in the OnClickListener
of the mConfirmButton of ReminderEditFragment. There, the app
responds to the user's Save button click. If the mRowId for the fragment
is 0, the user wants to add a new task. If the mRowId is greater than 0, the

user wants to edit an existing task. You first set up some parameters, ask a
ContentResolver to complete a create or update, and then process the
result and notify the user.

Add the following OnClickListener element to the mConfirmButton in
ReminderEditFragment.onCreateView():

```
mConfirmButton.setOnClickListener(new View.OnClickListener() {
    @Override
    public void onClick(View view) {
        ContentValues values = new ContentValues();                    →4
        values.put(ReminderProvider.COLUMN_ROWID, mRowId);             →5
        values.put(ReminderProvider.COLUMN_TITLE, mTitleText.getText()
                .toString());                                          →7
        values.put(ReminderProvider.COLUMN_BODY, mBodyText.getText()
                .toString());
        values.put(ReminderProvider.COLUMN_DATE_TIME,
                mCalendar.getTimeInMillis());                          →11

        if (mRowId == 0) {                                             →13
            Uri itemUri = getActivity().getContentResolver().insert(
                    ReminderProvider.CONTENT_URI, values);            →15
            mRowId = ContentUris.parseId(itemUri);                    →16
        } else {
            int count = getActivity().getContentResolver().update(
                    ContentUris.withAppendedId(
                            ReminderProvider.CONTENT_URI, mRowId),
                    values, null, null);                              →21
            if (count != 1)                                           →22
                throw new IllegalStateException("Unable to update "
                    + mRowId);
        }

        Toast.makeText(getActivity(),
                getString(R.string.task_saved_message),
                Toast.LENGTH_SHORT).show();                           →29
        getActivity().finish();                                       →30
    }
});
```

Here's how the code works:

→4 A query is run by ContentResolver that's ultimately served by
the ReminderProvider. Specifically, this line inserts or updates
a reminder. The ContentValues object indicates the record to
update and the data to use.

→5 The row ID for the reminder — 0 if the user is creating a new
record, or the specific ID of the task if the user is updating an
existing task.

→7 The title of the task, which is the value indicated by the user's input in the `mTitleText EditText` view. The app calls `mTitle Text.getText()` to get a `CharSequence` and then calls `toString()` to produce the string.

→11 Holds the date and time that the user selected for the reminder. It also calls `Calendar.getTimeInMillis()` and puts the result in a `ContentValues` object. (SQLite has no way to represent dates directly, so you must convert the object to a `long`.)

→13 Checks to see whether the user is adding a new task or updating an existing one. If `mRowID` is 0, the user is adding a new task. Otherwise, the user is updating an existing task.

→15 Calls `getContentResolver()` on the activity and then calls `insert()` to run the insert query. An insert requires two parameters: the data you want to insert and the URI of the table in which you're inserting it. In return, `insert()` gives you the full URI of the data it inserted.

→16 Parses the ID of the URI of the item that was inserted, by using `ContentUris.parseId()`, and sets `mRowId` to that value.

→21 Calls `update()` on `ContentResolver` to run an update. Rather than pass in the base URI, it passes the URI of the item being updated, which is obtained by calling `ContentUris.with AppendedId()` and passing the base URI and the reminder ID. The two last null parameters indicate that no fancy SQL queries need updating more than a single row at a time.

→22 Indicates how many records were updated. It should never be anything other than 1, so if no rows or multiple rows are updated, an error message is thrown.

→29 Calls `Toast.makeText()` to display a successful message for a short time. Then it calls `show()` so that the message appears onscreen.

→30 Calls `finish()` on the activity to close the edit activity and show the list activity again.

The entire ReminderProvider implementation

Sometimes seeing all elements at one time is better than seeing them piece-meal. Working with SQLite in the `ReminderProvider` class is no different. Listing 12-3 shows the entire implementation of the `ReminderProvider` so that you can get a feel for what you're working with.

Listing 12-3:   The Full Implementation of ReminderProvider

```
package com.dummies.android.taskreminder;

import android.content.ContentProvider;
import android.content.ContentResolver;
import android.content.ContentUris;
import android.content.ContentValues;
import android.content.Context;
import android.content.UriMatcher;
import android.database.Cursor;
import android.database.sqlite.SQLiteDatabase;
import android.database.sqlite.SQLiteOpenHelper;
import android.net.Uri;

public class ReminderProvider extends ContentProvider {
    // Content Provider Uri and Authority
    public static String AUTHORITY = "com.dummies.android.taskreminder.
            ReminderProvider";
    public static final Uri CONTENT_URI = Uri.parse("content://" + AUTHORITY
            + "/reminder");

    // MIME types used for searching words or looking up a single definition
    public static final String REMINDERS_MIME_TYPE = ContentResolver.CURSOR_DIR_
            BASE_TYPE
            + "/vnd.com.dummies.android.taskreminder.reminder";
    public static final String REMINDER_MIME_TYPE = ContentResolver.CURSOR_ITEM_
            BASE_TYPE
            + "/vnd.com.dummies.android.taskreminder.reminder";

    // Database Columns
    public static final String COLUMN_ROWID = "_id";
    public static final String COLUMN_DATE_TIME = "reminder_date_time";
    public static final String COLUMN_BODY = "body";
    public static final String COLUMN_TITLE = "title";

    // Database Related Constants
    private static final int DATABASE_VERSION = 1;
    private static final String DATABASE_NAME = "data";
    private static final String DATABASE_TABLE = "reminders";

    private static final String DATABASE_CREATE = "create table "
            + DATABASE_TABLE + " (" + COLUMN_ROWID
            + " integer primary key autoincrement, " + COLUMN_TITLE
            + " text not null, " + COLUMN_BODY + " text not null, "
            + COLUMN_DATE_TIME + " integer not null);";

    // UriMatcher stuff
    private static final int LIST_REMINDER = 0;
    private static final int ITEM_REMINDER = 1;
    private static final UriMatcher sURIMatcher = buildUriMatcher();
```

(continued)

Listing 12-3 *(continued)*

```
    private SQLiteDatabase mDb;

    /**
     * Builds up a UriMatcher for search suggestion and shortcut refresh
     * queries.
     */
    private static UriMatcher buildUriMatcher() {
        UriMatcher matcher = new UriMatcher(UriMatcher.NO_MATCH);
        // to get definitions...
        matcher.addURI(AUTHORITY, "reminder", LIST_REMINDER);
        matcher.addURI(AUTHORITY, "reminder/#", ITEM_REMINDER);

        return matcher;
    }

    @Override
    public boolean onCreate() {
        mDb = new DatabaseHelper(getContext()).getWritableDatabase();
        return true;
    }

    @Override
    public Cursor query(Uri uri, String[] ignored1, String ignored2,
            String[] ignored3, String ignored4) {                          →75

        String[] projection = new String[] { ReminderProvider.COLUMN_ROWID,
                ReminderProvider.COLUMN_TITLE, ReminderProvider.COLUMN_BODY,
                ReminderProvider.COLUMN_DATE_TIME };                         →79

        // Use the UriMatcher to see the query type and format the
        // db query accordingly
        Cursor c;
        switch (sURIMatcher.match(uri)) {                                    →84
        case LIST_REMINDER:                                                  →85
            c = mDb.query(ReminderProvider.DATABASE_TABLE, projection, null,
                    null, null, null, null);                                →87
            break;                                                          →89
        case ITEM_REMINDER:                                                 →90
            c = mDb.query(ReminderProvider.DATABASE_TABLE, projection,
                    ReminderProvider.COLUMN_ROWID + "=?", new String[] { Long
                        .toString(ContentUris.parseId(uri)) },              →92
                    null, null, null, null);
            if (c != null && c.getCount() > 0) {                            →94
                c.moveToFirst();                                            →95
            }
            break;
        default:                                                            →98
            throw new IllegalArgumentException("Unknown Uri: " + uri);
        }
```

```
        c.setNotificationUri(getContext().getContentResolver(), uri);    →102
        return c;                                                         →103
}


@Override
public Uri insert(Uri uri, ContentValues values) {                        →107
    values.remove(ReminderProvider.COLUMN_ROWID);                         →108
    long id = mDb.insertOrThrow(ReminderProvider.DATABASE_TABLE, null,→109
            values);
    getContext().getContentResolver().notifyChange(uri, null);            →111
    return ContentUris.withAppendedId(uri, id);                           →112
}


@Override
public int delete(Uri uri, String ignored1, String[] ignored2) {          →116
    int count = mDb.delete(ReminderProvider.DATABASE_TABLE,
            ReminderProvider.COLUMN_ROWID + "=?",
            new String[] { Long.toString(ContentUris.parseId(uri)) });→119
    if (count > 0)                                                        →120
        getContext().getContentResolver().notifyChange(uri, null);
    return count;                                                         →122
}


@Override
public int update(Uri uri, ContentValues values, String ignored1,
        String[] ignored2) {                                              →127
    int count = mDb.update(ReminderProvider.DATABASE_TABLE, values,
            COLUMN_ROWID + "=?",
            new String[] { Long.toString(ContentUris.parseId(uri)) });→130
    if( count>0 )
        getContext().getContentResolver().notifyChange(uri, null);        →132
    return count;                                                         →133
}


/**
 * This method is required in order to query the supported types. It's also
 * useful in our own query() method to determine the type of Uri received.
 */
@Override
public String getType(Uri uri) {
    switch (sURIMatcher.match(uri)) {
    case LIST_REMINDER:
        return REMINDERS_MIME_TYPE;
    case ITEM_REMINDER:
        return REMINDER_MIME_TYPE;
    default:
        throw new IllegalArgumentException("Unknown Uri: " + uri);
    }
```

(continued)

Listing 12-3 *(continued)*

```
    }

    // The SQLite DatabaseHelper code was omitted for brevity.
}
```

Here's how the code works:

→**75** The `query()` method retrieves a reminder or a list of reminders. Its URI can be either a list type or an item type.

→**79** Creates a variable named `projection` that tells various queries which columns of data the user wants to retrieve. Various queries include `ID`, `title`, `body`, `date`, and `time`.

→**84** Calls `URIMatcher.match()` to determine whether it's a list URI or an item URI.

→**85–87** For a list URI, this line calls `query()` on the SQLiteDatabase to retrieve all columns for all reminders.

The use of the SQLiteDatabase `query()` method and its parameters is explained in detail in the section "Understanding the query (read) operation," later in this chapter.

→**89-90** For an item URI, this line calls `query()` on the SQLiteDatabase to retrieve all columns for the specified reminder. It specifies the database table and the columns to retrieve.

→**92** The first parameter is a `COLUMN_ROWID=?` `String`, where the value of ? is supplied in the next parameter. The next parameter is an array of strings, where each one maps to a question mark. This parameter has one question mark, so it needs one string in the array, which is the ID of the task (from the URI).

→**94–95** If the call to the query succeeded and returned at least one value, it moves to the first value. The `moveToFirst()` method on the `Cursor` object instructs the cursor to move to the first record in the result set. This method is called only if the `Cursor` isn't null. The reason that the cursor isn't immediately positioned on the first record is that it's a result set. Before the app can work with the record, it must navigate to record. Think of the result set as a box of items: You can't work with an item until you take it out of the box.

→**98** Displays an error message if the URI was neither a list URI nor an item URI.

→**102** Calls `setNotificationUri()` on the `Cursor` object to associate the query result with the URI. It's passed to the `ContentResolver` and the `URI` that was updated.

A `ContentProvider` can notify users of changes in their data. For example, if one fragment has opened a list view for your reminders and another fragment is editing a specific reminder and you save it, the list view is notified that your content has changed and automatically updates it.

→103   Returns the `Cursor` object so that it can be used by the fragment to process the results.

→107   The method that's called when a user inserts a reminder into the database.

→108   Removes the ID parameter if it's there, because you can't specify an ID when you insert reminders. The database gives you the next available ID.

→109   Inserts the reminder into the database using whatever values were passed in.

The `insertOrThrow()` method usage and its parameters are explained in detail in the "Understanding the insert operation" section, later in this chapter.

→111   Calls `notifyChange()` on the `ContentResolver` for that URI; the counterpart to the `setNotificationUri()` call from line 102. When you modify the table by inserting an item, notify anyone who has a query open on that table that the query may have changed.

→112   Constructs the final item URI for this reminder by appending to the base URI the ID that was created.

→116   The `delete` method for the `ContentProvider`.

→119   Using the `ContentUris.parseId()` method to retrieve the task's `id` from the URI, calls the `delete()` method on the SQLite database to delete a task from the database.

The usage and parameters of the `delete()` method are described in detail in the "Understanding the delete operation" section, later in this chapter.

→120   If the database deleted anything, notifies everyone that the database was updated so that they can refresh their queries.

→122   Unlike `insert()`, `delete()` returns the number of rows that were deleted.

→127   The `update()` method is similar to the `delete()` method.

→130   The `update()` method is responsible for updating an existing task with new information.

The update() method usage and parameters are explained in detail in the "Understanding the update operation" section, later in this chapter.

→**132** If the database updated anything, notifies everyone that the database was updated so that they can refresh their queries.

→**133** Returns the count of rows that were modified.

A CRUD routine accepts a variety of parameters, which are explained in detail in the later sections "Understanding the insert operation," "Understanding the query (read) operation," "Understanding the update operation," and "Understanding the delete operation."

Understanding the insert operation

The insert operation is simple to complete because you're simply inserting a value into the database. You call insertOrThrow() instead of insert() because you want to get an exception if a problem occurs while inserting into the database. The insertOrThrow() method accepts these parameters:

✔ table: The name of the table to insert the data into. It uses the DATABASE_TABLE constant for the value.

✔ nullColumnHack: SQL doesn't allow inserting an empty row, so if the ContentValues parameter (the next parameter) is empty, this column is explicitly assigned a NULL value. It's passing null for this value.

✔ values: This parameter defines the initial values as defined as a ContentValues object. It's providing the initialValues local variable as the value for this parameter. This variable contains the key-value pair information for defining a new row.

Understanding the query (read) operation

The query operation is also known as the read operation because most of the time, the application is *reading* data from the database with the query() method. The query method is responsible for providing a result set based on a list of criteria you provide. This method returns a Cursor that provides random read-write access to the result set returned by the query.

The query method accepts these parameters:

✔ table: The name of the database table to perform the query against. The value comes from the DATABASE_TABLE constant.

✔ columns: A list of columns to return from the query. Passing null returns all columns, which is normally discouraged to prevent reading and returning unnecessary data. If you need all columns, it's valid to pass null. For this app, you can pass a string array of columns to return.

✔ selection: A filter describing what rows to return and formatted as an SQL WHERE clause (excluding the WHERE itself). Passing a null returns all rows in the table. If it's a list operation, you supply null because you want all rows returned. If it's a get operation to return a single reminder, you supply a COLUMN_ROWID=? query string. SQL knows that a question mark indicates a specific value of COLUMN_ROWID in the selectionArgs parameter.

✔ selectionArgs: Permissible to include question marks (?) in the selection string. These marks are replaced by the values from selection Args in the order they appear in the selection. These values are bound as string types. Depending on the situation, you either pass null or a String array containing the ID to be fetched.

✔ groupBy: A filter that shows only rows formatted as an SQL GROUP BY clause (excluding the GROUP BY). Passing null causes the rows not to be grouped. A null value is passed here because grouping the results is unnecessary.

✔ having: A filter that shows only row groups to include in the cursor, if row grouping is being used. Passing null causes all row groups to be included, and it's required when row grouping isn't being used, which is why a null value is required here.

✔ orderBy: The order of the rows, formatted as an SQL ORDER BY clause (excluding the ORDER BY itself). Passing null uses the default sort order, which may be unordered. You can pass a null value because the order in which the results are returned is unimportant.

✔ limit: Limits the number of rows returned by the query by using a LIMIT clause. Passing null states that you don't have a LIMIT clause. To avoid limiting the number of rows returned, you can pass null to return all rows that match your query.

Understanding the update operation

Updating a record in a database simply replaces incoming parameters in the destination cell that's inside the row specified (or in the rows, if many rows are updated). As in the following delete operation, the update can affect many rows. You should understand the update method's parameters and how they can affect the records in the database. The update() method accepts these parameters:

✔ table: The table to update. The value is provided by the DATABASE_ TABLE constant.

✔ values: The ContentValues object, which contains the fields to update.

✔ whereClause: The WHERE clause, which restricts which rows should be updated. You tell the database to update a row with a specific ID by providing the string value COLUMN_ROWID + "=?". The ID is specified in whereArgs.

✔ whereArgs: Additional whereClause arguments. You supply the ID that's plugged into the ? in the whereClause argument. In this case, the whereArgs is a String array containing the ID of the reminder to be updated. There should always be exactly one value in the array for each ? in the whereClause.

Understanding the delete operation

When using the delete() method, various parameters are used to define the deletion criteria in the database. A delete statement can affect none of the records in the database or all of them. You should understand the parameters of the delete call to ensure that you don't mistakenly delete data. The parameters for the delete() method are

✔ table: The table to delete the rows from. The value of this parameter is provided by the DATABASE_TABLE constant.

✔ whereClause: The optional WHERE clause to apply when deleting rows. If you pass null, all rows are deleted. This value is provided by manually creating the WHERE clause with the string COLUMN_ROWID + "=?".

✔ whereArgs: The optional WHERE clause arguments. You supply the ID that's plugged into the ? in the whereClause argument. In this case, whereArgs is a string array containing the ID of the reminder to be deleted. There should always be exactly one value in the array for each ? in the whereClause.

Loaders

When you're doing any kind of IO operation, such as reading from a network or from disk (reading a database, for example), you must do this work from a background thread. If you work from the main thread of the user interface, you run the risk of locking it up for an unknown period, which can cause it to feel jerky and unresponsive. Under particularly bad circumstances, it can even lead to displaying the dreaded Application Not Responsive dialog box, which can leave many users believing that your application has crashed.

The *loader* was introduced in Android 3.x to help solve this problem — it provides a mechanism by which you can launch background tasks (such as reading from your database) and then get a callback when those tasks finish so that you can update the user interface.

A typical example of a loader is a CursorLoader. You use a CursorLoader to load data from a SQLite database using a cursor. To add a CursorLoader to one of your list fragments, you implement the LoaderCallback interface in your callback and implement the three LoaderCallback methods:

✔ onCreateLoader(): This method is called in a background thread when you create a loader using initLoader(). In this method, you're responsible for creating a CursorLoader object and returning it. The CursorLoader uses a URI to ask a ContentProvider for data.

✔ onLoadFinished(): This method is called when the CursorLoader object finishes loading its data from the database. In this method, you're responsible for updating the UI to show the new data to the user.

✔ onLoaderReset(): This method is called when the loader is being reset or shutdown. When this happens you're responsible for making sure your fragment no longer uses the loader or its cursor.

To kick off a loader, you first obtain a LoaderManager from your activity by calling getLoaderManager() and then initLoader(). initLoader() starts loading data in the background by calling onCreateLoader(), and when it finishes it executes onLoaderFinished() in your LoaderCall back object.

You can use loaders for things other than loading data from a database, but all loaders must implement the same three methods regardless of whether they're loading their data from a database, a network, or somewhere else entirely.

Visit http://developer.android.com/guide/components/loaders. html for more information about loaders.

Returning all the tasks with a cursor

You can create a task, but what good is it if you can't see the task in the task list? None, really. You have to list the tasks that currently exist in the database in the ListView in the ReminderListFragment.

Listing 12-4 outlines the entire ReminderListFragment with the new code that can read the list of tasks from the database into the ListView.

Listing 12-4: The Entire ReminderListFragment with Database Access

```
package com.dummies.android.taskreminder;

import android.database.Cursor;
import android.os.Bundle;
import android.support.v4.app.ListFragment;
import android.support.v4.app.LoaderManager.LoaderCallbacks;
import android.support.v4.content.CursorLoader;
import android.support.v4.content.Loader;
```

(continued)

Listing 12-3 *(continued)*

```java
import android.support.v4.widget.SimpleCursorAdapter;
import android.view.View;
import android.widget.ListView;

import com.dummies.android.taskreminder.R.string;

public class ReminderListFragment extends ListFragment implements
        LoaderCallbacks<Cursor> {                                           →16

    private SimpleCursorAdapter mAdapter;

    @Override
    public void onCreate(Bundle savedInstanceState) {
        super.onCreate(savedInstanceState);

        // Create an array to specify the fields to display in the list
            // (only TITLE)
        String[] from = new String[] { ReminderProvider.COLUMN_TITLE };     →26

        // and an array of the fields to bind those fields to (in this
        // case, just text1)
        int[] to = new int[] { R.id.text1 };                                →30

        // Now create a simple cursor adapter and set it to display
        mAdapter = new SimpleCursorAdapter(getActivity(),
                R.layout.reminder_row, null, from, to, 0);                  →34
        setListAdapter(mAdapter);                                           →35

        getLoaderManager().initLoader(0, null, this);                       →37
    }

    @Override
    public void onViewCreated(View view, Bundle savedInstanceState) {
        super.onViewCreated(view, savedInstanceState);
        setEmptyText(getResources().getString(string.no_reminders));
        registerForContextMenu(getListView());
        setHasOptionsMenu(true);
    }

    @Override
    public void onListItemClick(ListView l, View v, int position, long id) {
        super.onListItemClick(l, v, position, id);
        startActivity(new Intent(getActivity(), ReminderEditActivity.class) →51
                .putExtra(ReminderProvider.COLUMN_ROWID, id));
    }

    @Override
    public boolean onContextItemSelected(MenuItem item) {                   →56
        switch (item.getItemId()) {
```

```
    case R.id.menu_delete:
        AdapterContextMenuInfo info = (AdapterContextMenuInfo) item
                .getMenuInfo();                                          →60
        getActivity().getContentResolver().delete(
                ContentUris.withAppendedId(ReminderProvider.CONTENT_URI,
                        info.id), null, null);                          →63
        return true;
    }
    return super.onContextItemSelected(item);
}


@Override
public Loader<Cursor> onCreateLoader(int ignored, final Bundle args) {  →70
    return new CursorLoader(getActivity(), ReminderProvider.CONTENT_URI,
            null, null, null, null);                                    →71
}


@Override
public void onLoadFinished(Loader<Cursor> loader, Cursor cursor) {      →75
    mAdapter.swapCursor(cursor);
}


@Override
public void onLoaderReset(Loader<Cursor> loader) {                      →80
    // This is called when the last Cursor provided to onLoadFinished()
    // above is about to be closed. Ensure that the adapter is no
    // longer using the cursor by setting it to null
    mAdapter.swapCursor(null);
}

// Menu code removed for brevity
}
```

This list describes the numbered lines of code for reading the list of tasks:

→**16** Adds the `LoaderCallbacks` interface to the list of interfaces.

For this line to work, you implement a few loader-related callbacks later in the class so that you can handle loading data in an asynchronous background thread. See the earlier section "Loaders" for more details.

→**26** Looks at the title field of the reminder.

→**30** Defines the array of views to bind to as the view for the row. The title then corresponds to a particular task ID, which is why the variable in line 26 is named `from` and the variable on this line is named `to`. The values from line 26 map to the values on line 30.

→**34**   Creates a `SimpleCursorAdapter` that maps columns from a `Cursor` to `TextViews` as defined in a layout XML file. Using this method, you can specify which columns to display and specify the XML file that defines the appearance of these views. Initially, the `SimpleCursorAdapter` is empty because it has no data yet.

            The use of a `SimpleCursorAdapter` and its associated parameters is described in the following section.

→**35**   Passes the `SimpleCursorAdapter` as the adapter parameter to the `setListAdapter()` method to inform the list view where to find its data.

→**37**   Asks the `LoaderManager` to start loading the loader with an ID of 0. When the loader is finished, it executes the callback methods in the `LoaderCallback` class that you pass in as the final parameter of this call (in this case, `"this"`).

→**51**   Places into the intent the ID of the task to be edited. The `ReminderEditActivity` inspects this intent and, if it finds the ID, attempts to allow the user to edit the task.

→**56**   Defines the method that handles the user context menu events that occur when a user first long-presses the task in the list view and then selects a menu item from the context menu.

→**60**   Uses the `getMenuInfo()` method of the item that was clicked to obtain an instance of `AdapterContextMenuInfo`. This class exposes various bits of information about the menu item and the item the user long-pressed in the list view.

→**63**   Gets a `ContentResolver` and requests that it delete the task whose ID is retrieved from the `AdapterContextMenuInfo` object's `id` field. This field contains the ID of the row in the list view, which is used to construct the URI for the row using `ContentUris.withAppendedId()`. When the reminder is deleted, the `ListView` automatically refreshes to show the latest data.

→**70**   When you call `initLoader()` on line 37, the `onCreateLoader()` method is called. Here, you create the loader that Android starts running in a background thread. Complicated fragments can have multiple loaders of different types, but you can use a single loader on this simple fragment and safely ignore the ID parameter of the `onCreateLoader()` method.

→**71**   Creates a new `CursorLoader`, which is used when you load items from a `ContentProvider` or `SQLiteDatabase`. The `CursorLoader` loads data using the `ReminderProvider`, so be sure to specify the `CONTENT_URI` of the `ReminderProvider`. It's a simple list operation, so you can ignore the optional projection, selection, `selectionArgs`, and `sortOrder` parameters to the `CursorLoader` constructor.

→75   When a loader finishes, calls the `onLoadFinished()` callback and returns the cursor containing the data that was loaded. Then the adapter swaps the new cursor for the old one and automatically refreshes the `ListView`.

→80   Calls `onLoaderReset()` when the last `Cursor` provided to `onLoadFinished()` is about to be closed. The adapter's cursor is set to null because it's no longer needed.

Understanding the SimpleCursorAdapter

Line 34 in Listing 12-4 creates a `SimpleCursorAdapter`. It does a lot of the work for you when you want to bind data from a `Cursor` object to a list view. To set up a `SimpleCursorAdapter`, provide these parameters:

- `getActivity()` - `Context`: The context associated with the adapter.

- `R.layout.reminder_row` - `layout id`: The layout resource identifier that defines the file to use for this list item.

- `null` - `Cursor`: The database cursor that the adapter uses to load data. You have no cursor yet, so use `null`.

- `from` - `from`: An array of column names that are used to bind data from the cursor to the view; defined on line 26.

- `to` - `to`: An array of view IDs that should display the column information from the `from` parameter. The To field is defined on line 30.

- `0` - `flags`: Any optional flags to be passed to the `SimpleCursorAdapter`. You don't need optional flags, so use `0`.

The `to` and `from` parameters create a map informing the `SimpleCursorAdapter` how to map data in the cursor to views in the row layout.

When you start the application now, you see a list of items you have created that are being read from the SQLite database. If you don't see this list, create one by pressing the menu and selecting the menu item to add a new task.

Deleting a task

To the user, deleting a task is as simple as long-pressing an item in the `ReminderListFragment` and selecting the delete action. To actually delete the task from the database, though, you use the `delete()` method on the SQLite database object. This method is called in Listing 12-3 on line 119.

The `ContentResolver delete ()` method is called from within the `onContextSelectedItem()` method call on line 63 of Listing 12-4. The only item that's needed before deleting the task from the database is the ID of the task in the database. To obtain the ID, you must use the `AdapterContextMenuInfo` object, which provides extra menu information. This information is provided to the context menu selection when a menu is opened for the `ListView`. Because you're loading the list with a database cursor, the `ListView` contains the ID you're looking for. Line 60 of Listing 12-4 obtains the `AdapterContextMenuInfo` object, and line 63 calls the `delete()` method with the ID as a parameter.

When you fire up the application in the emulator, you can now create, read, update, and delete tasks!

Chapter 13

Reminding the User with AlarmManager

....

In This Chapter

▶ Understanding scheduled tasks

▶ Planning permissions

▶ Setting up alarms

▶ Seeing how device reboots affect alarms

....

Many tasks need to happen daily, right? Wake up, take a shower, eat breakfast — we do all these things every day. These tasks comprise the standard Monday-through-Friday prework morning routine (or a variance of it). You may have an internal clock and awaken every day on time, but most people have to set alarms to wake up on time. At work, employees have calendars that remind them of upcoming events they need to attend, such as meetings and important server upgrades. Reminders and alarms are part of most everyday routines, and people rely on them in one way or another.

Building your own scheduled task system would be a pain. Thankfully Windows has scheduled tasks, Linux has `cron`, and Android has the `AlarmManager` class. Though Android is based on Linux, it doesn't have access to `cron` therefore, you have to set up scheduled actions via the Android `AlarmManager`.

Seeing Why You Need AlarmManager

The Task Reminder application has one key word in its name — *Reminder*. The user can set a task title, description, and reminder date and time to be reminded of a task, as in this example: A user adds a couple of tasks in the Task Reminder application (all due later today), puts his device away, and goes about his business. If he isn't reminded about the tasks, he might forget about them; therefore, he needs a way to be reminded of what should happen — which is where the `AlarmManager` class comes into play.

The `AlarmManager` class allows users to schedule a time when the Task Reminder application should be run. When an alarm goes off, an intent is broadcast by the system. Your application then responds to that broadcast intent and performs an action, such as opening the application, notifying the user via a status bar notification (which you can accomplish in Chapter 14), or performing another type of action.

Asking the User for Permission

You wouldn't let your next-door neighbor store holiday decorations in your shed without permission, would you? Probably not. Android is no different. Performing some actions on a user's Android device requires permission, as explained in the following sections.

Seeing how permissions affect the user experience

When a user installs an application from the Google Play Store, the application's manifest file is inspected for required permissions. Anytime your application needs access to sensitive components (such as external storage, the Internet, or device information), the user is notified and decides whether to continue the installation.

Don't request unnecessary permissions for your app — security-savvy users are likely to reject it. For example, the Silent Mode Toggle application (described in Part II) doesn't need GPS locations, Internet access, or hardware-related information.

If your application doesn't need a permission, yank it. The fewer number of permissions your application requests, the more likely the user is to install it.

Setting requested permissions in the AndroidManifest.xml file

When you need to request permissions, add them to the AndroidManifest.xml file in your project. You need to add the following permissions to the Task Reminder application:

- ✔ android.permission.RECEIVE_BOOT_COMPLETED: Allows the application to know when the device reboots so that it can re-register its alarms with the Alarm Manager.

- ✔ android.permission.WAKE_LOCK: Allows the device to remain awake during background processing for short periods of time.

Because AlarmManager holds a CPU wake lock as long as the alarm receiver's onReceive() method is executing, it guarantees that the device doesn't sleep until the app is finished working with the broadcast.

If your application needs access to the Internet or needs to write data to the SD card (the Task Reminder app doesn't), you would add these permissions, respectively:

- ✔ **Internet:** android.permission.INTERNET

- ✔ **SD Card:** android.permission.WRITE_EXTERNAL_STORAGE

You can add permissions to the AndroidManifest.xml file in one of two ways:

- ✔ The AndroidManifest.xml **Permissions Editor:** Choose Add⇨Uses Permission, and then select permission from the drop-down list.

- ✔ **The XML file:** Edit the file manually to add the uses-permission element to the manifest element. The XML permission request looks like this:

```
<uses-permission android:name="android.permission.WAKE_LOCK" />
```

If you haven't done so already, add the WAKE_LOCK and RECEIVE_BOOT_COMPLETED permissions to the Task Reminder application. To view a full list of available permissions, view the Android permission documentation at http://d.android.com/reference/android/Manifest.permission.html.

If you don't declare the permissions that your application needs, it won't function as expected on either a device or an emulator, and any runtime exceptions that are thrown may crash your application. Always ensure that your permissions are present.

Waking Up a Process with AlarmManager

To wake up a process with `AlarmManager`, you have to set the alarm first. In the Task Reminder application, the best place to do it is right after you save a task in the save button's `onClickListener()`. Before you add that code, however, you need to add four class files to your project:

- ✔ `ReminderManager.java`: This class is responsible for setting up reminders using `AlarmManager`. The code for this class is shown in Listing 13-1.

- ✔ `OnAlarmReceiver.java`: This class is responsible for handling the broadcast when the alarm goes off. The code for this class is shown in Listing 13-2. (See the section "Creating the OnAlarmReceiver class," later in this chapter.) You need to add the following line of code to the application element in the `AndroidManifest.xml` file for your application to recognize this receiver:

```
<receiver android:name=".OnAlarmReceiver" />
```

The leading-period syntax informs Android that the receiver is in the current package — the one that's defined in the application element of the `AndroidManifest.xml` file.

- ✔ `WakeReminderIntentService.java`: This abstract class is responsible for acquiring and releasing the wake lock. The code for this class is shown in Listing 13-3. (See the section "Creating the WakeReminderIntentService class," later in this chapter.)

- ✔ `ReminderService.java`: This class is an implementation of the `WakeReminderIntentService` that handles the building of the notification, as shown in Chapter 14. The code for this class is shown in Listing 13-4. (See the section "Creating the ReminderService class," later in this chapter.)

You need to add the following line of code to the application element in the `AndroidManifest.xml` file for your application to recognize `WakeReminderIntentService`:

```
<service android:name=".ReminderService" />
```

Creating the ReminderManager class

The `ReminderManager` class is responsible for setting up alarms using the `AlarmManager` class in Android. You place into this class all actions that pertain to setting alarms from `AlarmManager`.

Add the following line to the end of the `mConfirmButton`'s `onClick Listener()` in the `ReminderEditFragment` class to add an alarm for that task:

```
new ReminderManager(getActivity()).setReminder(mRowId,
        mCalendar);
```

This line of code instructs `ReminderManager` to set a new reminder for the task with a row ID of `mRowId` at the particular date and time as defined by the `mCalendar` variable.

Listing 13-1 shows the code for the `ReminderManager` class.

Listing 13-1:   The ReminderManager Class

```
public class ReminderManager {

private Context mContext;
private AlarmManager mAlarmManager;
public ReminderManager(Context context) {                              →5
    mContext = context;
    mAlarmManager =
        (AlarmManager)context.getSystemService(Context.ALARM_SERVICE);  →8
}

public void setReminder(Long taskId, Calendar when) {                  →11
    Intent i = new Intent(mContext, OnAlarmReceiver.class);            →12
    i.putExtra(RemindersProvider.COLUMN_ROWID, (long)taskId);          →13

    PendingIntent pi =
    PendingIntent.getBroadcast(mContext, 0, i,
                    PendingIntent.FLAG_ONE_SHOT);                       →17

    mAlarmManager.set(AlarmManager.RTC_WAKEUP, when.getTimeInMillis(), pi); →19
        }
}
```

The numbered lines of code are explained in this list:

→**5**   The `ReminderManager` class is instantiated with a `Context` object.

→**8**   An `AlarmManager` is obtained via the `getSystemService()` call.

→**11**   The `setReminder()` method is declared with the database ID of the task and the `Calendar` object of when the alarm should fire.

→**12**   A new `Intent` object is created and is responsible for specifying what should happen when the alarm goes off. In this instance, the line specifies that the `OnAlarmReceiver` receiver should be called.

→**13**   The `Intent` object is provided with extra information — the ID of the task in the database.

→**17**   The `AlarmManager` operates in a separate process, and for `AlarmManager` to notify an application that an action needs to be performed, a `PendingIntent` must be created. It contains an `Intent` object that was created on line 12. On this line, a `PendingIntent` is created with a flag of `FLAG_ONE_SHOT` to indicate that this `PendingIntent` can be used only once.

→**19**   The `AlarmManager`'s `set()` method is called to schedule the alarm. The `set()` method is provided with these parameters:

   • type: `AlarmManager.RTC_WAKEUP` is the wall-clock time in UTC. This parameter awakens the device when the specified `triggerAtTime` argument time elapses.

   • triggerAtTime: `when.getTimeInMillis()` is the time the alarm should go off. The `Calendar` object provides the `getTimeInMillis()` method, which converts the time into *long value,* which represents time in units of milliseconds.

   • operation: `pi` is the pending intent to act on when the alarm goes off. The alarm goes off at the requested time.

If an alarm is already scheduled with a pending intent that contains the same signature, the previous alarm is canceled and the new one is set up.

Creating the OnAlarmReceiver class

The `OnAlarmReceiver` class, shown in Listing 13-2, is responsible for handling the intent that's fired when an alarm is raised. This class acts as a hook into the alarm system because it's essentially a simple implementation of `BroadcastReceiver` — which can react to broadcast events in the Android system.

Listing 13-2: The OnAlarmReceiver Class

```
public class OnAlarmReceiver extends BroadcastReceiver {
        @Override
        public void onReceive(Context context, Intent intent) {
            long rowid =
                intent.getExtras().getLong(ReminderProvider.COLUMN_ROWID);   →5

                WakeReminderIntentService.acquireStaticLock(context);        →7

                Intent i = new Intent(context, ReminderService.class);       →9
                i.putExtra(ReminderAdapter.COLUMN_ROWID, rowid);             →10
                context.startService(i);                                     →11

        }
}
```

The numbered lines are explained in this list:

→**5**   This line retrieves the database ID of the task from the intent after the receiver has started handling the intent.

→**7**   The `WakeReminderIntentService` acquires a lock on the CPU to keep the device alive while work is performed.

→**9**   This line defines a new `Intent` object that starts the `ReminderService`.

→**10**   This line places the ID of the task into the intent that starts the service that does the work. This gives the `ReminderService` class the ID of the task that it needs to work with.

→**11**   This line starts the `ReminderService`.

The `OnAlarmReceiver`'s `onReceive()` is the first entry point for the alarm you've set. In this `BroadcastReceiver`, you don't want the device to go back to sleep during processing. Your task would never complete and could possibly leave your application in a broken state from data corruption in the database.

When an alarm goes off, the pending intent that's scheduled with the alarm is broadcast through the system, and any broadcast receiver capable of handling it handles it.

A `BroadcastReceiver` component does nothing but receive and react to system broadcast messages. It doesn't display a user interface; however, it starts an activity in response to the broadcast. The `OnAlarmReceiver` is an instance of a `BroadcastReceiver`.

When the `AlarmManager` broadcasts the pending intent, the `OnAlarm Receiver` class responds to the intent — because it's addressed to that class, as shown earlier, on line 12 of Listing 13-1. This class then accepts the intent, locks the CPU, and performs the necessary work.

Creating the WakeReminderIntentService class

The `WakeReminderIntentService` class is the base class for the `ReminderService` class, as shown in Listing 13-3. This class handles the management of acquiring and releasing a CPU wake lock, which keeps the device (but not necessarily the screen) on while work takes place. After the work is complete, this class releases the wake lock so that the device may return to sleep.

Listing 13-3:   The WakeReminderIntentService Class

```
public abstract class WakeReminderIntentService extends IntentService {
    abstract void doReminderWork(Intent intent);                          →2

    public static final String
        LOCK_NAME_STATIC="com.dummies.android.taskreminder.Static";       →5
    private static PowerManager.WakeLock lockStatic=null;                 →6

    public static void acquireStaticLock(Context context) {
        getLock(context).acquire();                                       →9
    }

    synchronized private static PowerManager.WakeLock
            getLock(Context context) {                                    →13
        if (lockStatic==null) {
            PowerManager
                mgr=(PowerManager)context
                    .getSystemService(Context.POWER_SERVICE);            →17

            lockStatic=mgr.newWakeLock(PowerManager.PARTIAL_WAKE_LOCK,
                            LOCK_NAME_STATIC);                            →20

        }
        return(lockStatic);                                               →23
    }

    public WakeReminderIntentService(String name) {                      →26
        super(name);
    }
```

```
    @Override
    final protected void onHandleIntent(Intent intent) {          →31
        try {
            doReminderWork(intent);                               →33
        } finally {
            getLock(this).release();                              →35
        }


    }
}
```

The numbered lines are explained in this list:

→**2**   This abstract method is implemented in any children of this
           class — such as in the child `ReminderService`, as shown a little
           later in this chapter, on line 7 of Listing 13-4.

→**5**   This is the tag name of the lock that acquires the CPU lock. This
           tag name assists in debugging.

→**6**   This is the private static wake lock variable, which is referenced
           and set later in this class.

→**9**   This calls the `getLock()` method. After that call is returned, the
           `acquire()` method is called to ensure that the device is on in the
           state you requested, a partial wake lock. This wake lock prevents
           the device from sleeping, but it doesn't turn on the screen.

→**13**   This line defines the `getLock()` method that returns the
           `PowerManager.WakeLock`, which lets you inform Android that
           you want the device to stay to do some work.

→**17**   This line retrieves the `PowerManager` from the `getSystem`
           `Service()` call. It's used to create the lock.

→**20**   This creates a new `WakeLock` using the `newWakeLock()` method
           call. This method accepts the following parameters:

           • `flags`: The `PARTIAL_WAKE_LOCK` tag informs Android that
             you need the CPU to be on, but the screen does not have to
             be on. You can provide other numerous tags to this call as
             well.

           • `tag`: `LOCK_NAME_STATIC` is the name of the class name
             or another string. It's used for debugging purposes. This
             custom string is defined on line 3.

→**23**   This returns the `WakeLock` to the caller.

→**26**   This is the constructor with the name of the child instance that
           has created it. This name is used for debugging only.

→**31**   This is the `onHandleIntent()` call of the `IntentService`. As soon as the service is started, this method is called to handle the intent that was passed to it.

→**33**   The service attempts to perform the necessary work by calling `doReminderWork()`.

→**35**   Regardless of whether the call to `doReminderWork()` is successful, ensure that `WakeLock` is returned. If you don't release it, the device can be left in the On state until the phone is rebooted, which is undesirable because of battery drain. That's why the `release()` method is called in the final portion of the `try-finally` block. The final portion of the `try-finally` block is always called, regardless of whether the try succeeds.

You must make sure that you always call `release()` on a wake lock exactly as many times as you call `acquire()`. You can put your `acquire()` and `release()` calls in a `try-finally` block to make sure that `release()` is always called whether an exception is thrown. Visit http://docs.oracle.com/javase/tutorial/essential/exceptions/finally.html for more information on `try-finally` blocks.

Although no implementation of `doReminderWork()` exists in the `ReminderService` yet, the Task Reminder application responds to alarms. Feel free to set up multiple tasks and to set break points in the debugger to watch the execution path break in the `ReminderService doReminderWork()` method.

The `AlarmManager` doesn't persist alarms — if the device is rebooted, the alarms must be set up again. Every time the phone is rebooted, the alarms need to be set up again.

Listing 13-3 demonstrates what is necessary to perform work on a device that might be asleep or locked. The code acquires the wake lock, and while the device is locked into a wakeful state, `doReminderWork()` is called, which is implemented in the `ReminderService`.

Creating the ReminderService class

The `ReminderService` class (see Listing 13-4) is responsible for doing the work when an alarm is fired. The implementation in this chapter simply creates a shell for work to take place. (You implement the status bar notification in Chapter 14.)

Listing 13-4:   The ReminderService Class

```
public class ReminderService extends WakeReminderIntentService {          →1
    public ReminderService() {
        super("ReminderService");
    }

    @Override
    void doReminderWork(Intent intent) {                                   →7
        Long rowId = intent.getExtras()
            .getLong(ReminderProvider.COLUMN_ROWID),                       →9

        //  Status bar notification Code Goes here.
    }
}
```

The numbered lines of code are explained in this list:

→**1**   This line defines the `ReminderService` class by inheriting from the `WakeReminderIntentService`.

→**7**   The abstract method `doReminderWork()` in the `WakeReminderIntentService` is implemented.

→**9**   This line retrieves the task ID that was inside the `Intent` object that passed in this class.

The `ReminderService` class contains no implementation — other than retrieving the ID of the task from the intent.

Rebooting Devices

You probably forget things from time to time. It's only human. The Android `AlarmManager` is no different. The `AlarmManager` doesn't persist alarms; therefore, when the device reboots, you must set up the alarms again.

If you don't set up your alarms again, they simply don't fire, because, to Android, they don't exist.

Creating a boot receiver

The `RECEIVE_BOOT_COMPLETED` permission allows your application to receive a broadcast notification from Android when the device is done booting and is eligible to be interactive with the user. Because the Android system can broadcast a message when this event is complete, you need to add another `BroadcastReceiver` to your project. This `BroadcastReceiver` is responsible for handling the boot notification from Android. When the broadcast is received, the receiver needs to retrieve the tasks from the `ReminderProvider` and loop through each task and schedule an alarm for it, to ensure that your alarms don't get lost in the reboot.

Add a new `BroadcastReceiver` to your application. For the Task Reminder application, the `BroadcaseReceiver` has the name `OnBootReceiver`. You also need to add the following lines of code to the application element in the `AndroidManifest.xml` file:

```xml
<receiver android:name=".OnBootReceiver" android:exported="false">
    <intent-filter>
        <action android:name="android.intent.action.BOOT_COMPLETED" />
    </intent-filter>
</receiver>
```

This snippet informs Android that `OnBootReceiver` should receive boot notifications for the `BOOT_COMPLETED` action. In layman's terms, it lets `OnBootReceiver` know when the device is done booting up.

The full implementation of `OnBootReceiver` is shown in Listing 13-5.

Listing 13-5: The OnBootReceiver Class

```
public class OnBootReceiver extends BroadcastReceiver {                    →1

    private static final String TAG = OnBootReceiver.class.getSimpleName();

    @Override
    public void onReceive(Context context, Intent intent) {               →6

        ReminderManager reminderMgr = new ReminderManager(context);       →8

        Cursor cursor = context.getContentResolver().query(
                ReminderProvider.CONTENT_URI, null, null, null, null);     →11

        if (cursor != null) {
            cursor.moveToFirst();                                          →14

            int rowIdColumnIndex = cursor
                    .getColumnIndex(ReminderProvider.COLUMN_ROWID);        →17
            int dateTimeColumnIndex = cursor
                    .getColumnIndex(ReminderProvider.COLUMN_DATE_TIME);    →19

            while (cursor.isAfterLast() == false) {                        →21

                long rowId = cursor.getLong(rowIdColumnIndex);            →23
```

```
            long dateTime = cursor.getLong(dateTimeColumnIndex);          →24

            Calendar cal = Calendar.getInstance();
            cal.setTime(new java.util.Date(dateTime));                    →27

            reminderMgr.setReminder(rowId, cal);                          →29

            cursor.moveToNext();                                          →31
        }
        cursor.close();                                                   →33
    }
  }
}
```

The numbered lines are detailed in this list:

→**1**   This is the definition of the `OnBootReceiver`.

→**6**   This is the `onReceive()` method that's called when the receiver receives an intent to perform an action.

→**8**   This sets up a new `ReminderManager` object that allows the user to schedule alarms.

→**11**   This obtains a cursor with all the reminders from the `ReminderProvider` via the `ContentResolver`. It's similar to the calls used to update and delete reminders in the `ReminderEditFragment` and `ReminderListFragment`.

→**14**   This moves to the first record in the `Cursor`.

→**17–19** Each row in the cursor contains several columns of data. Line 17 finds the index for the ID, and line 19 finds the index for the date and time.

            You want to find the ID of the row as well as the date and time so that you can schedule the reminder. To get this information, you need to find the index of the columns that contain this information.

→**21**   This sets up a `while` loop that checks to see whether the cursor has moved past the last record. If it equals false, the cursor moves to line 23. If this value is true, no more records are available to use in the cursor.

→**23–24** The ID and `dateTime` are retrieved from the cursor for this row using the column indices from lines 17–19.

→**27**   After the date is retrieved from the cursor, the `Calendar` variable needs to be updated with the correct time. This line sets the local `Calendar` object to the time of the task in the row.

→**29**   This schedules a new reminder with the row ID from the database at the time defined by the recently built `Calendar` variable.

→**31**   This line moves to the next record in the cursor. If no more records exist in the cursor, the call to `isAfterLast()` on line 21 returns `true`, which means that the `while` loop exits. Otherwise, the next row is processed.

→**33**   This line closes the cursor because it's no longer needed. `BroadcastReceivers` generally don't use loaders, so you need to close the cursor.

When you previously worked with the `Cursor` object in Chapter 12, you didn't have to close the cursor. This is because the `Loader` object was managing the cursor.

If you were to start the application, create a few reminders, and then reboot the device, you would see that the reminders persisted.

Checking the boot receiver

If you're unsure whether `OnBootReceiver` is working, you can place log statements into the `while` loop, like this:

```
Log.d("OnBootReceiver", "Adding alarm from boot.");
Log.d(TAG, "Row Id - " + rowId);
```

This snippet prints messages to the system log that are viewable via the Dalvik Debug Monitor Service, or DDMS. You can then shut down the emulator (or device) and start it again. Watch the messages stream in DDMS, and look for `OnBootReceiver` messages. If you have two tasks in your database, you should see two sets of messages informing you of the system adding an alarm from boot. Then the next message should be the ID for the task reminder. See Chapter 5 for more information about DDMS.

Chapter 14

Updating the Android Status Bar

Throughout this book, you discover various ways to grab the user's attention by using dialog boxes, toast messages, and new activities. Though these techniques work well in their respective situations, at other times you need to inform the user of something — without stealing his attention from the current activity. That's the purpose of the status bar.

Deconstructing the Status Bar

Figure 14-1 shows the *status bar,* the area where you can notify the user of an event. The status bar can hold many icons. The status bar shown in Figure 14-1 holds, starting on the left, a calendar notification announcing an appointment, and an icon signifying that USB debugging is enabled.

Status bar

Figure 14-1:
The status
bar, with
a couple
icons
present.

Users can also swipe the status bar downward to see more information, as
shown in Figure 14-2. Every status bar icon now has an expanded view, where
more information can be shown.

Figure 14-2:
Opening the
status bar.

You can inform users of various activities, such as device state, mail notifications, and even download progress, as shown in Figure 14-3.

Figure 14-3:
The progress loader on the status bar.

Adding an icon to the status bar isn't your only option for alerting the user to a notification. You can augment a notification using one — or more — of these three options:

- ✔ **Vibration:** The device vibrates briefly when a notification is received — useful when the device is in the user's pocket.

- ✔ **Sound:** An alarm sounds when the notification is received. A ringtone or a prerecorded tone that you install along with your application is useful when the user has cranked up the notification sound level.

- ✔ **Light:** The LED light on the device flashes at a given interval in the color you specify. (Many devices contain an LED that you can program.) If the LED supports only a single color, such as white, it flashes in that color and ignores your color specification. If the user has set the volume level to silent, the light provides an excellent cue that something needs attention.

Android 4.1 Jelly Bean introduces dramatic improvements to Android notifications. Devices that run Jelly Bean can have notifications with these features:

✔ **Expandable preview:** The user can expand a notification by using the pinch-and-zoom gesture. The expandable notification is a helpful way to show users an expanded preview of the notification content, such as a message preview for an e-mail application.

✔ **Action buttons:** A user has always been able to tap a notification to launch the app that created it. However, you can add as many as three additional buttons to a Jelly Bean app to make it perform whatever operations you want. One outstanding example in the Task Reminder app is having the Snooze button temporarily dismiss the notification and bring it back later.

✔ **Varied template styles:** Jelly Bean ships with three new styles of notifications, as shown in Figure 14-4:

  • `BigTextStyle`: Shows a multiline `TextView`

  • `BigInboxStyle`: Shows a list of information

  • `BigPictureStyle`: Shows an image

✔ **Larger size:** Jelly Bean notifications can be as tall as 256 dp.

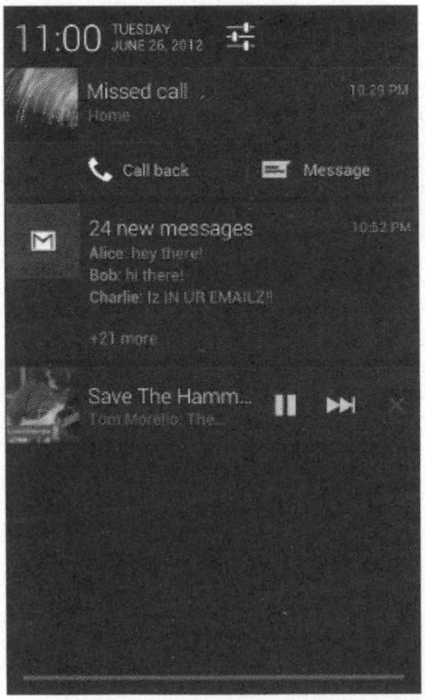

Figure 14-4:
Custom notifications in Jelly Bean.

These features aren't available on older devices, so you can't use them in versions earlier than 4.1. To give your notifications more impact in Jelly Bean, visit `http://developer.android.com/guide/topics/ui/notifiers/notifications.html` for more information.

Adding various options to your notification arsenal is immensely useful because they let the user know that the device needs attention even when the screen is turned off.

Using the Notification Manager

You use the Notification Manager to interact with the Android notification mechanism. Working with the Notification Manager is as simple as requesting it from the current context.

The following line of code obtains the `NotificationManager` object from the `getSystemService()` call of `Context`:

```
NotificationManager mgr = (NotificationManager)getSystemService(NOTIFICATION_
          SERVICE);
```

Creating a notification

The Task Reminder application needs a way to notify the user that a task needs attention, such as an alarm signifying that task. To set this notification on the status bar, you use the `NotificationManager`.

In the `doReminderWork()` method of the `ReminderService` class, type the code shown in Listing 14-1.

Listing 14-1: Implementation of doReminderWork()

```
Long rowId = intent.getExtras().getLong(ReminderProvider.COLUMN_ROWID);      →1

NotificationManager mgr =
          (NotificationManager)getSystemService(NOTIFICATION_SERVICE);      →4

Intent notificationIntent = new Intent(this, ReminderEditActivity.class);   →6
notificationIntent.putExtra(ReminderProvider.COLUMN_ROWID, rowId);          →7

PendingIntent pi = PendingIntent.getActivity(this, 0, notificationIntent,
          PendingIntent.FLAG_ONE_SHOT);                                     →9

Notification note=new Notification(android.R.drawable.stat_sys_warning,

          getString(R.string.notify_new_task_message),
          System.currentTimeMillis());                                     →14
```

(continued)

Listing 14-1 *(continued)*

```
note.setLatestEventInfo(this, getString(R.string.notify_new_task_title),
        getString(R.string.notify_new_task_message), pi);              →17

note.defaults |= Notification.DEFAULT_SOUND;                           →19
note.flags |= Notification.FLAG_AUTO_CANCEL;                           →20

// An issue can occur if the user enters more than 2,147,483,647 tasks (the
        maximum int value).

// Unlikely, but good to note.


int id = (int)((long)rowId);                                          →27
mgr.notify(id, note);                                                 →28
```

The numbered lines in Listing 14-1 are explained in this list:

→**1**   The intent that started the ReminderService contains the row ID of the task you're working with. This ID is necessary because you set it as part of the PendingIntent for the status. When the notification is selected from the status bar, the ReminderEditActivity starts with the row ID as part of the pending intent. That way, the ReminderEditActivity opens, reads the data about that particular row ID, and displays it to the user.

→**4**   This line gets an instance of the NotificationManager.

→**6**   This line builds a new intent and sets the class to ReminderEdit Activity. This activity starts when the user selects the notification.

→**7**   This line puts the row ID into the intent.

→**9**   This line sets up a pending intent to be used by the notification system. Because the notification system runs in another process, a PendingIntent is required. The FLAG_ONE_SHOT flag indicates that this pending intent can be used only once.

→**14**   This line builds the Notification that shows up on the status bar. The Notification class accepts these parameters:

- icon: android.R.drawable.stat_sys_warning is the resource ID of the icon to place on the status bar. This icon is an exclamation point enclosed in a triangle. Because it's a built-in Android icon, you don't have to worry about providing small-, medium-, high-, or extra-high-density graphics — they're already built into the platform.

- `tickerText: getString(R.string.notify_new_task_message)` is the text that flows by on the one-line status bar when the notification first appears.

- `when: System.currentTimeMillis()` is the time to show in the Time field of the notification.

  Eclipse may tell you that this constructor and the subsequent call to `setLatestInfo()` is deprecated and to use `Notification.Builder` instead. `Notification.Builder` is available only on API level 11 or later, so you can't use `Notification.Builder` on older devices.

→**17** This line sets the content of the expanded view with the standard Latest Event layout as provided by Android. For example, you can provide a custom XML layout to display. In this instance, you simply provide the stock notification view, not a custom layout. The `setLatestEventInfo()` method accepts these parameters:

- `context: this` is the context to associate with the event information.

- `contentTitle: getString(R.string.notifiy_new_task_title)` is the title that's displayed in the notification when it's expanded.

- `contextText: getString(R.string.notify_new_task_message)` is the text that's displayed below the title in the notification when it's expanded.

- `contentIntent: pi` is the intent to launch when the expanded view is selected.

→**19** You use this bitwise OR-ed in setting the `Notification` object to include sound during the notification process. It forces the default notification sound to be played if the notification volume is on. Visit `http://en.wikipedia.org/wiki/Bitwise_operation#OR` for more information about bitwise operators.

→**20** You use this bitwise OR-ed in setting the `Notification` object flag's property that cancels the notification after it's selected by the user.

→**27** This line casts the ID to an integer. The ID stored in the SQLite database is a long; however, this line casts it to an integer. A loss of precision is happening, but this application will likely never set up more than 2,147,483,647 tasks (the maximum number that an integer can store in Java). Therefore, this casting should be acceptable. The casting to an integer is necessary because the code on line 20 accepts an integer as the ID only for the notification.

→**28** Raises the notification to the status bar. The `notify()` call accepts two parameters:

- `id`: This ID is unique within your application. You use the task's row ID here.

- `Notification`: The `note` object you just created describes how to notify the user.

Viewing the workflow

Listing 14-1 allows this workflow to occur:

1. The user is active in another application, such as e-mail.

2. A task is due, and therefore the alarm fires. The notification is created on the status bar.

3. The user can elect to swipe the status bar downward and then select the notification or ignore it for now.

    If the user chooses to slide open the status bar and select an item, the pending intent within the notification is activated. This in turn causes the `ReminderEditActivity` to open with the given row ID of the task.

4. The notification is removed from the status bar.

5. The task information is retrieved from the database and displayed on the form in the `ReminderEditActivity`.

Adding string resources

You may notice that you need to add these two string resources to your `strings.xml` file:

- ✔ `notify_new_task_message`: The value is set to the text *A task needs to be reviewed!* This message has a dual purpose — in the expanded view and as the ticker text when the notification first arrives.

- ✔ `notify_new_task_title`: The value is set to *Task Reminder,* which is used as the title for the expanded view.

Updating a Notification

At some point, you might need to update the view of your notification, such as when your code runs in the background, to see whether tasks have been reviewed. This code checks to see whether any notifications are overdue. Suppose that after the 2-hour mark passes, you want to change the icon of the notification to a red exclamation point and quickly flash the LED in red. Thankfully, updating the notification is a fairly simple process.

If you call the notify() method again with an ID that's already active on the status bar, the notification is updated on the status bar. Therefore, to update the notification, you simply create a new Notification object with the same ID and text (but with a different red icon) and then call notify() again to update the notification.

Clearing a Notification

Users constitute an unpredictable group — whether they're first-time users or advanced power users, they can be located anywhere in the world. All Android users use their devices in their own, special ways. At some point, a user may see a notification and decide to open the app using the app launcher instead. If this happens while a notification is active, the notification persists. Even if the user looks at the task at hand, the notification still persists on the status bar. Your application should be able to simply recognize the state of the application and take the appropriate measures to cancel any existing notifications for the task. However, if the user opens your app and reviews a different task that has no active notification, your app shouldn't clear the notification.

Clear only the notification that the user is reviewing.

The NotificationManager makes it simple to cancel an existing notification by using the cancel() method. This method accepts one parameter — the ID of the notification. You may recall using the ID of the task as the ID of the note. The ID of the task is unique to the Task Reminder application. By doing this, you can easily open a task and cancel any existing notification by calling the cancel() method with the ID of the task.

At some point, you might also need to clear all previously shown notifications. To do this, simply call the cancelAll() method on the NotificationManager.

Chapter 15

Working with Android's Preferences Framework

. . . .

. . . .

Most programs need to be configured to suit a user's needs (for the most part), with individual settings or preferences. Allowing users to configure your Android application gives it a usability advantage. Thankfully, creating and providing a mechanism to edit preferences in Android are fairly easy processes.

Android provides, out of the box, a robust preferences framework that lets you declaratively — and programmatically — define preferences for your application. Android stores preferences as persistent key-value pairs of primitive data types for you. You aren't required to store the values in a file or database or in any other mechanism. The Android preferences framework commits the values you provide to internal storage on behalf of your application. You can use the preferences framework to store Boolean, float, int, long, and string elements. The data *persists* across user sessions — if the user closes the app and reopens it later, the preferences are saved and can be used, even if your application is killed.

This chapter delves into the Android preferences framework and describes how to incorporate it into your applications. You find out how to use the built-in `PreferenceActivity` to create and edit preferences and how to read and write preferences from code within your application. At the end of this chapter, you'll have integrated preferences fully into the Task Reminder application.

If you're using Android 3.x or later and you don't care to support older devices, consider using the new `PreferenceFragment` instead of `Preference Activity`. However, the `PreferenceFragment` isn't yet available as part of the support library, so you cannot use `PreferenceFragment`s on older devices. For this reason, this chapter sticks with using the tried-and-true `PreferenceActivity`.

Understanding the Android Preferences Framework

One outstanding quality of the Android preferences framework is the simplicity of developing a screen that allows users to modify their preferences. Most of the heavy lifting is done for you by Android because developing a preferences screen is as simple as defining it in the XML located in the `res/xml` folder of your project. Though these XML files aren't the same as layout files, there are specific XML definitions that define screens, categories, and actual preferences. Common preferences that are built into the framework include

- `EditTextPreference`: Stores plain text as a string
- `CheckBoxPreference`: Stores a Boolean value
- `RingtonePreference`: Allows the user to store a preferred ringtone from those available on the device
- `ListPreference`: Allows the user to select a preferred item from a list of items in the dialog box

If the built-in preferences don't suit your needs, you can create your own preference by deriving it from the base `Preference` class or `DialogPreference`. A `DialogPreference` is the base class for preferences that are dialog-box-based. Tapping one of these preferences opens a dialog box showing the preference controls. Examples of built-in `DialogPreference`s are `EditTextPreference` and `ListPreference`.

Android also provides a `PreferenceActivity` in which you can load a preferences screen in the same manner as you load a layout for a basic `Activity` class. This base class allows you to tap into the `PreferenceActivity` events and perform advanced work, such as setting an `EditTextPreference` to accept only numbers.

Understanding the PreferenceActivity Class

The responsibility of the PreferenceActivity class is to show a hierarchy of Preference objects as lists, possibly spanning multiple screens, as shown in Figure 15-1.

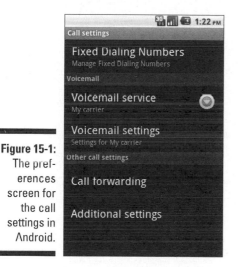

Figure 15-1: The preferences screen for the call settings in Android.

When preferences are edited, they're stored using an instance of Shared Preferences. The SharedPreferences class is an interface for accessing and modifying preference data returned by getSharedPreferences() from any Context object.

A PreferenceActivity is a base class that's similar to the Activity base class. However, the PreferenceActivity behaves a bit differently. One of the most important features that the PreferenceActivity handles is the displaying of preferences in the visual style that resembles the system preferences. This gives your application a consistent feel across the board in regard to Android user interface components. You should use the PreferenceActivity when dealing with preferences screens in your Android applications.

Persisting preference values

Because the Android framework stores preferences in the Shared Preferences, which automatically stores the preference data in internal storage, you can easily create a preference. When a user edits a preference, the value is automatically saved for you; you don't have to do any persisting yourself.

Figure 15-2 shows a preference being set in the Task Reminder application. After the user taps OK, Android persists the value to SharedPreferences. Android does all the heavy lifting in regard to persisting the preference values.

Figure 15-2:
Setting a
preference.

Laying out preferences

Working with layouts in Android can sometimes be a painstaking process of alignment, gravity, and other complicating factors. Building layouts is almost like building a website with various tables all over the place. Sometimes it's easy; sometimes it isn't. Thankfully, laying out Android preferences is much simpler than defining a layout for the application screen.

Android preferences screens are broken into these categories:

✔ PreferenceScreen: Represents a top-level preference that's the root of a preference hierarchy. You can use a PreferenceScreen in these two places:

- *In a* PreferenceActivity: The PreferenceScreen isn't shown because it shows only the containing preferences within the PreferenceScreen definition.

- *In another preference hierarchy:* When present in another hierarchy, the PreferenceScreen serves as a gateway to another screen of preferences (similar to nesting PreferenceScreen declarations inside other PreferenceScreen declarations). Though this concept might seem confusing, you can think of it as XML, where you can declare an element and any element can contain the same parent element. At that point, you're nesting the elements. The same statement applies to the PreferenceScreen. By nesting PreferenceScreens, you're informing Android that it should show a new screen when selected.

✔ PreferenceCategory: This preference is used to group preference objects and provide, above the group, a title that describes the category.

✔ Preference: A preference that's shown onscreen. This preference can be any common preference or a custom one that you define.

By laying out a combination of the PreferenceScreen, Preference Category, and Preference in XML, you can easily create a preferences screen that looks similar to Figure 15-1.

Creating Your Preferences Screen

Creating preferences using the PreferenceActivity and a preference XML file is a fairly straightforward process. The first thing you do is create the preference XML file, which defines the layout of the preferences and the string resource values that show up onscreen. These string resources are presented as TextViews onscreen to help the user determine what the preference does.

Your PreferenceScreen should give users the chance to set the default time for a reminder (in minutes) and a default title for a new task. As the application stands now, the default title is empty and the default reminder time is set to the current time. These preferences allow the user to save a couple of steps while building new tasks. For example, if the user normally builds tasks with a reminder time of 60 minutes from the current time, the user can now specify it in the preferences. This new value becomes the value of the reminder time when the user creates a new task.

Building the preferences file

To build your first preferences screen, create a `res/xml` folder in your project. Inside the `res/xml` folder, create an XML file and name it `task_preferences.xml`. Add the code in Listing 15-1 to the file.

Listing 15-1: The task_preferences.xml File

```
<?xml version="1.0" encoding="utf-8"?>
<PreferenceScreen                                                          →2
   xmlns:android="http://schemas.android.com/apk/res/android">
        <PreferenceCategory                                                →4
          android:key="@string/pref_category_task_defaults_key"            →5
          android:title="@string/pref_category_task_defaults_title">       →6
          <EditTextPreference                                              →7
             android:key="@string/pref_task_title_key"                     →8
             android:dialogTitle="@string/pref_task_title_dialog_title"    →9
             android:dialogMessage="@string/pref_task_title_message"       →10
             android:summary="@string/pref_task_title_summary"             →11
             android:title="@string/pref_task_title_title" />              →12
        </PreferenceCategory>
        <PreferenceCategory                                                →13
          android:key="@string/pref_category_datetime_key"                 →14
          android:title="@string/pref_category_datetime_title">            →15
           <EditTextPreference                                             →16
              android:key="@string/pref_default_time_from_now_key"         →17
    android:dialogTitle="@string/pref_default_time_from_now_dialog_title"  →18
 android:dialogMessage="@string/pref_default_time_from_now_message"        →19
    android:summary="@string/pref_default_time_from_now_summary"           →20
    android:title="@string/pref_default_time_from_now_title" />            →21
     </PreferenceCategory>
</PreferenceScreen>
```

Quite a few string resources are introduced in Listing 15-1 (see the next section). Each numbered line of code is explained as follows:

→**2**   This is the root-level `PreferenceScreen`; it's the container for the screen itself. All other preferences live below this declaration.

→**4**   This is a `PreferenceCategory` that defines the category for task defaults, such as title or body. As you may have noticed, line 13 declares another `PreferenceCategory` for the default task time. Normally, you place these two items into the same category; they're split here to show how to use multiple `PreferenceCategory` elements on one screen.

→**5**   This line defines the key that's used to store and retrieve the preference from the `SharedPreferences`. This key must be unique.

→**6**   This line defines the category title.

→**7**   This line contains the definition of the EditTextPreference, which is responsible for storing the preference for the default title of a task.

→**8**   This line contains the key for the default title text EditText Preference.

→**9**   The EditTextPreference is a child class of Dialog Preference. When a user selects the preference, he sees a dialog box similar to the one shown in Figure 15-2. This line of code defines the title for that dialog box.

→**10**   This line defines the message that appears in the dialog box.

→**11**   This line defines the summary text that's present on the preferences screen, as shown in Figure 15-1.

→**12**   This line defines the title of the preference on the preferences screen.

→**13**   This line defines the PreferenceCategory for the default task time.

→**14**   This line defines the category key.

→**15**   This line defines the title of the category.

→**16**   This line is the start of the definition of the EditText Preference, which stores the default time in minutes (digits) that the task reminder time defaults to from the current time.

→**17**   This line defines the key for the default task time preference.

→**18**   This line defines the title of the dialog box that opens when the preference is selected.

→**19**   This line defines the message that's present in the dialog box.

→**20**   This line defines the summary of the preference that's present on the main preferences screen, as shown in Figure 15-1.

→**21**   This line defines the title of the preference on the preferences screen.

Adding string resources

For your application to compile, you need the string resources for the preferences. In the res/values/strings.xml file, add these values:

```
<!-- Preferences -->
<string name="pref_category_task_defaults_key">task_default_category</string>
<string name="pref_category_task_defaults_title">Task Title Default</string>
<string name="pref_task_title_key">default_reminder_title</string>
<string name="pref_task_title_dialog_title">Default Reminder Title</string>
<string name="pref_task_title_message">The default title for a reminder.</
        string>
<string name="pref_task_title_summary">Default title for reminders.</string>
<string name="pref_task_title_title">Default Reminder Title</string>
<string name="pref_category_datetime_key">date_time_default_category</string>
<string name="pref_category_datetime_title">Date Time Defaults</string>
<string name="pref_default_time_from_now_key">time_from_now_default</string>
<string name="pref_default_time_from_now_dialog_title">Time From Now</string>
<string name="pref_default_time_from_now_message">The default time from now (in
        minutes) that a new reminder should be set to.</string>
<string name="pref_default_time_from_now_summary">Sets the default time for a
        reminder.</string>
<string name="pref_default_time_from_now_title">Default Reminder Time</string>
```

You should now be able to compile your application.

Working with the PreferenceActivity Class

Defining a preferences screen is fairly simple: Provide the values to the necessary attributes and you're done. Though the preferences screen may be defined in XML, simply defining it in XML doesn't mean that it will show up onscreen. To display your preferences screen, you create a PreferenceActivity.

The PreferenceActivity shows a hierarchy of preferences onscreen according to a preferences file defined in XML — such as the one you may have just created. The preferences can span multiple screens (if multiple PreferenceScreen objects are present and nested). These preferences are automatically saved to SharedPreferences. As a bonus, the preferences that are shown automatically follow the visual style of the system preferences, which allows your application to have a consistent user experience in conjunction with the default Android platform.

To inflate and display the PreferenceScreen you may have just built, add an activity that derives from PreferenceActivity to your application and name it TaskPreferences. Add the code in Listing 15-2.

Listing 15-2:   The TaskPreferences File

```
public class TaskPreferences extends PreferenceActivity {          →1
    @Override
    protected void onCreate(Bundle savedInstanceState) {
        super.onCreate(savedInstanceState);
        addPreferencesFromResource(R.xml.task_preferences);        →5

        EditTextPreference timeDefault = (EditTextPreference)
    findPreference(getString(R.string.pref_default_time_from_now_key));   →8
 timeDefault.getEditText().setKeyListener(DigitsKeyListener.getInstance());  →9
  }
}
```

That's all the code needed to display, edit, and persist preferences in
Android. The numbered lines of code are explained in this list:

→1   The `TaskPreferences` class file is defined by inheriting from the
        `PreferenceActivity` base class.

→5   The call to `addPreferencesFromResource()` method is pro-
        vided with the resource ID of the `task_preferences.xml` file
        that's stored in the `res/xml` directory. This method is depre-
        cated in favor of `PreferenceFragment` from the support library
        so Eclipse may give you a warning that you can ignore.

→8   This line retrieves the `EditTextPreference` for the default
        task reminder time by calling the `findPreference()` method
        and providing it with the key that was defined in the `task_`
        `preferences.xml` file. This method is also deprecated in favor
        of `PreferenceFragment` from the support library so Eclipse may
        give you a warning that you can ignore.

→9   This line obtains the `EditText` object, which is a child of the
        `EditTextPreference`, using the `getEditText()` method. This
        object sets the key listener, which is responsible for listening to key-
        press events. The `setKeyListener()` method sets the key listener,
        and by providing it with an instance of `DigitsKeyListener`, the
        `EditTextPreference` allows digits to be typed in the `EditText`
        `Preference` only for the default reminder time.

        You don't want users to enter string values such as `foo` or `bar`
        into the field because it isn't a valid integer value. Using the
        `DigitsKeyListener` ensures that the only values passed into
        the preferences are digits.

At this point, you can use your activity. This `PreferenceActivity` allows
users to edit and save their preferences. As you can see, this implementation
requires only a snippet of code. The next step is displaying the preferences
screen by adding a menu item.

Add your new `PreferenceActivity` to the `AndroidManifest.xml` file by using this line of code:

```
<activity android:name=".TaskPreferences" android:label="@string/app_name" />
```

Opening the PreferenceActivity class

To open this new activity, you add a menu item to the `ReminderList Activity`. To add a new menu item, you add a new menu definition to the `list_menu.xml` file that's located in the `res/menu` directory. Updating this file updates the menu on the `ReminderListActivity`. The updated `list_menu.xml` file is shown here with the new entry in bold:

```
<?xml version="1.0" encoding="utf-8"?>
<menu
    xmlns:android="http://schemas.android.com/apk/res/android">
    <item android:id="@+id/menu_insert"
        android:icon="@android:drawable/ic_menu_add"
        android:title="@string/menu_insert" />
        <item android:id="@+id/menu_settings"
            android:icon="@android:drawable/ic_menu_preferences"
            android:title="@string/menu_settings" />
</menu>
```

The last item adds a menu item for settings, which uses the built-in Android Settings icon and the `menu_settings` string resource. You add a new string resource named `menu_settings` with a value of `Settings` in your string resources.

Handling menu selections

After your menu is updated, the app needs to respond whenever the user taps a menu item. To make it do this, you add code to the `onOptions ItemSelected()` method in the `ReminderListFragment`. The code to handle the settings menu selection is bold in this snippet:

```
@Override
public boolean onOptionsItemSelected (MenuItem item) {
      switch(item.getItemId()) {
          case R.id.menu_insert:
              ((OnEditReminder) getActivity()).editReminder(0);
              return true;
          case R.id.menu_settings:
              Intent i = new Intent(getActivity(), TaskPreferences.class);
              startActivity(i);
              return true;
          }
      return super.onOptionsItemSelected(item);
}
```

This code creates a new `Intent` object with a destination class of `Task Preferences`. A user who selects the Settings menu item is shown the preferences screen, to edit his preferences. If you start the app and select Settings, you should see a screen similar to the one shown in Figure 15-3.

Figure 15-3:
The pref-
erences
screen.

Working with Preferences in Your Activities at Runtime

Though setting preferences in a `PreferenceActivity` is useful, it provides no value in the end unless you can read the preferences from the `SharedPreferences` object at runtime and use them in your application. Thankfully, Android makes the process fairly simple.

In the Task Reminder application, you read these values in the `Reminder EditFragment` to set the default values when a user creates a new task. Because the preferences are stored in `SharedPreferences`, you can access the preferences across various activities in your application.

Retrieving preference values

Open the `ReminderEditFragment` and navigate to the `onCreateView()` method. It determines whether the task is an existing task or a new task. If the task is new, you pull the default values from `SharedPreferences` and load them into the activity for the user. If for some reason the user has never specified her preferences, they're empty strings and you ignore the defaults. You use the preferences only if the user has set them.

To retrieve preference values, you use the SharedPreferences object, as shown in Listing 15-3. Add the bold code to the very bottom of onCreate View().

Listing 15-3:   Retrieving Values from SharedPreferences

```
if (mRowId == 0) {                                              →1
    // This is a new task - add defaults from preferences if set.
    SharedPreferences prefs = PreferenceManager               →3
            .getDefaultSharedPreferences(getActivity());
    String defaultTitleKey = getString(R.string.pref_task_title_key);→5
    String defaultTimeKey = getString(R.string.pref_default_time_from_
        now_key);                                             →7
    String defaultTitle = prefs.getString(defaultTitleKey, null);  →8
    String defaultTime = prefs.getString(defaultTimeKey, null);    →9

    if (defaultTitle != null)
        mTitleText.setText(defaultTitle);                     →12

    if (defaultTime != null && defaultTime.length()>0)
        mCalendar.add(Calendar.MINUTE, Integer.parseInt(defaultTime));
        →15

    updateButtons();                                          →17

} else {

    // Fire off a background loader to retrieve the data from the
    // database.
    getLoaderManager().initLoader(0, null, this);

}
```

Each new line of code is explained in this list:

→**1**   The if statement handles the logic for a new task.

→**3**   This line retrieves the SharedPreferences object from the static getDefaultSharedPreferences() call on the PreferenceManager object.

→**5**   This line retrieves the key value for the default title preference from the string resources. This same key is used in Listing 15-1 to define the preference.

→**7**   This line retrieves the key value for the default time offset, in minutes, from the preferences.

→**8**   This line retrieves the default title value from the preferences
with a call to getString() on the SharedPreferences object.
The first parameter is the key for the preference, and the second
parameter is the default value if the preference doesn't exist (or
hasn't been set). In this instance, the default value is null if the
preference doesn't exist.

→**9**   This line retrieves the default time value from the preferences,
using the same method as described on line 8 with a different key.

→**12**   This line sets the text value of the EditText view — which is the
title of the task. This value is set if the preference wasn't equal to
an empty string.

→**15**   This line increments time on the local Calendar object by calling the add() method with the parameter of Calendar.MINUTE
if the value from the preferences wasn't equal to an empty string.
The Calendar.MINUTE constant informs the Calendar object
that the next parameter should be treated as minutes and the
value should be added to the calendar's Minute field. If the minutes force the calendar into a new hour or day, the Calendar
object updates the other fields for you.

For example, if the calendar was originally set to 2012-08-
31 11:45 p.m. and you added 60 minutes to the calendar, the
new value of the calendar is 2012-09-01 12:45 a.m. Because
EditTextPreference stores all values as strings, the string
parses the minute value to an integer with the Integer.parse
int() method. By adding time to the local Calendar object,
the time picker and button text associated with opening the time
picker are updated as well.

→**17**   This line updates the time button text to reflect the time that was
added to the existing local Calendar object.

When you start the application, you can now set the preferences and see
them reflected when you choose to add a new task to the list. Try clear-
ing the preferences and then choosing to create a new task. Notice that the
defaults no longer apply — easy!

Setting preference values

Though updating preference values via Java isn't done in the Task Reminder
application, at times you might need to in your own apps. Suppose that you
develop a help desk ticket system application that requires users to enter
their current departments. You have a preference object for the default
department, but the user never uses the preferences screen and therefore
repeatedly enters the department into your application manually. Using logic

that you define and write, you determine that the user is entering the same department for each help desk ticket (assume that it's the Accounting department), so you prompt him to determine whether he wants to set the default department to Accounting. If he chooses Yes, you programmatically update the preferences for him.

To edit preferences programmatically, you need an instance of `Shared Preferences`. You can obtain it via `PreferenceManager`, as shown in Listing 15-4. After you obtain an instance of `SharedPreferences`, you can edit various preferences by obtaining an instance of the preference `Editor` object. After the preferences are edited, you need to commit them, also demonstrated in Listing 15-4.

Listing 15-4:   Programmatically Editing Preferences

```
SharedPreferences prefs =
    PreferenceManager.getDefaultSharedPreferences(this);       →1
Editor editor = prefs.edit();                                  →2
editor.putString("default_department", "Accounting");          →3
editor.commit();                                               →4
```

The numbered lines of code are explained in this list:

→1   An instance of `SharedPreferences` is retrieved from the `PreferenceManager`.

→2   An instance of the preferences `Editor` object is obtained by calling the `edit()` method on the `SharedPreferences` object.

→3   This line edits a preference with the key value of `default_department` by calling `putString()` method on the `Editor` object. The value is set to "`Accounting`". Normally, the key value is retrieved from the string resources and the value of the string is retrieved via your program or user input. The code snippet remains simple for brevity.

→4   After changes are made to any preferences, you must call the `commit()` method on the `Editor` object to persist them to `SharedPreferences`. The commit call automatically replaces any value stored in `SharedPreferences` with the key given in the `putString()` call.

If you don't call `commit()` on the `Editor` object, your changes don't persist and your application doesn't function as you expect.

Part IV
Tablets

The 5th Wave   By Rich Tennant

"Until we work the kinks out, David will be providing the audio portion of our App demonstration."

In this part . . .

Part IV introduces you to the world of Android tablet development. Android tablets are a different sort of beast than Android phones, and this part walks you through all the changes you need to make to your Task Reminder application to make it run on Android tablets.

Should you like to go beyond the realm of standard Google Android tablets, you find everything you need to know to add support for Android-based (but non-Google) devices, such as the Amazon Kindle Fire, in Chapter 18.

Chapter 16

Developing for Tablets

In This Chapter

▶ Zeroing in on why a tablet is a different digital beast

▶ Modifying your existing app to run on tablets

*Y*ou need to master some tricks of the trade to make your apps work on tablets and on phones. In this chapter, you can get an overview of the differences in phones and tablets, and then find out how to design the Task Reminder application to work on both types of devices.

Considering the Difference Between Phones and Tablets

Android tablets and Android phones have some obvious differences, and size immediately comes to mind, but there are a few other differences:

- ✔ Android tablets tend to be much larger than their phone counterparts.

- ✔ Tablets are designed to be held in two hands, whereas phones are designed for only one.

- ✔ Android tablet screens tend not to extend past the 7-to-10-inch range, and the largest phones max out around 5 inches.

  The line between tablet and phone can blur at the 5-inch mark. Some "tweener" devices are marketed as phones, and others with nearly the same specs are marketed as tablets.

- ✔ Tablet orientation varies depending on usage, whereas almost all Android phones have settled on portrait orientation for their screens.

  Many Android tablets are designed for wide-screen media viewing, so they favor landscape orientation. Others, such as the Nexus 7 and Kindle Fire, are designed primarily for use in Portrait mode. That's not to say that you can't run an app in Portrait mode on a landscape tablet (or vice versa), but be aware that many users may run your app in an orientation other than the one in which you completed most of your testing.

Tablets and phones also have some differences in hardware design and operation that affect app design. This list describes them from the tablet perspective:

- ✔ Tablets often lack always-on 3G or 4G data connections.

- ✔ Tablets tend to be larger, use larger batteries, and benefit from much longer battery life than their phone counterparts.

- ✔ Tablets may have cheaper cameras — or no cameras — because tablet cameras typically get less use than phone cameras.

- ✔ Tablets often lack such common phone capabilities as GPS location service.

In addition, don't be surprised if you have to design your app (or tweak an existing one) to accommodate new tablet features. Both the original 3.0 and later 4.0 versions of Android tablets support fragments, the user interface element known as the action bar, and the holographic theme (named Holo). Users expect you to add these new tools to your arsenal as you upgrade your app to add tablet support.

Tweaking the Task Reminder App for Tablets

To help accommodate the differences, you use a few techniques to upgrade the Task Reminder app so that it can work on both tablets and phones.

Use these strategies every time you design an Android application because it's likely that most of your apps target users of both types of devices.

Anticipating screen size with a flowing layout

Go with the flow when you're designing your layout to fit multiple screen sizes. A flowing layout skips a lot of hassle and frustration for both the designer and the user.

If you're familiar with iOS development, you know that you have only two screen sizes to worry about: iPhone and iPad. Each size requires both low- and high-resolution images, but that's easy enough to handle: Design for iPhone first, and *then* for iPad, and then plug in the low- and high-resolution images in the respective versions and you're done.

Android isn't quite as simple to design for. Layouts in Android need to "flow" — that is, resize and rearrange themselves — so that they can accommodate minor (and sometimes major) differences in the width and height of users' devices. Where iOS has only two different sizes, Android has dozens or hundreds.

It's similar to designing for websites — when you're building a website, you can't assume that all users will view it in browser windows that are exactly the same size (800x600pixels). Users may view the site from bigger (or sometimes smaller) browser windows; your design must be flexible enough to give a good experience to the whole range of sizes. Designing for Android makes the same requirement.

So how do you perform this bit of magic? For openers, don't try to use fixed dimensions (such as `10px` or `120dp`) in your layouts. Instead, favor *relative* dimensions, such as `"wrap_content"` and `"fill_parent"` as much as possible. The idea is to achieve a *flowing* layout that can resize to fit the device.

The following code shows a layout that makes too many assumptions about the device it's on:

```
<?xml version="1.0" encoding="utf-8"?>
<TextView xmlns:android="http://schemas.android.com/apk/res/android"
    android:layout_width="300px"
    android:layout_height="match_parent"
    android:lines="1"
    android:text="Occurrences of the word &apos;Internet&apos; in the Gettysburg
            Address: 0 (unverified)" />
```

The code has multiple problems:

✔ It uses a fixed sized `TextView` rather than flexible dimensions, like `wrap_content` and `fill_parent`.

✔ It uses pixels (px) to measure size, which doesn't scale automatically across different devices, as dp (device-independent pixels) would.

✔ It hard-codes the number of lines in `TextView` to 1 and doesn't tell Android what to do with any overflow.

✔ It doesn't use `ScrollView`, so if your layout is taller than the device screen there's no way to see the offscreen views.

Generally speaking, many of your layouts should be wrapped in a single `ScrollView` to handle unanticipated overflow off the bottom of the screen. Exceptions include layouts that already handle scrolling, such as `ListView`, which shouldn't be wrapped in a `ScrollView`. The Task Reminder app needs only a single `TextView`, but more complicated layouts should consider them.

Though "fill_parent" was renamed to "match_parent" in Android 2.2, older devices don't support "match_parent". As long as your minSdk Version is set to a value lower than 8, however, you should use "fill_ parent" instead of "match_parent".

Figure 16-1 shows the TextView in Listing 16-1. It abruptly cuts off text mid-sentence because of the fixed size. If the developer had used a flowing layout, the text wouldn't have been cut off.

Figure 16-1:
A nonflow-
ing layout.

Fixing this particular example is easy by changing the width of the TextView and replacing android:lines="1" with android:maxLines="3":

```
<?xml version="1.0" encoding="utf-8"?>
<TextView xmlns:android="http://schemas.android.com/apk/res/android"
    android:layout_width="match_parent"
    android:layout_height="match_parent"
    android:maxLines="3"
    android:text="Occurrences of the word &apos;Internet&apos; in the Gettysburg
              Address: 0 (unverified)" />
```

When you're designing your layouts, always consider the maximum size of each item in your layout. The app content can take up more space than you expect, and it's important to anticipate these situations and plan for them rather than end up with an app that looks ugly.

Adding more fragments

If you're like many developers, you might expect Google — as the fount of all knowledge— to know *everything*. But one thing the folks at Google didn't know when they started building Android was how popular tablets would become in five years. But tablets did become popular and brought with them all that onscreen space to fill.

Android 3.0 Honeycomb introduced fragments to help you deal with this newfound real estate. The basic idea is that a typical phone activity centers on one, two, or three distinct groups of reusable onscreen items. Put each of these groups into its own fragment and it becomes easy to reuse across multiple activities.

You're going to do exactly this in Chapter 17 — you'll add the `Reminder EditFragment` and the `ReminderListFragment` from your two phone activities into a single new activity that tablet users will enjoy.

Figure 16-2 shows how Reminder fragments lay out on a phone and on a tablet.

Figure 16-2:
Fragments
can handle
a single
activity on
a phone
(left) or two
activities
on a tablet
(right).

Without fragments, you'd have to reinvent the wheel every time you want to make an activity that shows a list of tasks. Using fragments, just write the code once and you can reuse it as many times as you want.

Creating different layouts for different devices

The fragment is a handy feature for the designer, but how do you slice and dice fragments to show the right experience for the right device? The tablet's relatively vast screen real estate (compared to a phone) can show one or two more fragments on a single activity.

You can use one layout containing a single activity for your phone and another layout containing multiple fragments for your tablet. For example, here's the `ReminderListActivity` layout for the phone size in the Task Reminder app:

```xml
<?xml version="1.0" encoding="utf-8"?>
    <fragment
      xmlns:android="http://schemas.android.com/apk/res/android"
            android:name="com.dummies.android.taskreminder.ReminderListFragment"
            android:layout_width="fill_parent"
            android:layout_height="fill_parent"
        />
```

And here's how you might modify the code using two fragments to create a 2-column layout on a tablet:

```xml
<?xml version="1.0" encoding="utf-8"?>
<LinearLayout xmlns:android="http://schemas.android.com/apk/res/android"
        android:layout_width="fill_parent"
        android:orientation="horizontal"
        android:layout_height="fill_parent">

    <fragment
            android:id="@+id/list_fragment"
            android:name="com.dummies.android.taskreminder.ReminderListFragment"
            android:layout_width="0dp"
            android:layout_weight="1"
            android:layout_height="fill_parent"
        />

    <fragment
            android:id="@+id/edit_fragment"
            android:name="com.dummies.android.taskreminder.ReminderEditFragment"
            android:layout_width="0dp"
            android:layout_weight="1"
            android:layout_height="fill_parent"
        />

</LinearLayout>
```

You can find an explanation for how this code works in Chapter 17.

Using the action bar

User interfaces change continually, and Android is no exception. One convenient example is the action bar — standard on all Android 3.0 and 4.0 devices. If you're targeting tablets, you'll definitely make use of this new element.

Before Android 3.0, all Android phones had a dedicated Menu button. (For more about the Menu button, see Chapter 10.) This button isn't in Android 3.0 devices and later. The items on the menu are on the action bar.

The action bar makes these functions (for example, how to add or delete a task or access an app's settings) significantly easier to find. The important ones are onscreen at all times; less important ones are tucked away on a submenu, as shown in Figure 16-3.

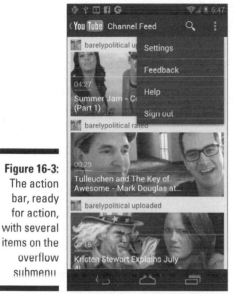

Figure 16-3: The action bar, ready for action, with several items on the overflow submenu

As the developer, you get to choose which actions are the most important, and Android tries to keep them onscreen. You can add three different actions to your menu items:

- ✔ android:showAsAction="ifRoom": This XML is for unimportant items that you prefer to have on the action bar if it has room, but Android can move into the overflow menu.

- ✔ android:showAsAction="always": This XML is for the first couple of items that you know you want to always have onscreen, and for items you always want showing on the action bar.

- ✔ android:showAsAction="never": Use this XML for the items you can safely position on the overflow menu.

It's tempting to list all of your actions as `android:showAsAction=`
`"ifRoom"` or `"always"`, but don't clutter the action bar with too many
actions. Consider putting many actions, such as `"Settings"`, on the overflow
submenu using `"never"`.

The best part about the action bar is that you don't have to do anything
to add it to your app. All menus magically turn into action bar items when
they're run on Android 3.x devices or later.

Using the Support Library and ActionBarSherlock

Of course, not everybody snaps up the latest technology right away. At the
time this book was written, a large number of devices are still running older
versions of Android (earlier than 4.0). You had better take them into account.

Know your target audience! Visit `http://developer.android.com/`
`about/dashboards` to see the latest statistics on which versions of Android
your users are most likely to be running. At the time of this writing, Android
2.3.3 (Gingerbread) has the most users, but its lead is shrinking.

You want to make use of fragments and the action bar, but if most of your
users' devices are running Android 2.x, those older devices don't support
these newfangled features yet. What's a developer to do?

Luckily, these tools can help:

- ✔ **Android Support Library (from Google):** Brings fragments to your pre-4.0 apps.

- ✔ **ActionBarSherlock, by Jake Wharton:** Lets you use the action bar
  for pre-4.0 apps. Go to `http://actionbarsherlock.com` for more
  details.

Chapter 17

Porting Your App to Android Tablets

*Y*our phone app is poised to conquer the tablet, and the situation is getting exciting. Here's where this chapter shows you how to modify the Task Reminder application (developed in Part III) to work on an Android tablet.

Configuring a Tablet Emulator

First things first —you need a tablet on which to test your application. If you already have a tablet, you're well on your way; if you don't, then you need an emulator to simulate an Android device on your computer. Google calls these Android Virtual Devices (AVDs). Follow these steps to get the Google Nexus 7 AVD:

1. **Click the Android AVD Manager icon on the Eclipse toolbar.**

2. **Click New.**

   The Create New Android Virtual Device dialog box opens, as shown in Figure 17-1.

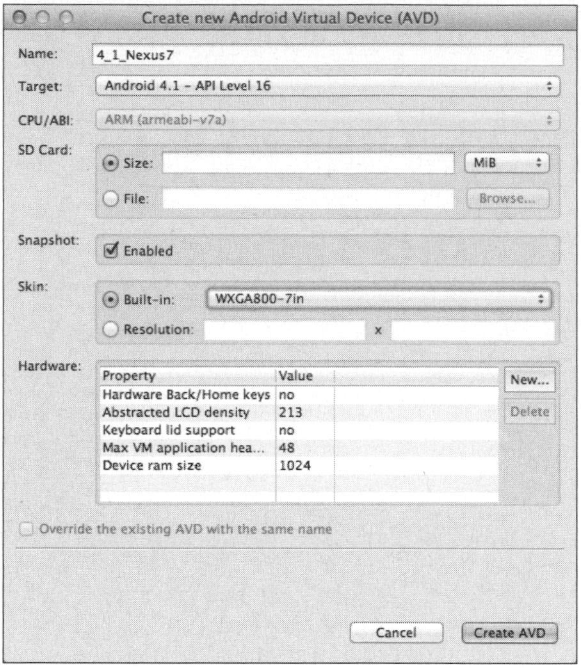

○ ○ ○   Create new Android Virtual Device (AVD)

Name: 4_1_Nexus7

Target: Android 4.1 – API Level 16

CPU/ABI: ARM (armeabi-v7a)

SD Card:
    ⊙ Size: MiB
    ○ File: Browse...

Snapshot: ☑ Enabled

Skin:
    ⊙ Built-in: WXGA800–7in
    ○ Resolution: x

Hardware:

Property	Value	
Hardware Back/Home keys	no	New...
Abstracted LCD density	213	
Keyboard lid support	no	Delete
Max VM application hea...	48	
Device ram size	1024	

☐ Override the existing AVD with the same name

Cancel   Create AVD

Figure 17-1:
Create a
Nexus 7 tab-
let emulator.

3. **Choose Android 4.1 – API Level 16 from the Target drop-down list.**

   The Nexus 7 uses Android 4.1.

4. **From the Skin section, select the Built-In radio button and choose WXGA800-7 from the drop-down menu.**

5. **Click the Create AVD button.**

6. **Choose the AVD you just created from the list of AVDs and click the Start button to launch it.**

Updating the AndroidManifest File

You need to tell Android that your app works on the large and extra-large screens of tablets. Without it, your app runs in Compatibility mode as though it was on a smaller screen, and Android expands your app so that it fills the screen. Your app can look "jaggy" and ugly.

Edit the `AndroidManifest.xml` file to add the following lines to the `supports-screens` element inside the `<manifest>` element before the `<application>` element:

```
<supports-screens
        android:largeScreens="true"
        android:normalScreens="true"
        android:smallScreens="true"
        android:xlargeScreens="true" />
```

You might think that setting one of these attributes to false prevents your app from being downloaded by devices of that size, but that isn't necessarily the case. If `xlargeScreens="false"`, for example, your app is still download-able on extra-large devices, but it runs in Compatibility mode and Android scales it up to fit the screen. On the other hand, while it's easy to expand an app, it's hard to shrink it, so if `smallScreens="false"` your app isn't down-loadable by small screen devices.

Programming Activities for Tablets

After you update your `AndroidManifest` file, the next step is to begin coding the new activities that are unique to the tablet version of your app.

Creating the ReminderListAndEditorActivity

The tablet version of your app needs a new, main activity. One that works for phones doesn't work with tablets because you want to retain that activity so that your app continues to work on phones. Create a `ReminderListAndEditorActivity.java` file and add this code to it:

```
package com.dummies.android.taskreminder;

import android.os.Bundle;
import android.support.v4.app.FragmentActivity;                          →4

public class ReminderListAndEditorActivity extends FragmentActivity {
    @Override
    public void onCreate(Bundle savedInstanceState) {
        super.onCreate(savedInstanceState);
        setContentView(R.layout.reminder_list_and_editor);              →10
    }
}
```

Here's how the code works:

→4   This line ensures you use the `FragmentActivity` from the sup-
      port library rather than the one built into Android 3.x and later.
      Otherwise your code doesn't work on earlier versions of Android.

→10   The `R.layout.reminder_list_and_editor` layout, which
      defines the layout for this activity doesn't exist yet, but you create
      it later in this chapter.

Add the new activity to the `AndroidManifest.xml` file beneath the
`ReminderEditActivity` that already exists for phones:

```
<activity android:name=".ReminderListAndEditorActivity" android:label="@string/
          edit_reminder_title"/>
```

Give the activity a title. Open `strings.xml` and add a string for `edit_`
`reminder_title`, such as `Task Reminder - Edit`.

Choosing the right activity

The Task Reminder application now has two different main activities — one
for phones and one for tablets. When the user launches your app, which one
will Android choose?

At the moment, Android chooses the phone activity because that's the only
one associated with the `android.intent.action.MAIN` intent filter.
Because there's no way for the app to automatically choose the correct
activity for you, you need to detect it manually when the app starts and then
switch to the tablet version, if necessary.

Add the following method to your `ReminderListActivity` class:

```
private Boolean isTablet() {
    int sizeMask = getResources().getConfiguration().screenLayout &
            Configuration.SCREENLAYOUT SIZE MASK;
    boolean large = (sizeMask == Configuration.SCREENLAYOUT_SIZE_LARGE);
    boolean xlarge = (sizeMask == 4);
    return large || xlarge;
}
```

This code detects whether the device has a screen in large or extra-large format. If it does, it returns true.

Why `sizeMask == SCREENLAYOUT_SIZE LARGE` for the `large` Boolean, but `sizeMask -- 4` for the `xlarge` Boolean? On later versions of Android, `SCREENLAYOUT_SIZE_XLARGE` is equal to 4, so you might think you could replace the 4 with `SCREENLAYOUT_SIZE_XLARGE`. However, `SCREENLAYOUT_SIZE_XLARGE` did not appear in Android until API level 9, so if you try to use this constant on an older device the device will crash. Because the Task Reminder app supports devices older than API level 9, you can't use the `SCREENLAYOUT_SIZE_XLARGE` constant directly. See `http://d.android.com/reference/android/content/res/Configuration.html` for more information about `SCREENLAYOUT_SIZE_XLARGE`.

Beginning with Android 3.2, the `SCREENLAYOUT_SIZE_MASK` has been deprecated in favor of a new system of device size qualifiers. The system is much more reliable for choosing whether to show a phone or tablet layout, but because it isn't available before version 3.2 (even with the support library), it's beyond the scope of this book. Visit `http://developer.android.com/guide/practices/screens_support.html` for details about the new size qualifiers.

In your `onCreate()` method, add the code shown in bold before the call to `setContentView()`:

```
@Override
public void onCreate(Bundle savedInstanceState) {
    super.onCreate(savedInstanceState);

    // Switch to Tablet activity and finish this one if we're on a tablet.
    if (isTablet()) {
        startActivity(new Intent(this, ReminderListAndEditorActivity.class));
        finish();
        return;
    }

    setContentView(R.layout.reminder_list);
}
```

The idea is that if this code runs on a tablet, the ReminderListActivity immediately quits and starts the ReminderListAndEditorActivity instead. This way, if a user opens your app on a phone, your app works optimally for the phone size. But if a user opens your app on a tablet, it runs optimally for a tablet. A slight overhead cost is involved in doing this kind of switching, but it should be unnoticeable to your users.

Creating the activity layout

After you have the activity, you need to create its layout.

At this point, you already know the basic idea of what this layout will look like: a list fragment and an edit fragment placed side by side.

Create a reminder_list_and_editor.xml file in your res/layout directory and add the following code to it:

```
<?xml version="1.0" encoding="utf-8"?>
<LinearLayout xmlns:android="http://schemas.android.com/apk/res/android"
    android:layout_width="fill_parent"
    android:layout_height="fill_parent"
    android:orientation="horizontal" >                                →5

    <fragment
        android:id="@+id/list_fragment"                               →8
        android:name="com.dummies.android.taskreminder.ReminderListFragment" →9
        android:layout_width="0dp"                                    →10
        android:layout_height="fill_parent"                           →11
        android:layout_weight="1" />                                  →12

    <FrameLayout
        android:id="@+id/edit_container"                              →15
        android:layout_width="0dp"
        android:layout_height="fill_parent"
        android:layout_weight="1" />                                  →18

</LinearLayout>
```

Here's how the code works:

→5   The line wraps your two fragments in a full-screen, horizontal LinearLayout so that they appear side by side.

→8–9   These lines designate the first fragment as the list fragment, called "@+id/list_fragment", and specify its full class name as com. dummies.android.taskreminder.ReminderListFragment.

→**10** This line gives the layout of a width 0dp. See line 12 to find out why zero width is a benefit.

→**11** This line tells the list fragment to occupy half the screen horizontally and the full screen vertically.

→**12–18** LinearLayouts support the special "layout_weight" parameter, which can be used to flexibly split the screen between two or more views. To use it, set the widths or heights of the children of LinearLayout to 0dp, and then set a weight for each one. The LinearLayout adds all the weight values and assigns each child the proportion that the individual child's weight represents.

Line 12 designates list_fragment and edit_container views have a weight of 1 so that each view occupies half the screen.

You can also make the list_container have a value of 1 and the edit_container have a value of 2, in which case the list_fragment occupies a third of the screen and the edit_container takes the remaining two-thirds.

Note that this strategy works only for LinearLayouts, though it can be quite handy.

→**15** This line designates a placeholder ("@+id/edit_container") for ReminderEditFragment. A placeholder is preferable because, even though list view is always onscreen, edit view may come and go, depending on whether a user is editing an item. If an item isn't being edited, it would be confusing to the user to see an empty edit fragment on the screen.

Run your application on both your phone and the tablet emulator. Though the new ReminderListAndEditorActivity shows up on the tablet emulator, it won't on the phone emulator.

Working with Fragments on Tablet Applications

You create a new activity for your table app, and now you have to add fragments to it. There's no need to write new fragments to use with the tablet activity. However, you need to make some changes to your fragments to make sure they work properly in this new environment.

Communicating with fragments

Allowing fragments to communicate with each other by using activities as their intermediaries is a common best practice when using fragments. Visit http://developer. android.com/guide/components/ fragments.html for more details on this important pattern. Anytime you need to interact with another fragment, you should always use a method in the fragment's activity rather than access the other fragment directly. The only time it makes sense to access one fragment from another is when you *know* that you won't need to reuse your fragment in another activity. However, life is always full of surprises — you should almost always write fragments assuming that you'll reuse them rather than hard-code them to each other.

Communicating between fragments

If you try to add a task with your tablet application, it doesn't show the edit fragment next to the list fragment as you expect, but instead opens a new activity to add a task.

The reason that your app opens the edit fragment in a new activity, rather than adjacent to the list fragment, is that it's still doing exactly what it was told. It's still executing the old phone behavior, which is to start a new activity for each fragment.

The code that does it is this line in ReminderListFragment:

```
startActivity(new Intent(this, ReminderEditActivity.class).putExtra(
        ReminderProvider.COLUMN_ROWID, id));
```

It should be easy to change, right? Not so fast. If you change this line to make it work for tablets, you "break" your existing phone app. The problem is that you want one behavior (the existing one) for phones and another behavior for tablets.

To solve this problem, you create an abstract method named edit Reminder() that does one thing for phones and another thing for tablets. You then replace the existing call to startActivity() with this updated method.

 Don't be so quick to put the new editReminder() method in the Reminder ListFragment. The fragment doesn't know whether it's running on a phone or a tablet. It has a method that it can call — editReminder() — that lets the user edit a reminder.

The key is to realize that because you need one version of editReminder() for phones and one for tablets, you need to put the editReminder() in *two* places — one that runs on phones and one that runs on tablets. Where does one class run on phones and another class run on tablets? In the activity, of course. So you put editReminder() in the phone and tablet Activity classes.

To create the editReminder() callback for your fragment to call, follow these steps:

1. **Create a new** OnEditReminder.java **interface, and put the** edit Reminder() **method in it, like this:**

```
package com.dummies.android.taskreminder;

public interface OnEditReminder {
    public void editReminder(long id);
}
```

2. **Implement this method in the** ReminderListActivity **for the phones.**

   Modify ReminderListActivity by adding the bits in bold:

```
package com.dummies.android.taskreminder;

import android.content.Intent;
import android.os.Bundle;
import android.support.v4.app.FragmentActivity;

public class ReminderListActivity extends FragmentActivity implements
        OnEditReminder {

    @Override
    public void onCreate(Bundle savedInstanceState) {
        super.onCreate(savedInstanceState);
        setContentView(R.layout.reminder_list);

        // Switch to tablet activity and finish this one if user is on a
            tablet.
        if (isTablet()) {
            startActivity(new Intent(this, ReminderListAndEditorActivity.
            class));
            finish();
            return;
        }
    }

    @Override
    public void editReminder(long id) {
        startActivity(new Intent(this, ReminderEditActivity.class).
            putExtra(
                ReminderProvider.COLUMN_ROWID, id));
    }
}
```

The editReminder() call is identical, line-for-line, to what you had in the ReminderListFragment, except that now it's in the ReminderListActivity instead.

3. **Call this method from the fragment:**

Visit ReminderListFragment and modify the onOptionsItem Selected() and onListItemClick() methods as follows:

```
@Override
public boolean onOptionsItemSelected(MenuItem item) {
    switch (item.getItemId()) {
    caseR.id.menu_insert:
            ((OnEditReminder) getActivity()).editReminder(0);
            return true;
    caseR.id.menu_settings:
    startActivity(new Intent(getActivity(), TaskPreferences.class));
    return true;
        }

    return super.onOptionsItemSelected(item);
    }


@Override
public void onListItemClick(ListView l, View v, int position, long id) {
    super.onListItemClick(l, v, position, id);
    ((OnEditReminder) getActivity()).editReminder(id);
    }
```

Now, rather than call startActivity() directly in each method, the app calls getActivity() to get the activity, casting it to an OnEditReminder and then calling editReminder().

Casting is normally frowned on in Java because it's often unsafe. However, it's safe to cast the result of getActivity() to an OnEdit Reminder because the ReminderListFragment will always be in either ReminderListActivity or ReminderListAndEditor Activity, and both implement OnEditReminder. If ever you want to add the fragment to another activity, ensure that it, too, implements OnEditReminder.

4. **Implement the same** OnEditReminder **interface in your** ReminderListAndEditorActivity **for tablets.**

Add the code in bold to your ReminderListAndEditorActivity:

```
public class ReminderListAndEditorActivity extends FragmentActivity
        implements OnEditReminder {

    @Override
    public void onCreate(Bundle savedInstanceState) {
        super.onCreate(savedInstanceState);
        setContentView(R.layout.reminder_list_and_editor);
    }

    @Override
    public void editReminder(long id) {
        // TBD
    }
}
```

Check out the next section to see exactly how to implement `edit Reminder()` for the tablet app.

Before you do that, you need to address one more subtle interaction between fragments. Take a look at the `OnClickListener` for the `mConfirmButton` in `ReminderEditFragment` and you'll see this line:

```
getActivity().finish();
```

No good. Calling `getActivity().finish()` from the phone app returns the user to the list activity, but calling it from the tablet app closes the app. Clearly, from the tablet app you want to remove the edit fragment, not finish the entire activity.

To fix this problem, follow these steps:

1. **Create a new interface named** `OnFinishEditor`, **and make it look like this:**

   ```
   package com.dummies.android.taskreminder;

   public interface OnFinishEditor {
       public void finishEditor();
   }
   ```

2. **Modify the** `ReminderEditFragment` **to call this interface instead of calling** `finish()` **directly.**

   Replace both instances of `getActivity().finish()` with the following (there should be two):

   ```
   ((OnFinishEditor) getActivity()).finishEditor();
   ```

3. **Modify the two activities of** `ReminderEditFragment` **to add this interface and implement the** `finishEditor()` **method.**

Add the following to your `ReminderEditActivity`:

```
public class ReminderEditActivity extends FragmentActivity implements
        OnFinishEditor {

    @Override
    public void finishEditor() {
        finish();
    }
}
```

This is the same code that used to be called in your `OnClickListener` and `onLoadFinished()`.

4. **Add the following code to** `ReminderListAndEditorActivity`:

```
public class ReminderListAndEditorActivity extends FragmentActivity
        implements
        OnEditReminder, OnFinishEditor {

    @Override
    public void finishEditor() {
        FragmentManager fragmentManager = getSupportFragmentManager();
          →6
        FragmentTransaction transaction = fragmentManager.
          beginTransaction();  →7
        Fragment previousFragment = fragmentManager
          .findFragmentByTag(ReminderEditFragment.DEFAULT_EDIT_FRAGMENT_
          TAG);        →9
        transaction.remove(previousFragment);     →10
        transaction.commit();    →11
    }

}
```

As before, you're using the `FragmentManager` and a `Fragment Transaction` to manage the adding and removing of fragments from the activity. Here's what the code does:

→6   Asks the `FragmentActivity` for the `FragmentManager`.

→7   Starts the `FragmentTransaction` by calling `begin Transaction()`.

→9   Asks the `FragmentManager` to find the previous fragment named `DEFAULT_EDIT_FRAGMENT_TAG`, if any. This name must agree with the name that you used when you initially added the fragment in `editReminder()`.

→**10**   Removes the fragment. If `previousFragment` was `null`, this line does nothing.

→**11**   Commits the transaction. Remember that every call to `begin Transaction()` must end with a call to `commit()`.

Adding fragment transactions

Fundamentally, `editReminder()` should show an edit fragment for the task that the user tapped. Or it should show an empty edit fragment if the user tapped the Add button on the action bar so that the user can add a new task. If a user taps several tasks in a row, `editReminder()` should replace the existing edit fragment with a new one representing the last item.

You've already put fragments into activities using XML in your `reminder_list.xml` layout. Because you want to dynamically add and remove fragments, this time you use Java instead of XML. The process isn't hard; it's just a little different from XML.

When you want to add or remove fragments in Java, you need to use the `FragmentManager` to begin a `FragmentTransaction`. You then make your changes and call `commit()` on the `FragmentTransaction`, much like you might do when interacting with a database transaction.

Inside `editReminder()`, add the following code:

```
/**
 * Set the edit fragment, replacing the existing fragment if there's one
 * already there.
 */
@Override
public void editReminder(long id) {
    ReminderEditFragment fragment = new ReminderEditFragment();          →7
    Bundle arguments = new Bundle();                                     →8
    arguments.putLong(ReminderProvider.COLUMN_ROWID, id);               →9
    fragment.setArguments(arguments);                                    →10

    FragmentTransaction transaction = getSupportFragmentManager()
            .beginTransaction();                                         →13
    transaction.replace(R.id.edit_container, fragment,
            ReminderEditFragment.DEFAULT_EDIT_FRAGMENT_TAG);            →15
    transaction.addToBackStack(null);                                   →16
    transaction.commit();                                               →17
}
```

Here's how the code works:

→7　　Creates a new `ReminderEditFragment` fragment.

　　　Fragments must have no-argument constructors. All arguments go into a bundle.

→8–10　Tells the fragment which task is being edited. An ID of `0` indicates that a new fragment is being created.

→13　　Gets the `FragmentManager` by calling `FragmentActivity.` `getSupportFragmentManager()`, and then calls `begin` `Transaction()` to start a new fragment transaction.

→15　　Calls `FragmentTransaction.replace()` to replace the existing fragment with the new fragment. The `edit_container` view tells you where to place the fragment, `fragment` tells you which fragment to use, and `ReminderEditFragment.DEFAULT_EDIT_` `FRAGMENT_TAG` reveals the fragment name.

→16　　Calls `addToBackStack()` and passes `null` for the optional state name.

　　　This line requires a little explanation. Think about what happens whenever you start a new activity — it is added to the activity stack and, if users tap the Back button, they return to the previous activity. This standard interaction is expected by users for almost all activities.

　　　The default behavior for fragments, though, is the opposite. By default, when you add a fragment to an activity, it doesn't go on the back stack. So a user who taps the Back button exits the activity rather than removes the fragment you just added. This may not be what you want to happen. If you want the Back button to remove the fragment, you need to call `addToBackStack()`.

　　　When adding fragments dynamically, think about what your users are most likely to expect the Back button to do. In this case, when the user taps a list item to display an edit fragment, it's reasonable for him to expect to be able to tap the Back button to close the edit fragment.

→17　　Every call to `beginTransaction()` must be accompanied by a call to `commit()`. This is where Android does the actual work to add fragments to, or remove them from, your activity.

Congratulations — you should now have a fully implemented version of your phone application running on your tablet.

Chapter 18

Moving beyond Google

- -

- -

For Android, Google may be the biggest game in town — but it isn't the only one. Because Google makes every release of Android open to the public via the Android Open Source Project, many companies produce their own, custom versions of the Android source code.

One version that you may be familiar with, Amazon, chose Android to run on its tablet, the Kindle Fire.

The Android-based Kindle can run apps with few or no modifications. It has no access to the Google Play Store, though, which means that if you want Kindle Fire users to be able to download your application, you have to publish your app to the Amazon Appstore for Android. In this chapter, you find out how to port your application to the Kindle Fire and then publish it via Amazon.

One reason you may want to port to the Kindle Fire is to reach more users. But only you can decide whether the additional users you'll acquire are worth the extra effort that's necessary. Do your homework and read relevant statistics on how many users each new platform has before you commit to expending the effort.

Working Around Google Features

Because the Kindle Fire isn't a "true" Android device (it doesn't use the official Google Android source code but instead uses its custom version), it doesn't have access to any of the closed-source Google services that you might already be using. In addition, the device itself may not have certain features that you're accustomed to:

- **Google Maps:** If you're using the Google Maps library to bring maps to your Android application, you can't use this library on the Kindle Fire.

- **Location services:** You cannot use Maps, and neither do you have access to location services on the Kindle Fire. It has no GPS or Wi-Fi–based location services, so you have no way to tell where the device is physically located.

- **Google Play Store in-app purchasing:** If your app uses in-app purchasing to allow users to purchase from inside it, you can't use this same API in your Kindle Fire app. Luckily, Amazon has a version of in-app purchasing that you can use on the Kindle Fire.

- **Camera, microphone, Bluetooth, 3G, external storage:** The Kindle Fire has none of these items, so if your app uses them, either find a way around the limitation or consider not releasing your app on the Kindle Fire.

- **Honeycomb, Ice Cream Sandwich, Jelly Bean:** Amazon uses the version of Android source code before Honeycomb was released, so the Kindle Fire has no access to any of the features in these three versions. In particular, you'll notice that the Kindle Fire has a unique look and feel that is unlike any other Android tablet. See Chapter 1 for the features that come with these three Android versions.

Even without these features and services, *many* Android applications work on the Kindle Fire with little or no modification. If this includes your app, read on.

Setting Up Your Kindle Fire or Emulator

If you want to develop for the Kindle Fire, you need either the Kindle Fire itself to test your app with or an emulator that can act as a surrogate. Because the Kindle Fire is its own breed of Android, you can't use the same ADB you use with other Android devices unless you make a few configuration changes.

Creating Kindle-like emulator

If you don't have access to a Kindle Fire, you need to create an emulator for one. The process for doing so is slightly different than it is for a regular Android emulator because the Kindle Fire runs its own version of Android. Follow these steps:

1. **Install the Android 2.3.3 (API Level 10) SDK using the SDK Manager.**

   Check out Chapter 2 for more details on how to use the SDK Manager.

2. **In the SDK Manager, choose Tools⇨Manage Add-on Sites.**

   The Add-on Sites dialog box opens, as shown in Figure 18-1.

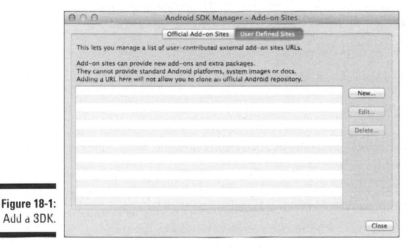

3. **On the User Defined Sites tab, click the New button.**

4. **Enter the URL** `http://kindle-sdk.s3.amazonaws.com/addon.xml` **and click Close.**

   The Android SDK Manager dialog box opens, as shown in Figure 18-2.

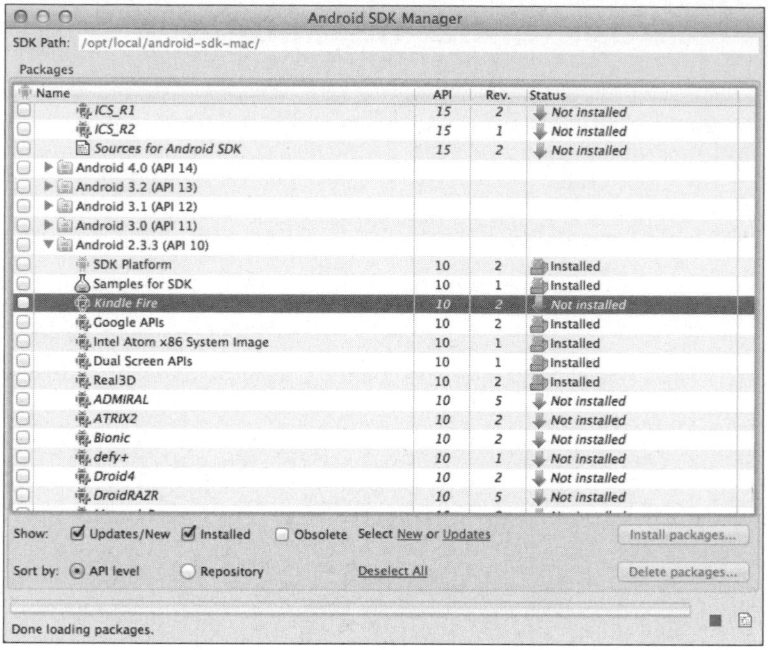

Figure 18-2:
Install the
Kindle Fire
emulator.

5. **Scroll down to Android 2.3.3 (API 10), select Kindle Fire, and then click the Install Packages button.**

6. **Accept the license agreement and click Install again.**

7. **Open the AVD Manager and click the New button.**

8. **Select Target Kindle Fire (Amazon) – API Level 10.**

   The Create New Android Virtual Device dialog box opens, as shown in Figure 18-3.

9. **Enter a name for your emulator and click Create AVD.**

10. **Select the 2_3_3_Kindle_Fire AVD you just created and click Start, and then click the Launch button to run your new emulator.**

    The Kindle Fire emulator is now running in a window. See Figure 18-4.

○ ○ ○　　　Create new Android Virtual Device (AVD)

Name:	2_3_3_Kindle_Fire
Target:	Kindle Fire (Amazon) – API Level 10
CPU/ABI:	ARM (armeabi)

SD Card:
- ● Size: [   ] MiB
- ○ File: [   ] Browse...

Snapshot:
- ☐ Enabled

Skin:
- ● Built-in: Default (KindleFire)
- ○ Resolution: [   ] x [   ]

Hardware:

Property	Value	
SD Card support	yes	New...
Hardware Back/Home keys	no	Delete
Abstracted LCD density	169	
DPad support	no	
LCD pixel height	1024	
Cache partition size	251	
Initial data partition		

☐ Override the existing AVD with the same name

Cancel　　Create AVD

Figure 18-3:
Name your
emulator.

Figure 18-4:
The emula-
tor running
Kindle Fire.

Now you can run your Android application from Eclipse in your Kindle Fire emulator.

Configuring ADB (Mac)

If you're using a real Kindle Fire device (as opposed to the emulator), you can't connect to a Kindle Fire directly out of the box using ADB without making a few modifications first. Follow these steps:

1. **On your Mac, edit the** `adb_usb.ini` **file in the** `.android` **folder of your home directory.**

   Add the following lines to the bottom of the file:

   ```
   0x1949
   0x0006
   ```

2. **Plug in your Kindle Fire and restart ADB:**

   ```
   adb kill-server
   adb devices
   ```

You now see your Kindle Fire listed in the output from the `adb devices` command.

Configuring ADB (Windows)

As on a Mac, you can't connect to a Kindle Fire device directly out of the box using ADB, without making a few modifications first.

1. **On your Windows machine, edit the** `adb_usb.ini` **file in the** `.android` **folder of your home directory.**

   Add the following line to the bottom of the file:

   ```
   0x1949
   ```

2. **Edit the** `android_winusb.inf` **file.**

   Add the following two lines to both the Google.NTx86 and Google.NTamd64 sections:

   ```
   ;Kindle Fire
   %SingleAdbInterface% = USB_Install, USB\VID_1949&PID_0006
   %CompositeAdbInterface% = USB_Install, USB\VID_1949&PID_0006&MI_01
   ```

3. **Plug in your Kindle Fire and, when prompted, choose to install the driver manually.**

4. **Browse to the** `android_winusb.inf` **file you just edited and install it.**

5. **Restart ADB by running the following commands in a command window:**

```
adb kill-server
adb devices
```

You now see your Kindle Fire in the output from the `adb devices` command.

Publishing to Amazon Appstore for Android

Publishing to the Android Appstore for Android is similar to publishing to the Google Play Store: You create an account, and then you may need to pay a developers' fee.

Unlike the Google Play Store, apps must be reviewed on the Amazon Appstore for Android, so plan a few days between the day you submit your app and the day it becomes available on the store.

Follow these steps:

1. **Go to** `https://developer.amazon.com/welcome.html`.

2. **Sign in using your Amazon login, or create a new account.**

3. **Click the Accept and Continue button to accept the developer's license agreement.**

4. **Fill out the monetization information if you intend to charge for your app or for in-app purchases. Then click Save.**

   See Figure 18-5.

5. **Click the Add a New App button.**

6. **Enter your app's title, form factor (phone, tablet, or both), and contact information on the General Information tab. Click Save when you're done.**

   Feel free to fill in the other optional fields such as SKU if it's useful to you. See Figure 18-6.

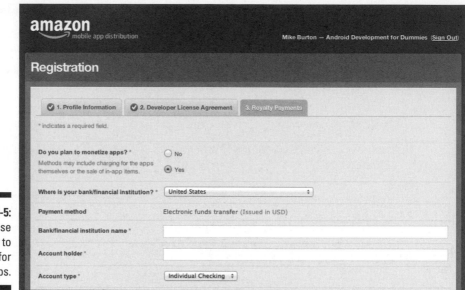

Figure 18-5:
Choose
whether to
charge for
your apps.

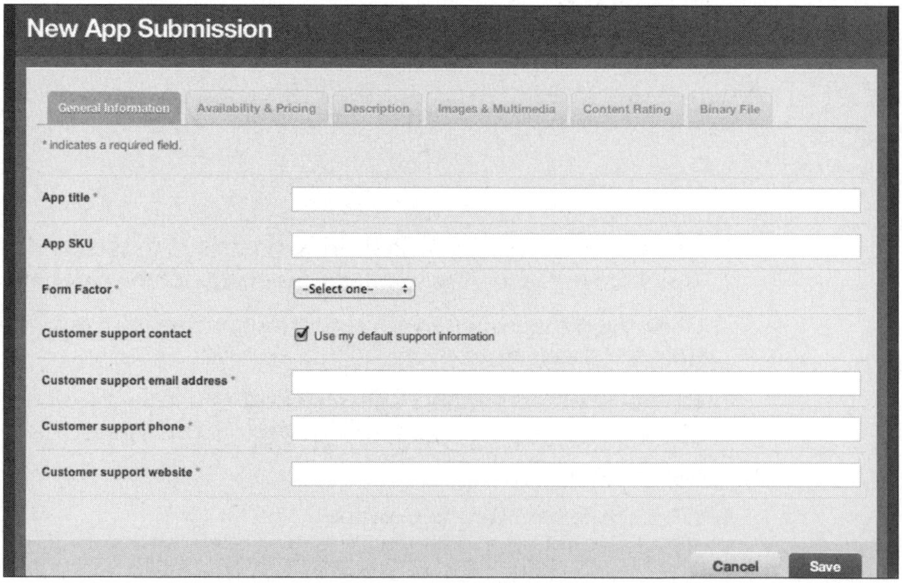

Figure 18-6:
Give
Amazon the
details of
your app.

7. **Choose in which countries to make your app available — and its price.**

8. **Choose a category for your app, the language it uses, its title, and short and long descriptions. Then click Save.**

   See Figure 18-7.

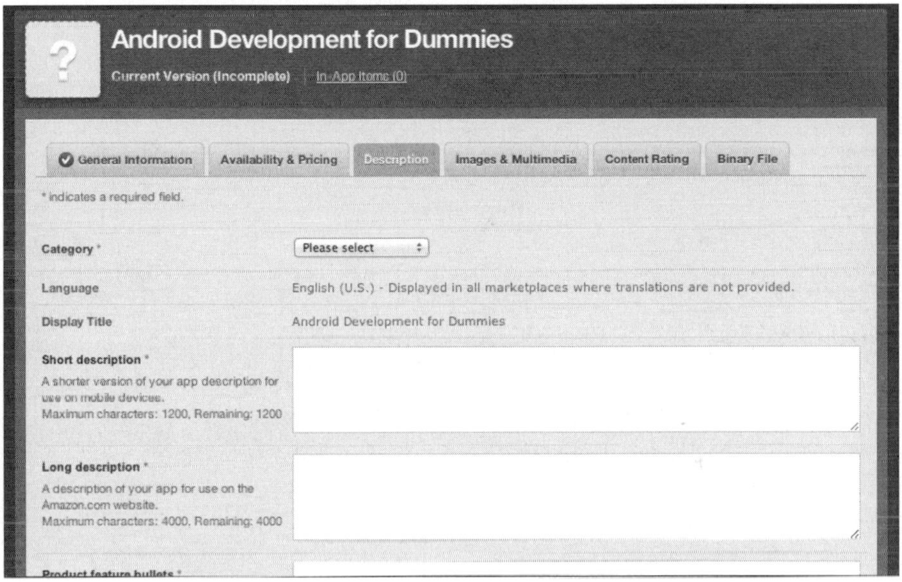

Figure 18-7:
Select a
category
and lan-
guage for
your app.

9. **Upload a small icon, a large icon, screenshots to include in your app description, and a promotional screenshot. Then click Save.**

10. **Choose your app's content rating and age restrictions by clicking the appropriate radio buttons. Then click Save.**

11. **Upload your app's binary code. Then click Save.**

    See Chapter 8 for more information about how to build and upload your app's APK file.

12. **Click the Submit App button.**

The review process can take anywhere from hours to days to weeks. However, when your app launches in the app store, you can find it in the Amazon Appstore for Android alongside other apps as shown in Figure 18-8.

Figure 18-8:
The Amazon
Appstore for
Android.

Part V
The Part of Tens

The 5th Wave   By Rich Tennant

"This is a bill from a record label, Deb. Tell me you didn't commission Sir Elton John to compose a song for your application."

In this part . . .

Part V consists of some of the best secret-sauce-covered Android nuggets that you acquire only after having been in the development trenches for quite some time. Chapter 19 lists some of the best sample applications that can help springboard you on your way to creating the next hit application. These applications range from database-oriented apps to interactive games to applications that interact with third-party Web application programming interfaces (APIs).

Part V closes with a list of professional tools and libraries that can help streamline and improve the productivity of your application development process and make your life as a developer much easier.

Chapter 19

Ten Free Sample Applications and SDKs

● ●

*W*hen you develop Android apps, you may run into various roadblocks based on the code. Perhaps you want an app to communicate with a third-party API that returns JSON or to perform collision detection in a game. You can usually search the web for sample code because someone else has likely already written it. Then all you have to do is review the code, alter it to fit your needs, and continue with development.

Reviewing sample code increases your knowledge even if you don't need the code in an application. In fact, a good way to find out how to program for Android is to look at sample code. Sure, it comes supplied with the Android SDK — in the API Demos, for example (see Chapter 2) — but a truly cool plethora of real world application code is freely available on the web. You can find on the Internet plenty of high-quality open source applications to serve as examples, thanks to the open source nature of Android.

Most of the ten excellent open source applications and samples in this chapter are real world Android applications that you can install from the Google Play Store. Try an application on your device, and then crack open its source code to see how the gears turn.

The Google I/O 2012 App

```
http://code.google.com/p/iosched
```

Every year, throngs of Google developer groupies descend on Moscone Center in San Francisco for a multiday conference to discuss all things Google. The official conference app is written for Android devices, and the app serves as an example of how to write good applications for the platform.

LOLcat Builder

```
http://code.google.com/p/apps-for-android
```

LOLcat shows you how to manipulate images in Android — how to take a picture using the device's camera, add captions to the picture, and then save the resulting file on the SD card. You can see how to create various intents, which allow you to send the image in multimedia message service (MMS) format or as an e-mail attachment.

Amazed

```
http://code.google.com/p/apps-for-android
```

The fun game Amazed demonstrates the use of a device's built-in accelerometer to navigate a 2D marble through various obstacles inside increasingly difficult levels of a maze. If you're interested in accelerometer-based applications, reviewing its Amazed source code can help you immensely. The application not only shows you how to use the accelerometer but also demonstrates other game development fundamentals, such as collision detection and the game loop principle.

API Demos

The `samples` folder of the Android SDK holds the source code for the API Demos app, which demonstrates how to use various Android APIs via small, digestible, working examples. You can find tons of simple, straight-to-the-point examples in the API Demos source code. Incorporating animation into your project or playing an audio file inside your app is easy because API Demos provides examples of both. If you have a lot of ideas but not a lot of time, you should definitely install this demo app on your device and play with its numerous examples to see exactly what they can do.

HoneycombGallery

If you want your app to run well on phones and tablets, check out the HoneycombGallery example in the Android SDK because it can save you hours of debugging and positioning views of the user interface. The working sample app shows how to support multiple screen sizes and resolutions, and it demonstrates the proper way to use fragments on different sized devices. You can find the source code in the samples folder of your Android SDK.

K-9 Mail

```
http://code.google.com/p/k9mail/
```

K-9 Mail is a popular e-mail client for Android that used to ship with Android before it became a separate app. It's an extraordinarily full-featured open-source application, with functionality such as search, push, sync, flagging, signatures, and more.

Agit

```
https://github.com/rtyley/agit
```

Git is a popular open-source Distributed Version Control System (DVCS). Agit lets you view, from the palm of your hand, all your favorite Git repositories located on GitHub.com. The application demonstrates how to use the GitHub API as well as the RoboGuice framework.

Facebook SDK for Android

```
http://github.com/facebook/facebook-android-sdk
```

If you're feeling ambitious, you can tackle the task of creating the next popular Facebook application, even if you don't know where to begin. Use the Facebook Android SDK to easily integrate Facebook functionality into your application — authorize users, make API requests, and much more. Integrate all the goodness of Facebook without breaking a sweat.

Replica Island

```
http://code.google.com/p/replicaisland
```

Perhaps you want to make a 2D, side-scrolling game for the Android platform but have no clue how to get started. Well, it's your lucky day because the cool side-scrolling game Replica Island features none other than the little green android (BugDroid) that developers know and love. Replica Island is not only a popular, free game on the Google Play Store, it's also an open source learning tool for game developers.

Notepad Tutorial

```
http://d.android.com/guide/tutorials/notepad/index.html
```

If you're interested in understanding the basic principles of SQLite without all the fluff of services, background tasks, and other technical concepts, Notepad Tutorial is for you. Although simple in its execution and usage, the source code and tutorial that go along with it are helpful.

Chapter 20

Ten Tools to Simplify Your Development Life

. . . .

As a developer, you inherently build tools to become more productive — for example, to assist in asynchronous communication, XML and JSON parsing, date and time utilities, and much more. Before you write a ton of helper classes or frameworks to handle items for you, seek out tools that already exist. This chapter lists ten tools and utilities that can simplify your development life by increasing your productivity and ensuring that your app is up to snuff.

droid-fu and ignition

```
http://github.com/kaeppler/droid-fu
https://github.com/kaeppler/ignition
```

The droid-fu open source library has a handful of methods to help you apply a karate chop to slice your development time drastically. The library is composed of utility classes that do all the mundane heavy lifting for you, such as handling asynchronous background requests, retrieving images from the web, and, most amazingly, enhancing the application life cycle.

Also check out ignition, a replacement for droid-fu by the same authors but now in the alpha stage.

RoboGuice

```
http://code.google.com/p/roboguice
```

No, RoboGuice isn't the latest and greatest energy drink marketed to developers — it's a framework that uses the Google Guice library to streamline dependency injection. *Dependency injection* handles the initializing of variables at the right time so that you don't have to. This concept cuts down the amount of code you have to write overall, and it makes maintaining your application a breeze.

Translator Toolkit

```
http://translate.google.com/toolkit
```

If you want to increase the number of people who can use your app, there's almost no better way to do it than to translate your app into other languages. The answer is to use Google to find helpers to translate your app for you. The translations aren't as clean as if you found a native speaker to translate for you, but they're a great place to start on the cheap. You might consider getting the initial translations done by Google, then reaching out to your user community to find volunteers to edit the translations for you, or using an outsourcing website such as ODesk to find translators. Even craigslist can be a great resource!

Draw 9-patch

```
http://developer.android.com/tools/help/draw9patch.html
```

The Draw 9-patch utility lets you easily create scalable images for Android. You use this utility to embed instructions in an image to tell the operating system where to stretch images so that they display as crisply and cleanly as possible regardless of the size or resolution of the device screen.

Hierarchy Viewer

```
http://developer.android.com/tools/help/hierarchy-viewer.
          html
```

Working with various views inside the layout file to create a user interface isn't always a straightforward process. Hierarchy Viewer, located in the Android SDK `tools` directory, lets you see exactly how your widgets are laid out onscreen graphically. This format lets you clearly see a widget's boundaries so that you can determine what's going on inside the layout. Hierarchy Viewer, the ultimate tool to make a pixel-perfect user interface, also lets you magnify the display in the pixel-perfect view to ensure that images and UIs display flawlessly on all screen sizes and at all densities.

UI/Application Exerciser Monkey

```
http://developer.android.com/tools/help/monkey.html
```

Don't worry: The UI/Application Exerciser Monkey doesn't need to be fed bananas to remain happy! You use Exerciser Monkey to stress-test your application. It simulates random touches, clicks, and other user events to ensure that abnormal usage doesn't make the app explode. Exerciser Monkey can be used to test apps on either your emulator or your own device.

zipalign

```
http://developer.android.com/tools/help/zipalign.html
```

The zipalign tool aligns all uncompressed data in an APK. Running zipalign minimizes memory consumption during runtime. If you're using the ADT in Eclipse, your application always gets zip-aligned when you export a signed application, as demonstrated in Chapter 8.

layoutopt

```
http://developer.android.com/tools/help/layoutopt.html
```

The layoutopt command-line tool analyzes layouts and reports any problems or inefficiencies. It's a helpful tool to run against all your layouts and resource directories because it identifies problems that may slow down your app and cause problems later on.

Git

```
http://git-scm.com
```

Git — a superfast, free, and open-source-distributed version control system — manages repositories quickly and efficiently, making it painless to back up work. Don't let a system crash ruin your day by not having a version control system for your next spectacular app. Git makes working with branching simple and effective, and it integrates into your workflow easily. Eclipse plug-ins exist to help manage your Git repository from within the Eclipse IDE. Although Git is distributed, you'll likely want a remote location where the Git repository is stored. You can obtain a free, private Git repository from Projectlocker (`http://projectlocker.com`) or Unfuddle (`https://unfuddle.com`). If your code is open source, you can create free repositories on Github.com.

Paint.NET and GIMP

```
www.getpaint.net
www.gimp.org
```

You will work with images at some point during Android development. Most professionals use Adobe Photoshop, but you may not be able to shell out much money for an image editing program. Therefore, you have two free alternatives: Paint.NET and GIMP.

The Paint.NET image manipulation program was written on top of the .NET Framework. Paint.NET, which is targeted for Windows, works great and is used by many developers around the world.

The GIMP open source program is similar to Photoshop. GIMP can be installed on Windows, Linux, or Mac.

Index

Apple & Mac

iPad 2 For Dummies,
3rd Edition
978-1-118-17679-5

iPhone 4S For Dummies,
5th Edition
978-1-118-03671-6

iPod touch For Dummies,
3rd Edition
978-1-118-12960-9

Mac OS X Lion
For Dummies
978-1-118-02205-4

Blogging & Social Media

CityVille For Dummies
978-1-118-08337-6

Facebook For Dummies,
4th Edition
978-1-118-09562-1

Mom Blogging
For Dummies
978-1-118-03843-7

Twitter For Dummies,
2nd Edition
978-0-470-76879-2

WordPress For Dummies,
4th Edition
978-1-118-07342-1

Business

Cash Flow For Dummies
978-1-118-01850-7

Investing For Dummies,
Edition
978-0-470-90545-6

Job Searching with Social
Media For Dummies
978-0-470-93072-4

QuickBooks 2012
For Dummies
978-1-118-09120-3

Resumes For Dummies,
6th Edition
978-0-470-87361-8

Starting an Etsy Business
For Dummies
978-0-470-93067-0

Cooking & Entertaining

Cooking Basics
For Dummies, 4th Edition
978-0-470-91388-8

Wine For Dummies,
4th Edition
978-0-470-04579-4

Diet & Nutrition

Kettlebells For Dummies
978-0-470-59929-7

Nutrition For Dummies,
5th Edition
978-0-470-93231-5

Restaurant Calorie Counter
For Dummies,
2nd Edition
978-0-470-64405-8

Digital Photography

Digital SLR Cameras &
Photography For Dummies,
4th Edition
978-1-118-14489-3

Digital SLR Settings
& Shortcuts
For Dummies
978-0-470-91763-3

Photoshop Elements 10
For Dummies
978-1-118-10742-3

Gardening

Gardening Basics
For Dummies
978-0-470-03749-2

Vegetable Gardening
For Dummies,
2nd Edition
978-0-470-49870-5

Green/Sustainable

Raising Chickens
For Dummies
978-0-470-46544-8

Green Cleaning
For Dummies
978-0-470-39106-8

Health

Diabetes For Dummies,
3rd Edition
978-0-470-27086-8

Food Allergies
For Dummies
978-0-470-09584-3

Living Gluten-Free
For Dummies,
2nd Edition
978-0-470-58589-4

Hobbies

Beekeeping
For Dummies,
2nd Edition
978-0-470-43065-1

Chess For Dummies,
3rd Edition
978-1-118-01695-4

Drawing For Dummies,
2nd Edition
978-0-470-61842-4

eBay For Dummies,
7th Edition
978-1-118-09806-6

Knitting For Dummies,
2nd Edition
978-0-470-28747-7

Language &
Foreign Language

English Grammar
For Dummies,
2nd Edition
978-0-470-54664-2

French For Dummies,
2nd Edition
978-1-118-00464-7

German For Dummies,
2nd Edition
978-0-470-90101-4

Spanish Essentials
For Dummies
978-0-470-63751-7

Spanish For Dummies,
2nd Edition
978-0-470-87855-2

Math & Science

Algebra I For Dummies,
2nd Edition
978-0-470-55964-2

Biology For Dummies,
2nd Edition
978-0-470-59875-7

Chemistry For Dummies,
2nd Edition
978-1-1180-0730-3

Geometry For Dummies,
2nd Edition
978-0-470-08946-0

Pre-Algebra Essentials
For Dummies
978-0-470-61838-7

Microsoft Office

Excel 2010 For Dummies
978-0-470-48953-6

Office 2010 All-in-One
For Dummies
978-0-470-49748-7

Office 2011 for Mac
For Dummies
978-0-470-87869-9

Word 2010
For Dummies
978-0-470-48772-3

Music

Guitar For Dummies,
2nd Edition
978-0-7645-9904-0

Clarinet For Dummies
978-0-470-58477-4

iPod & iTunes
For Dummies,
9th Edition
978-1-118-13060-5

Pets

Cats For Dummies,
2nd Edition
978-0-7645-5275-5

Dogs All-in One
For Dummies
978-0470-52978-2

Saltwater Aquariums
For Dummies
978-0-470-06805-2

Religion & Inspiration

The Bible For Dummies
978-0-7645-5296-0

Catholicism For Dummies,
2nd Edition
978-1-118-07778-8

Spirituality For Dummies,
2nd Edition
978-0-470-19142-2

Self-Help & Relationships

Happiness For Dummies
978-0-470-28171-0

Overcoming Anxiety
For Dummies,
2nd Edition
978-0-470-57441-6

Seniors

Crosswords For Seniors
For Dummies
978-0-470-49157-7

iPad 2 For Seniors
For Dummies, 3rd Edition
978-1-118-17678-8

Laptops & Tablets
For Seniors For Dummies,
2nd Edition
978-1-118-09596-6

Smartphones & Tablets

BlackBerry For Dummies,
5th Edition
978-1-118-10035-6

Droid X2 For Dummies
978-1-118-14864-8

HTC ThunderBolt
For Dummies
978-1-118-07601-9

MOTOROLA XOOM
For Dummies
978-1-118-08835-7

Sports

Basketball For Dummies,
3rd Edition
978-1-118-07374-2

Football For Dummies,
2nd Edition
978-1-118-01261-1

Golf For Dummies,
4th Edition
978-0-470-88279-5

Test Prep

ACT For Dummies,
5th Edition
978-1-118-01259-8

ASVAB For Dummies,
3rd Edition
978-0-470-63760-9

The GRE Test For
Dummies, 7th Edition
978-0-470-00919-2

Police Officer Exam
For Dummies
978-0-470-88724-0

Series 7 Exam
For Dummies
978-0-470-09932-2

Web Development

HTML, CSS, & XHTML
For Dummies, 7th Edition
978-0-470-91659-9

Drupal For Dummies,
2nd Edition
978-1-118-08348-2

Windows 7

Windows 7
For Dummies
978-0-470-49743-2

Windows 7
For Dummies,
Book + DVD Bundle
978-0-470-52398-8

Windows 7 All-in-One
For Dummies
978-0-470-48763-1